Clothes and Monasticism in Ancient Christian Egypt

This book is an exploration of the ideals and values of the ascetic and monastic life, as expressed through clothes. Clothes are often seen as an extension of us as humans, a determinant of who we are and how we experience and interact with the world. In this way, they can play a significant role in the embodied and material aspects of religious practice.

The focus of this book is on clothing and garments among ancient monastics and ascetics in Egypt, but with a broader outlook to the general meaning and function of clothes in religion. The garments of the Egyptian ascetics and monastics are important because they belong to a period of transition in the history of Christianity and very much represent this way of living. This study combines a cognitive perspective on clothes with an attempt to grasp the embodied experiences of being clothed, as well as viewing clothes as potential actors. Using sources such as travelogues, biographies, letters, contracts, images, and garments from monastic burials, the role of clothes is brought into conversation with material religion more generally.

This unique study builds links between ancient and contemporary uses of religious clothing. It will, therefore, be of interest to any scholar of religious studies, religious history, religion in antiquity, and material religion.

Ingvild Sælid Gilhus is Professor of the Study of Religion, University of Bergen, Norway. She works in the areas of religion in late antiquity and New Age religion. Her publications include *Laughing Gods, Weeping Virgins* (Routledge 1997); *Animals, Gods and Humans: Changing Attitudes to Animals in Greek, Roman and Early Christian Ideas* (Routledge 2006); *Evolution, Cognition, and the History of Religion: A New Synthesis* (edited with Anders K. Petersen, Luther H. Martin, Jeppe S. Jensen, and Jesper Sørensen, 2019); and *The Archangel Michael in Africa: History, Cult, and Persona* (edited with Alexandros Tsakos and Marta Camilla Wright, 2019).

Routledge Studies in Religion

Asian Philosophies and the Idea of Religion
Beyond Faith and Reason
Edited by Sonia Sikka and Ashwani Kumar Peetush

Orthodox Christian Identity in Western Europe
Contesting Religious Authority
Sebastian Rimestad

Spirit Possession and Communication in Religious and Cultural Contexts
Edited by Caroline Blyth

Blasphemies Compared
Transgressive Speech in a Globalised World
Edited by Anne Stensvold

Religion, Family, and Chinese Youth Development
An Empirical View
Jerf W. K. Yeung

Contemporary Christian-Muslim Dialogue
Twenty-First Century Initiatives
Douglas Pratt

Heresy and Borders in the Twentieth Century
Edited by Karina Jakubowicz and Robert Dickins

Clothes and Monasticism in Ancient Christian Egypt
New Perspective on Religious Garments
Ingvild Sælid Gilhus

For more information about this series, please visit: www.routledge.com/religion/series/SE0669

Clothes and Monasticism in Ancient Christian Egypt

New Perspective on Religious Garments

Ingvild Sælid Gilhus

Routledge
Taylor & Francis Group

LONDON AND NEW YORK

First published 2021
by Routledge
2 Park Square, Milton Park, Abingdon, Oxon OX14 4RN

and by Routledge
52 Vanderbilt Avenue, New York, NY 10017

Routledge is an imprint of the Taylor & Francis Group, an informa business

British Library Cataloguing-in-Publication Data
A catalogue record for this book is available from the British Library

Library of Congress Cataloging-in-Publication Data
Names: Gilhus, Ingvild Sælid, author.
Title: Clothes and monasticism in ancient Christian Egypt : new
    perspective on religious garments / Ingvild Sælid Gilhus.
Description: Abingdon, Oxon ; New York : Routledge, 2021. |
    Includes bibliographical references and index.
Identifiers: LCCN 2020046053 (print) | LCCN 2020046054 (ebook) |
    ISBN 9780367505479 (hardback) | ISBN 9781003050308 (ebook)
Subjects: LCSH: Desert Fathers—Clothing. | Clothing and dress—
    Religious aspects—Christianity. | Clothing and dress—Social
    aspects.
Classification: LCC BR190 .G55 2021 (print) | LCC BR190 (ebook) |
    DDC 271/.02062—dc23
LC record available at https://lccn.loc.gov/2020046053
LC ebook record available at https://lccn.loc.gov/2020046054

ISBN: 978-0-367-50547-9 (hbk)
ISBN: 978-1-003-05030-8 (ebk)

Typeset in Sabon
by Apex CoVantage, LLC

Contents

Acknowledgments

The background to this book about monastic clothes was an invitation to a seminar on religion, law, and justice, arranged by my colleagues Håkan Rydving and Stefan Olsson in 2014. After racking my brain to summon up what I knew about the topic and coming up with little, I remembered the Pachomian Rules. I had read these monastic rules in a Coptic version when I was studying the language many years ago, and this gave me an opportunity to revisit them. Very soon, I was hooked. Through the study of the Rules, the importance of artifacts in monasteries, and in particular monastic clothes, became more and more obvious. I decided to focus on them and expand the source material. The topic turned out to be much more interesting and with many more dimensions than I had imagined.

In recent years, I participated in several conferences, where I presented my project. At these conferences, colleagues offered invaluable criticism of various aspects of the work. I am especially grateful for the helpful comments I got from participants at a research seminar at the Norwegian Institute at Athens (February 25–26, 2020): Moa Airijoki, David Brakke, Jan Bremmer, Christian Bull, Laura Feldt, Anders Klostergaard Petersen, Dimitris J. Kyrtatas, Samuel Rubenson, Einar Thomassen, Alexandros Tsakos, and Jorunn Økland.

I am especially indebted to Hugo Lundhaug, who read and critiqued the entire manuscript. His expertise in the textual culture and early monastic tradition of Egypt and keen comments have been extremely helpful.

Special thanks are due to Jan Bremmer, Laura Feldt, and Siv Ellen Kraft, who read and commented on some chapters. Their great knowledge and expertise helped me improve the manuscript. I would also like to express my sincere thanks to Christian Bull for his advice on the Hermetic texts and to Lisbeth Mikaelsson, Torunn Selberg, Einar Thomassen, and Sissel Undheim for fruitful discussions.

Kari Normo at the University of Bergen Library has, as always, offered invaluable help and obtained interlibrary loans faster than I thought it was possible for books to travel from one end of Europe to the other. For his meticulous editing, useful comments, and active involvement in the preparation of this manuscript for publication, Dimitri Kakos is warmly thanked.

Many thanks are due to the Norwegian Research Council and the Department of Archaeology, History, Cultural Studies and Religion of the University of Bergen for offering me an extra sabbatical as part of the Evaluation of the Humanities in Norway. I am also deeply grateful to my department for the excellent working conditions and my wonderful colleagues for a lively and fruitful research environment and for their interest, helpful comments, and general encouragement in the progress of this work.

The last part of Chapter 6 has earlier been published in Ingvild Sælid Gilhus. 2018. "Sheepskins, Hair Shirts and Tunics of Palm Leaves: Charismatic Authority and Monastic Clothing in Egypt in Late Antiquity." *Temenos* 54 (1): 79–102.

Finally, I wish to thank my beloved husband, Nils Erik Gilhus, for his firm support in all phases of this work, from the first ideas to the finished manuscript.

Bergen, September 2020
Ingvild Sælid Gilhus

1 Introduction

The crocodile and the habit

> A brother going to Scete arrived at the Nile worn out by the journey. At the heat of the day, he took his clothes (*himation*) off and went down to bathe. Then an animal called a crocodile rushed in and seized him. Now an elder who had the second sight (*dioratikos*) passed by and saw that the brother had been seized. He shouted at the animal, saying, "Why did you eat the *abba*?" In a human voice, the beast said to him, "I did not eat an *abba*. I found a worldling (*kosmikos*) and ate him; the monk is there," and it nodded toward the habit (*schema*). The elder went his way grieving over what had taken place.
>
> (*AP* S 18.53)[1]

Because a monastic goes bathing having removed all his clothes and leaving them on the shore, the crocodile mistakes him for a secular person and eats him.[2] The crocodile has the power of speech and wants to justify what it has just done. It obviously thinks that it is legitimate to eat secular people but not to gorge itself on monastics. With its statement, the crocodile points to the special status of the monastics, while at the same time stressing the indecency and inconsistency of monks who appear in the nude.[3] But the animal makes an additional point, which is the importance of clothes for the monastic identity. Pushed to their logical conclusion, the crocodile's words indicate that the identity of the monastic is inseparably connected to his habit. Without his clothes, he is no longer considered a monk. It is doubtful whether the reptile is the best judge of what constitutes human identity, and we, humans, might be unwilling to accept that clothes are us or represent us. Clothes are rarely a matter of life and death and rarely involve clairvoyant crocodiles, but they are essential to the lived life of humans. The present study aims to offer a more comprehensive view on clothes. It is driven by a double interest—a special interest in ascetic and monastic clothes and a general interest in clothes as an integrated part of embodied existence: What were the meanings and functions of ascetic and monastic clothes in ancient Christian Egypt? How did they interact with their wearers? Why are clothes so significant?

Humans are not so much naked apes as the dressed species. Clothes are present most of the time, forming a layer between us and the world at the same time as they constitute a medium through which the world is filtered. Clothes reduce the stress of being in the world, interact with the body, express its identity, and participate in the continuous interplay between humans and the surrounding world. Roughly speaking, humans are defined not only by their bodies but even more by how these bodies are dressed. Clothes are an integral part of being human, and their ability to form us is often not realized. In the words of Virginia Woolf in her novel *Orlando*:

> Vain trifles as they seem, clothes have, they say, more important offices than merely to keep us warm. They change our view of the world and the world's view of us. . . . Thus, there is much to support the view that it is clothes that wear us and not we them; we may make them take the mould of arm or breast, but they mould our hearts, our brains, our tongues to their liking.
>
> (Woolf 1977: 179)

One might object that if we, along with the crocodile and Virginia Woolf, give so much importance to clothes, we universalize something from which there are clear exceptions. There are and have been human cultures where clothes are not in general use. It can be argued that in some cases, the psychosocial functions that clothes usually have can be taken care of in other ways, for instance by means of decorations directly on the body, such as tattoos and piercings, as well as jewelry, which make the body "dressed" albeit not clothed.[4] And even if clothes are not worn in some cultures, in most they have been in use on a regular basis for thousands of generations, which means that they have become a largely universal characteristic of being human.

The opposite of being clothed is being naked. In cultures where clothing is the norm, a human being without clothes stands very much out. In antiquity, there were different views on nakedness. In the ancient Near East and in Israel/Palestine, "male nudity was first and foremost a sign of the *lack or loss of status, (physical or military) defeat, humiliation, depravation, and death*" (Pyschny 2019: 142). The *Book of Jubilees* (ca. 150 BC), a Jewish work well-known to Christians, says that just as God clothed Adam and Eve, so Jews must "cover their shame and should not uncover themselves as the Gentiles uncover themselves" (3: 31). On the other hand, the nakedness of Greek athletes, probably practiced from the late eighth century BC (McDonnell 1991: 182), was a celebration of male power, the human form at its most splendor. When the desert ascetics of late antiquity sometimes appeared naked and were compared to the athletes (*AP* S 15.117), their aged and skinny bodies had a different meaning than the heroic nakedness of the young athletes: they referred to the prelapsarian nakedness of Adam and offered a glimpse of the future body of the Resurrection.

The naked bodies, whether those of athletes or ascetics, got their meaning from being exceptions to a norm, in other words, from the significant absence of clothes (Entwistle 2015: 6–8). Two types of nakedness are thematized in Genesis: before and after the fall of the first two humans. Before the fall, the nakedness of Adam and Eve was part of their childlike innocence; after the fall, when "the eyes of both were opened, and they knew that they were naked" (Gen. 3:7a), it was intertwined with sin and shamefulness.

Prelapsarian nakedness was sometimes seen as an ideal, but to pull it off was something quite different. In his *Lausiac History*,[5] a narrative of his travels to monastic settlements in Egypt and Syria and his visits to famous ascetics, written in 419–420 AD, Palladius tells the story of the holy man Serapion Sindonios. According to his account, Serapion got his moniker because he was only clad in a sheet (*sindon*), and he sometimes dispensed with the sheet as well. Serapion, Palladius tells us, once visited Rome, where he heard about a virgin who had been living a holy life and had not left her house for 25 years, claiming that she had died to the world. Serapion challenged her to come out of her house undressed: "Take off all your clothes (*himatia*) (as I am doing); put them on your shoulders and pass through the city center, with me going before you in the same guise (*schema*)" (*LH* 37.15). The virgin declined, admitting that she had not yet reached the level of holiness required for prelapsarian nakedness to feel like a natural state.

The crocodile, on the other hand, did not count nakedness as a real option. It simply did not find it *comme-il-faut* for a monastic to appear in the nude. The reptile obviously viewed the habit, the *schema*, as a defining and integral part of the monastic. The meaning of *schema* is "shape, form," with the extended meaning of "clothing, habit," so the meaning of the term is semantically in line with the importance the crocodile placed on the abandoned garment.[6] It constitutes the hapless monastic's shape or form. When the term is used in the story of the virgin and nakedness as the superior form, it shows that *schema* is a term denoting a uniform type of dressing and that it gives a shape to its wearer.

The stories about the crocodile who ate the naked monastic and the holy woman who refused to walk about without any clothes point to the importance of being dressed. In this study of ascetic and monastic clothes in Egypt in late antiquity, clothes are seen as mediators between their wearers and the world, and sometimes as actors, because of their potential to restrain as well as enable those who wore them.

The long history of clothes and their influence on humans

Before we proceed, we will briefly see the clothes of the monastics, and sometimes the lack thereof, in light of the long history of the evolution of clothes. The brief survey of their prehistory is intended to show the general significance of clothes in human life and to provide a background of their importance in human culture and especially in ascetic and monastic societies in Egypt in late antiquity.

Why do humans wear clothes? When did they start wearing them? What does the wearing of clothes imply for the human experience of being in the world in the first place? These questions have been long discussed (Gilligan 2010a). One problem is that no really old remnants of clothes, say, tens of thousands of years old, have been found, which means that one must rely on circumstantial evidence to re-create the history of humanity's oldest garments. The indirect evidence for Paleolithic clothes is, in addition to climatology, of a biological and technological/archaeological kind. Such indirect evidence comes, for instance, in the form of tiny insects, namely lice, and in the form of tools that were presumably used to transform animal skins and fibers into textiles and garments.[7]

In his study of the evolution of clothes, archaeologist Ian Gilligan combines climate changes, the use of tools, and the introduction of agriculture to tease out the prehistory of clothing (2019). Gilligan particularly stresses the physiological functions and effects of clothes. The genetic mutation that led to the loss of hair covering most of the human body happened more than a million—some suggest three million—years ago, long before humans started to wear clothes (Reed et al. 2015: 204; Rantala 2007; Gilligan 2010a: 32). However, later climate changes bringing about lower temperatures made clothes absolutely necessary for survival. Gilligan points to the thermal motive as crucial for the invention of clothes. Clothing evolved because of climate change with the onset of ice and as a means to keep warm (Gilligan 2019: 10). The limited biological defense against cold can be fatal, and, in addition to fire and shelter, clothing was the most important behavioral adaption to meet the new challenges. As clothes became necessary for survival, humans started to protect themselves with skins taken from flayed animals. Gilligan suggests that clothing came into continuous use in some human groups around 90,000–100,000 years ago (2010a: 32). When complex clothing was developed, he argues, shame and modesty came into being as well (Gilligan 2019: 27), and the need for clothing became independent of climate (2019: 67).[8]

Clothes protect the body and skin, balance blood circulation, and help to regulate temperature. They interact with the chemistry of the brain and the physiology of the body and have influenced the evolution of skin pigmentation (Jablonski 2004: 610). In addition to such changes, it is fruitful to see the use and development of clothes in relation to human cultural evolution in a broader perspective, because it is helpful for developing a more comprehensive view of clothes. An interesting approach to cultural evolution is made by Merlin W. Donald in his book *Origins of the Modern Mind: Three Stages in the Evolution of Culture and Cognition* (1991; see also Donald 2001). According to Donald, the human cognitive architecture comprises biological memory as well as external memory fields, which consist of specific technologies and media. Donald divides the cultural development of symbolic capacity into three major stages of transition, which changed human consciousness. After what he calls the mimetic stage, with the development of mimetic skills, and the mythic stage with the invention of language and symbolic representations, comes the last stage, the theoretic. This stage marks the transition to an external symbolic universe where culture and cognition interact and where "a huge number of external symbolic devices to store and retrieve cultural knowledge" come into use (Donald 2001: 262; see also Geertz 2010). Donald (2001: 262) estimates that this stage goes back about 40,000 years, but it could be even older.[9]

Donald's approach can be combined with an awareness of the development of clothes. The discovery of approximately 40,000-year-old eyed needles indicates that more complex clothing had already been invented by then. Weaving cloths and making garments represent an advanced stage of human development and a major leap forward in cultural evolution. This transition is dependent on what has been called "the string revolution," which took place at least 20,000 years ago and perhaps more.[10] Elizabeth W. Barber points to what happened when "humans started to invent and make new things at a tremendous rate" and speaks about "the string revolution," when "some genius hit upon the principle of twisting handfuls of little weak fibers together into long, strong thread" (1994: 43; cf. Barber 1991). The term "the string revolution" refers to the development of the necessary technological skills to process fibers from plants and animals into thread.[11]

The hypothesis of the origin of clothes as a protection against the cold has its opponents. Michael Carter has adopted a critical approach to explanations of the invention of clothes as "first and foremost a technological object, a useful tool, something capable of providing the wearer with protection against the cold" (2017: 92). Carter suggests instead that clothing and bodily decoration have common roots and that, accordingly, "dress may be an essential component of transforming the human body into forms other than those bestowed by nature" (2017: 93). He sees dress and dressmaking as part of a much broader human reworking of the world. Carter offers an alternative account of what he calls "the coming into being of the dressed body" (Carter 2017: 116). He argues that

> the 'body' emerges as the adjustments of dress get made. That is, it comes into being as part of a field of symbolic marks and materials. It adds to, and draws upon, those alternative and imaginary worlds that play such a large role in the life of Homo sapiens.
>
> (Carter 2017: 116)

Carter sees dress as constitutive of the social body: "What "we call 'dressing' was, and still is, something that lies at the heart of what it is to be human" (2017: 117). Carter's hypothesis that the development of dress is an integral part of the development of a human world of imagination and symbols—in short, an integral part of the development of what it means to be human—offers a fruitful perspective on wearing clothes.

Clothes are indeed part of the external symbolic storages that humans had started to develop. Complex clothes incite psychosocial motivations for wearing them. They mark status, class, age, sex, social belonging, cultural difference, and origin (Corrigan 2008: 161–162). Clothes cater to the wish to stand apart from the rest of the biological world and contribute to create a feeling of shame connected to nakedness (Gilligan 2010a: 17, 27).[12] They function, among other things, as material memories (see Chapter 5; see also Jones and Stallybrass 2000: 269), and, in line with this view, they constitute a form of external symbolic storage. Storage, however, does not mean inalterability. On the contrary, this type of storage is a cultural reservoir that invites continuous interpretation and change, and artifacts such as clothes play an active role in this process (Malafouris 2013: 73; Sutton 2008: 39–44).[13]

Another side of the human cognitive evolution, which is highly relevant for the creation and use of clothes, is the development of metaphorical thinking. According to George Lakoff and Mark Johnson, basic experiences of the body and the physical environment are source domains used to understand abstract areas of experience; these areas are labeled "target domains" (1980). In Near Eastern literature, vestimentary metaphors figure prominently in hymns and prayers. In Old Babylonian hymns, Ishtar is dressed in her exuberance and fertility, while Yahweh is "clothed with honour and majesty, wrapped in light as with a garment."[14] Because clothes are worn from birth to death, and even thereafter, and are intimately connected with what it means to be a human, vestimentary metaphors must have been used from an early time to think about human identity and about humans as complex psychological and material beings (Mihas 2012; Cairns 2016). The wearing of clothes thus made more complex thoughts possible about being human.

Ancient Christianity applied vestimentary imagery to its full extent. The garments that God gave Adam and Eve in Genesis were part of their fallen condition and sometimes interpreted as their new fleshly body (see Chapter 2). The idea of resurrection after death when the biological condition is transcended and the dead is transformed into an immortal being was expressed by means of elaborate imagery based on clothing. Paul's ideas about the resurrection body are expressed by means of such imagery:

> For this perishable body must put on imperishability, and this mortal body must put on immortality. When this perishable body puts on imperishability, and this mortal body puts on immortality, then the saying that is written will be fulfilled: 'Death has been swallowed up in victory'.
>
> (1 Cor. 15: 53–54)

The Greek term used in this key scriptural passage denoting the transformation from mortality to immortality is *endúno*. It is translated as "to put on" and "to clothe oneself" and implies that the soul becomes invested with a new dimension as with a garment (see Chapter 8). Clothes are obviously tools to think with.

Paul and his successors, as well as his opponents, speak of the human compound of spirit, soul, and body and use clothes metaphorically to approach the secrets of the resurrection and the continued existence of humans after death (see Chapter 8). With this in mind, let us return briefly to the talking crocodile. It is dubious whether the reptile has the slightest grasp of the inner constitution of humans, let alone the theological debate in Egypt in late antiquity and the strong opinions concerning resurrection and the discussion about what part of humans will rise after death. The crocodile is preoccupied with the external form as expressed by the monastic garments. If, however, we combine the anthropology of Paul with the crocodile's observation, we are left with a human being, consisting of not only spirit, soul, and body, but also his clothing or habit. What theoretical approaches do we need to understand the meaning and functions of garments as integral parts of monastics as clothed beings?

Theoretical perspectives and recent research

Clothes have been studied in many ways and have invited various theoretical approaches. If we take a bird's-eye view, we can discern at least two aspects: the material and the immaterial.[15] Clothes are physical things that not only affect physically those wearing them, but they are also part of discourse and communication as well as of systems of symbols and metaphors.

What are clothes when they appear in discourse? Do they constitute a language and, if so, what sort of language? Are clothes good to think with? An influential voice is the literary theorist and philosopher Roland Barthes (1915–1980), who, in line with his Saussurean and semiotic perspective, made a famous and influential analysis of the meaning of fashion (Barthes [1967] 2010). Barthes also wrote shorter articles and gave interviews about the more general meaning of clothes. This is what he has to say about clothes in one of his articles:

> Man invented clothing for three reasons: as protection against harsh weather, out of modesty for hiding nudity and for the ornamentation to get noticed. This is all true. But we must add another function, which seems to me to be more important: the function of meaning. Man has dressed himself to carry out a signifying activity. The wearing of an item of clothing is fundamentally an act of meaning that goes beyond modesty, ornamentation, and protection. It is an act of signification and therefore a profoundly social act right at the very heart of the dialectic of society.
>
> (Barthes 2013: 92–93)

In his book *Système de la Mode* (*The Fashion System*), Barthes treats fashion as a system, in line with the so-called "linguistic turn" ([1967] 2010).[16]

Garments are seen in relation to other garments, which together constitute the collective system of clothing. He metaphorically describes this system as a language. In this structural linguistic approach, the meanings of the various garments are read in relation to each other. Barthes distinguishes between "written clothing," "image clothing," and "real clothing" (Barthes 2010: 3–7; see Chapter 3). Barthes's focus is on "written clothing" and more specifically on fashion as presented in French fashion magazines in the 1950s.

Barthes's approach presupposes that the fashion system has language-like properties and communicates by means of a code. These presuppositions have been questioned and modified. Grant D. McCracken pointed out that, while it is important to understand clothing as a means of communication, it is more fruitful to study the *differences* between language and clothing (1985: 103). According to McCracken, clothing in actual use reads more like a puzzle than a sentence with a linear meaning. In interpreting what people wear, the aim is to fit the different pieces of an outfit into a preconceived model and not to tell a new story. In empirical tests, novelties in an outfit were regarded as problems and were not "read" in ways that created new messages. According to McCracken, "clothing provides society with a fixed set of messages" and "clothing is a conservative code" (1985: 120). In a later study, McCracken and Victor J. Roth (1989) stressed that clothing is a means of communication, which relies on a code shared by the addressor and the addressee of a clothing message, but the knowledge of this code is unevenly distributed in society, which also distinguishes clothing from language. In other words, compared to verbal language, the meaning of dress is unclear (Entwistle 2015: 67).

These are valuable observations; clothes are obviously used for communication, but not in the same way as linguistic messages. It is also important to realize that the communicative aspect of clothes in no way exhausts what clothes are and what they do (Carter 2012). One characteristic is that in addition to being good to think with, they also have strong affective dimensions. They play on emotions, as when the favorite sweater of a beloved, long-dead relative turns up in a drawer. Another thing is that they have specific functions by virtue of being material objects.

Since it is impossible to do fieldwork in ancient cultures, we are dependent on empirical studies of the contemporary use of clothes to try to understand how they work, both cognitively and affectively. Experimental psychological studies raise and try to answer questions of how clothes contribute to construct images of other people and of oneself. For instance, it has been shown that subtle changes in clothing styles influence the impression made. Men's suits and posture are interpreted as statements of competence (Howlett et al. 2012, 2015; cf. Gurney et al. 2017). Even

> minor modifications to clothing style can have a major impact on the information conveyed to the perceivers. Unfastened buttons on

a woman's blouse, for instance. People are judged on their overall head-to-toe appearance within seconds, and the fundamental role that choice of apparel plays in creating a positive first impression cannot be underestimated.

(Howlett et al. 2012: 47)

Clothes influence cognition more broadly and change how objects, people, and events are construed (Slepian et al. 2015: 661–662). This means that the formality of clothing influences not only how others perceive a person and how this person perceives himself or herself, but also how decisions are made (Slepian et al. 2015: 666).

Cognition is conceived as the mental act of acquiring knowledge and understanding through thought, experience, and the senses and, more specifically, it can be seen as "embrained, embodied, encultured, extended and distributed" (Geertz 2010: 304). In addition, cognition is also "enclothed," because wearing certain clothes nourishes certain mentalities, and clothes influence the wearers' perception and meaning-making (Gilhus 2019). Recent studies have combined the symbolic meaning of clothes with the actual experience of wearing them and with how clothing cues influence people. Empirical work on dress practices is done both by anthropologists and by social psychologists (Entwistle 2015: 75). Adam and Galinsky have coined the term "enclothed cognition" to denote the "systematic influence of clothes on the wearer's psychological processes and behavioural tendencies" (Adam and Galinsky 2012: 919). This is a new take on what is usually called "embodied cognition." Enclothed cognition involves "the co-occurrence of two independent factors—the symbolic meaning of the clothes *and* the physical experience of wearing clothes" (Adam and Galinsky 2012: 918; see also López-Pérez et al. 2016).[17] In relation to the monastic clothes, enclothed cognition means that the material priming effects of clothes must be seen in consonance with their symbolic meanings (Gilhus 2019). According to this line of research, we will expect that monastics " 'embody' the clothing and its symbolic meaning" (Adam and Galinsky 2012: 919).[18] Accordingly, when the habit was worn, seen, and felt, it influenced the psychological processes of the monastics.

Recent anthropological approaches have made it possible to see an even more active role of clothes in life and society. These approaches more explicitly counterbalance the impulse to treat things, including clothes, solely as language and text; they take material things seriously and treat them as mediators and even as actors.[19] The theories of Birgit Meyer, Bruno Latour, Daniel Miller, and Lambros Malafouris have also inspired this study. Meyer's approach is to treat things as media, while Miller, Latour, and Malafouris view things as actors. Their theories help us understand how monastic clothes shape and direct the ways monastics act, feel, and think (see also Kloss 2016: 20–22). Importantly to this study, the affective functions of monastic clothes are essential, because they provide direction and stability to the monastic and ascetic life.

According to Birgit Meyer, religion is formed and mediated through cultural forms (2009: 6–11). One of Meyer's insights is that a community does not exist a priori and manifests itself to the world through fixed symbols; rather, a community—in our case, a monastic community—comes into being when common cultural forms are circulated and used. Among such cultural forms are the clothes of the ascetics and the monastics. In the context of this study, Meyer's approach implies that monastic clothes create and transmit the ascetic life of the Egyptian monasteries and desert cells to the surrounding society and to the monastics and ascetics themselves. Meyer has put forth the notion of "aesthetic formation," which helps to move beyond fixed social groups and toward processes of forming social entities through shared things and imagination (2009: 7). Her extended concept of media offers a framework for the study of ascetic and monastic clothes (Meyer 2009: 11).

Other recent approaches treat things as actors. According to anthropologist Daniel Miller, "things make people just as much as people make things" (2010: 135). In his book *Stuff*, Miller explains "how the sari wears the Indian woman, how it makes her what she is—both woman and Indian" (Miller 2010: 23). He goes on to describe not only how it feels to wear a sari, but also how one part of the sari, the *pallu*, which falls over the shoulder, is used as a kind of a third hand to lift hot vessels, wipe a seat, collect money in a purse-like knot, clean spectacles, and protect the face from smoke and smog (Miller 2010: 25). For a child, it is a sort of extension of his mother (Miller 2010: 26). Miller notes the interplay of modesty and eroticism, which are potentially present in the garment (2010: 27). The sari has an emotional repertoire (Miller 2010: 28). It is not easy to wear and has to be mastered; but when mastered, it "turns a woman into a person who interacts with others and with the self through this constantly shifting material" (Miller 2010: 31). Miller ends his subchapter on the sari with the general observation that "there are a multitude of different expectations and experiences that are a direct result of wearing a particular item of clothing" (2010: 31).

Bruno Latour has proposed what he calls Actor Network Theory (ANT). He sees things as actors and as parts of networks. His most famous example is that of a hotel key that, because of its added weight, hinders the guests from putting it in their pockets and taking it with them. The physicality of the key resists attempts to steal it, which, according to Latour, makes the key an actor in its own right (Latour 1991: 104; Malafouris 2013: 124ff). Applying this to clothes, we observe, for instance, that high-heeled shoes change the posture of the body. They lift it up, make the hind part more prominent, make the legs look longer, transmit sexual signals, and hinder fast walking and running. High-heeled shoes are actors and communicators at the same time and part of a strongly gendered hierarchy. The monastic hood, when drawn down so that it covers much of the face, limits the wearer's view of the surroundings and acts directly on his or her range of perception.

Lambros Malafouris has taken the material actor approach to a new level, proposing an ambitious theory about the extended mind and material engagement, which he calls Material Engagement Theory (2013). In his view, things take a direct part in human cognitive processes. He sees material objects and cultural artifacts "as continuous integral parts of the human cognitive architecture" (Malafouris 2010: 266). He returns repeatedly to a classic example, used, for instance, by Maurice Merleau-Ponty and Gregory Bateson, about the blind man and his stick. Malafouris asks the pertinent question: "Where does the blind man's self end and the world begin?" The point is that the stick becomes part of the blind man's perceptual system and transforms touch into sight (Malafouris 2013: 5). Malafouris uses this example to show the plasticity of the human mind and the continuity between minds and things (2013: 243–244). The human mind extends beyond the body and interacts with things.

Malafouris points out not only that things take part in cognitive processes but also that the mind does not necessarily need mental representations when it thinks through things in action. This is what he calls "enactive signification." This type of signification, he contends, liberates agency from the notion of intentionality traditionally associated with it. Accordingly, a material sign should not be reduced to a linguistic sign. In the book at hand, Malafouris's insights are used to counteract reducing clothes to their linguistic meanings, as well as to shed light on possible functions that the processes of making thread, textiles, and garments had in the life of the Egyptian monastics (see Chapter 5).

In addition to theoretical perspectives that focus on the communicative aspect of clothes, combined with theories about their psychological functions and agency, this book has been inspired by studies of clothes. Before the 1980s, studies on clothes were very rare.[20] Clothes have traditionally been regarded as relatively unimportant as study objects. It is perhaps telling that in studies of clothes, the percentage of female authors and editors is particularly high (Kloss 2016: 22). According to Ian Gilligan, in "archaeology, clothing is the invisible invention of the invisible sex—so at least it has been, until quite recently" (2019: 17). The lack of general interest represents, of course, a gross underestimation of the implications and the significance of what it means to be the only clothed species.

After the 1980s, there has been a growing research interest, not only generally in clothes but also in specific periods, such as antiquity and the Middle Ages. Anthropological studies on dress and clothes in contemporary societies have increased as well (see Hansen 2004). I will not present a broad research history here but content myself with mentioning some of the books that have been especially helpful to this study. Additional books and articles are referred to throughout this book. The academic literature on clothes that is of special relevance for this study can be divided into three groups: (1) studies of clothes in present-day societies, which include two subgroups, anthropological studies of clothes and studies of fashion; (2) studies of clothes in antiquity; and (3) studies with a special focus on clothes, worn by ancient Christians, including monastic garments.

In recent studies on clothes, one can observe a clear tendency to combine their symbolic interpretation with explanations of their material functions and how they operate, as well as viewing the state of being dressed as an embodied experience. According to sociologist Joanne Entwistle (2000: 344),

> the study of dress as situated practice requires moving between, on the one hand, the discursive and representational aspects of dress and the way the body/dress is caught up in relations of power, and on the other hand, the embodied experience of dress and the use of dress as one means by which individuals orientate themselves to the social world.

According to Anna-Karina Hermkens, "clothing is intertwined with gender, social, and ethnic identity" and "actually gives material form to social categories and hierarchies" (Hermkens 2010: 231–232).[21]

Regarding the study of ancient clothes in particular, there is a growing field of research on clothes as well as on ancient textile industries, trading centers, and trade routes for wool, linen, textiles, and clothes. Examples of recent studies on ancient clothes are Kristi Upson-Saia's *Early Christian Dress: Gender, Virtue, and Authority* (2011), a commentary on authority connected to hierarchy and gender, and N. K. Rollason's analysis of ancient clothing gifts in *Gifts of Clothing in Late Antique Literature* (2016). In addition, a small and highly specialized research literature on Coptic textiles and clothing is also to be noted. Monastic clothes constitute a subfield, mainly seen in works by scholars who are especially interested in the material aspects of dress, such as Anne Boud'hors and Maria Mossakowska-Gaubert (Boud'hors 2009; Mossakowska-Gaubert 2004, 2015, 2017), who studied actual garments and tried to determine more specifically to which garments the various vestimentary terms refer.

Equally important are recent attempts to theorize dress and to see it as having agency. According to Carly Daniel-Hughes, scholars of religions have been "overlooking the possibility that dress, and embodied practice generally, is not imitative of religious identity and culture, but in fact, productive of it as well" (Daniel-Hughes 2011: 12). In Introduction to the edited volume *Dressing Judeans and Christians in Antiquity*, Alicia J. Batten, Carly Daniel-Hughes, and Kristi Upson-Saia state that "the study of dress enables us to understand the values, worldviews, and priorities of ancient people, as well as the social dynamics and structures of their communities, which are expressed in and negotiated through styles and modes of dressing" (2014: 7). There is a growing interest in how dress mediates between individual and society (Upson-Saia et al. 2014: 9). Rebecca Krawiec has fruitfully pursued this approach in the study of the clothes of ancient Egyptian monastics (2009, 2014). According to her, "Monastic dress—like the monastic body itself—brings to the fore the paradox between transcendent perfection and material imperfection in the monastic life" (2009: 126). She stresses that monastic clothing "for both male and female monks, indicates paradoxically both the monks' humility and their religious authority" (Krawiec 2009: 131; see also 133).[22]

The book

The theme of this book is clothing and garments among ancient monastics and ascetics in Egypt, but with a broader outlook to the general meaning and function of clothes as well as to their long history. Clothes are seen as an extended part of humans, the outer form, which shape who we are and how we experience and interact with the world. The study is built on the presupposition that there was a close connection between the monastics and ascetics and their clothing. When clothes are scarce and the monastic habit functions as a uniform and an external form of the monastic, it is reasonable to assume that they were experienced as a significant part of the person wearing them to a high degree.[23]

I agree with Roland Barthes when he says that clothing "concerns all of the human person, all the body, all the relationships of Man to body as well as the relationships of the body to society" (Barthes 2013: 90), but I want to combine an interpretation of the meaning of clothes with an attempt to grasp embodied experiences of being clothed and, to a certain extent, also view clothes as actors. Accordingly, clothes are conceived of as something that is made, a medium through which the world is experienced, objects to which things happen, actors acting on their wearers and their surroundings, and, finally, signs that communicate and are interpreted.

Why choose monastic clothes in late antiquity as a subject of study? What does this period and the clothing of ancient ascetics have to offer to the general study of religion and the study of clothes? What makes ancient monks and nuns especially interesting in a study of the function and meaning of clothes?

Late antiquity is a period of religious change, when a new religion, Christianity, evolved and gradually became dominant. The official recognition of Christianity in the fourth century was parallel to the establishment of desert asceticism as an ideal practice and to the growth and institutionalization of monasticism (Frankfurter 2018: 6). The institutionalization of monasticism included the development of a monastic habit, a process that implied continuity as well as innovation.

When referring to the first centuries of its development, "Christianity" can be considered an umbrella term for a wide range of groups and doctrines, partly in conflict with each other, as reflected, for instance, in the flourishing Christian genre of heresiology. An extreme and durable figure, the ascetic, developed gradually and spread across various groups and doctrines. Along with restrictions on food and sleep, a striking characteristic of the ascetics is their renunciation of sexuality and procreation. Renunciation is directly associated with the goal of transcending the earthly existence and becoming a spiritual, angelic kind of being.

The ancient ascetics and monastics were the religious heroes who incorporated these new ideals. The monk was a type of Christian male who renounced procreation—a type of male that Mathew Kuefler labelled "the manly eunuch" (Kuefler 2001).[24] Female monastics and ascetics have been subject to much research, but they are harder to interpret, as ancient females usually are, because they are part of men's descriptions.[25] This means that they are often seen negatively and, though in some cases also idealized and highly praised, simply ignored usually.

While certain types of clothes were associated with ancient ascetics, the creation of a specific monastic dress was intricately connected to more profound social and religious developments, including a routinization of asceticism. Ascetic groups were created and kept together not only by means of sacred texts and holy rituals, but also through the things that circulated in the monasteries and among the ascetics (Gilhus 2018a). The ideal principle of the ascetic and monastic groups was to own very little, which means that the things they had were the most significant, necessary, and basic. Among those things were books and clothes as well. And while clothes tend to withdraw from awareness, this is not necessarily so with monastic clothes, which are frequently brought into focus in various genres of ancient sources.

The ascetic and monastic groups of Egypt and Syria had a lasting influence on monastic life and on the types of garments that became part of it. What Pachomius and his followers wore and the ideals that their garments incorporated and conveyed are the ancestors of the garbs of present-day monastics. Accordingly, the garments of the Egyptian monastics are important because they belong to a period of transition in the history of Christianity, are part of the origin of an extreme way of living, embody this way of living, and have an enduring influence on an elite type of Christian life. Basic functions and meanings of wearing clothes are reflected in the ways of dressing of the monastics. These clothes are also interesting because they are early examples of how clothes evolved into a uniform closely connected to their wearer.

Christianity is marked by an attempt at transcending the human biological category and establishing a new categorization of the world and living beings. The extended great chain of being is a theoretical model of the world where all beings, including superhuman ones, are ranked in a typological hierarchy. If humans are presupposed to be able to move higher up in the chain, how are clothes affected? While the use of clothes separates humans from animals, there exists a higher brand of clothing. The polar opposite of the garments of shame—the clothes that God made for Adam and Eve after they had eaten the forbidden fruit, which are sometimes interpreted as their physical bodies—are the garments of incorruptibility and salvation (see Chapters 2 and 8). The dress history of an individual Egyptian monastic, male or female, starts with the newborn baby, which—like all babies—was born naked but was then "very soon covered with clothes and thereby wrapped into culture" (Utriainen 2004: 135), went through transitions, through Egyptian secular clothing, journeyed to monastic habits, then to clothed and shrouded corpses, and finally to the glory of the heavenly dress.

The relevant sources are mainly sayings, travelogues, biographies, and normative texts, as well as images of dressed monastics and garments from monastic burials (see Chapter 3). The literary sources tend to present clothes in action: not only what the monastics were wearing, but also how their clothes interacted with them and how the monastics acted by means of their clothes. The clothes of ascetics and monastics contributed to produce monastic bodies and communities. We will analyze monastic clothes as part of ascetic communication and investigate their meanings and functions. At the same time, we will treat them as material things and explore how they interact with their wearers and their surroundings.

The book moves from the biblical and Near Eastern mythological background to ascetic and monastic clothes. It proceeds to the interaction between clothes and monastics and discusses the cognitive aspect of crafting and incorporating memories in clothes, discourse on clothes, clothes as mediators of authority, and vestimentary deviances and anomalous dressing. It ends with the dresses of the dead and clothes of salvation and with an attempt to pull the threads together.

After Chapter 1, the Introduction, Chapter 2 introduces the ancient Near Eastern mythological background of wilderness garments. It presents the use of clothes in the *Epic of Gilgamesh*, an epic connected to Uruk, one of the oldest cities in the world; continues with Genesis and the creation of the first two humans and their clothes; and concludes with the narratives in Kings about the sheepskin mantle (*melote*) of Elijah, inherited by Elisha, and how it got a new life among Egyptian monastics and ascetics. What are the functions and meanings of clothes in ancient Near Eastern mythology as reflected in these texts, and how are they relevant to ascetic and monastic conceptions of clothes?

Chapter 3 explores the monastic and ascetic life in Egypt in the fourth and fifth centuries. It investigates the complexity and varieties of ascetic life and the kinds of monastic dresses and items of clothing that were part of this life. It also discusses the various categories of sources and the relations between them, such as the relation between the normative description of clothes in the monastic rules and the depiction of clothes in action in the literary sources, and it discusses the origin of the monastic habit.

Chapter 4 examines how intimately monastic clothes were connected to the body, in what ways they interacted with the monastics, and what they did to their bodies. The chapter discusses the ritual life of clothes, their role when monastics were punished, and in the end how specific monastic clothes functioned as extensions of and restrictions to their bodies.

Chapter 5 discusses the production of textiles and clothes and the cognitive aspects of crafting. Its focus is on the interplay between the monastic mind and handiwork, such as making ropes, basketwork, weaving textiles, and making clothes, seen as a significant part of the monastic meditative life. The chapter further describes healing garments, and it discusses clothes as material memories. The chapter discusses how monastic memory was transmitted by means of clothes.

Chapter 6 investigates the values and ideals of the ascetic and monastic communities and the economy of salvation. This spiritual economy of salvation has a different value system than the economy of this world, but the two economies coexist in the ascetic and monastic communities, sometimes in cooperation and sometimes in conflict. As part of both economies, what roles did clothes play? A special focus is on clothes and authority and on how the tension and conflict between various types of authorities were generated and expressed through ascetic and monastic clothes.

Chapter 7 is about anomalous dressing and deviances from norms. It discusses ascetic nakedness, disguises, and cross-dressing. The chapter delves into the tension between orthodoxy and heresy to explore how this tension was channeled through clothes. What did it take for clothes to become heretic? How important were clothes as markers of heresy?

Chapter 8 deals with the clothes of the dead monastics and the clothes of the afterlife. Clothes in archaeological finds are witnesses to the moment of inhumation, when the dead body was clothed for eternity, shrouded, and disposed of in the grave. These finds show real clothes, but ones that are no longer part of this life. How was the monastic body dressed in death? Why was it dressed? What was the function of the shrouds that swaddled the dead body? When was the deceased buried naked? The second part of the chapter looks into the body seen as a garment, clothes of transition, and clothes of salvation.

The last chapter is the epilogue. It returns to the crocodile. The position of the crocodile is used as a point of departure for some final comments. The epilogue presents four dimensions of dress, which reflect the multiplicity of meanings and functions of clothes, including their metaphorical applications.

Notes

1 This apophthegm is recorded in one manuscript from the twelfth century (Bibliotheca Ambrosiana, Milan, C-30-Inf).
2 The elder's second sight, literally, his description as "clear-sighted" (*dioratikos*), explains why he understands what the crocodile says, though it does not explain why the crocodile has the power of speech in the first place. *Dioratikos* is used in patristic literature of prophetic insight or "second sight" of demons (Lampe 1997: 373).

3 On bathing and nakedness, see *Praecepta* 92 and the *Instructions of Horsiesios* 7.10 (see Chapter 7).

4 According to Terence S. Turner (2012: 486), "Man is born naked but is everywhere in clothes (or their symbolic equivalents)." His study of the Kayapo tribal people in the Amazon Rainforest has shown that, while they do not use clothing, they "possess a quite elaborate code of what could be called 'dress'" (Turner 2012: 487). "A closer look at Kayapo bodily adornment discloses that the apparently naked savage is as fully covered in fabric of cultural meaning as the most elaborately draped Victorian lady or gentleman" (Turner 2012: 488).

5 So called because it was written at the request of Lausus, a high-ranking official at the court of the Byzantine Emperor Theodosius II.

6 Additional meanings are "frame," "form," "attitude of body," "position," "action," "rank," and "appearance" (Lampe 1997: 1358–1359).

7 Recent research has shown that head lice underwent genetic mutations that can be explained by the introduction of clothes. According to David L. Reed and colleagues (2015), body lice diverged from their ancestors, the head lice, between 83,000 and 170,000 years ago, which means that sometime during this period, the purposeful parasites installed themselves in human garments; and they stayed there. One of the stories about Egyptian monastics warns against telling anybody "to remove lice from your beard, your head or your clothing" (*AP* N 592.64). While the reason for the prohibition is that this sort of intimate contact could lead to sexual acts, the account is also telling of the success story of *Pediculus humanus humanus*.

8 Skin taken from animals is very different from textiles that are fitted to shape, sewn, and made into clothes. It makes an enormous difference whether clothes are draped or fitted and whether they are layered or not. Gilligan describes "the widespread postglacial shift to the use of woven textiles" and sees global warming as a condition creating the need for new types of clothes in addition to or instead of the animal hide that was the earliest clothing material (2010b: 68, 2019). The new warm and humid climate made people sweat and created the need to rid themselves of moisture. Systematic fiber production and woven fabrics were responses to superfluous moisture as they provided enhanced permeability to perspiration. Gilligan suggests an alternative rationale for the transition to agriculture and farming where the production of fibers for textile clothing from domesticated plants and animals, for instance wool, plays a key role. In his view, the introduction of agriculture was more about textile than about food production (Gilligan 2007, 2019: 131ff.). Both sedentism and agriculture change humans' relationship to nature and the environment, and "the psychological connection with clothing is that sedentism, like agriculture, acts as a kind of enclosure" (Gilligan 2019: 209).

9 Armin W. Geertz has suggested 70,000 years (2010: 312), and recent finds in the Blombos Cave in South Africa suggest that an earlier date is more correct (Henshilwood et al. 2018). In the cave, the researchers found an abstract drawing where red ocher pigment was intentionally applied to a ground silcrete flake. The drawing is an estimated 73,000 years old (Henshilwood et al. 2018).

10 Traces of fibers of flax and wool have been detected in the Dzudzuana Cave in the Caucasus. According to carbon analyses, these strands are 36,000 years old (Balter 2009: 1329).

11 Textiles tend to succumb to the ravages of time and disappear. The oldest preserved woven fabric is from Peru and dates back to 11,000 years. Textile fragments from Neolithic times, made of flax, have been found in Egypt, as has the oldest known woven garment in the world, the Tarkhan dress, made of linen— cut, tailored, and fitted—and dating back to more than 5,000 years (Stevenson and Dee 2016).

12 In prehistoric Australia, clothes seem to have been used only occasionally and then basically as protection against the cold, while psychosocial functions were assigned to decorating the naked body (Gilligan 2010b).
13 According to Merlin Donald, artifacts "are static things, and undoubtedly serve as static storage devices, but their functions in the larger cultural matrix go well beyond mere storage, because they are in a dynamic interaction with the entire cognitive-cultural system in any living culture." (Donald 1998: 184).
14 Psalm 104:1b—2; RA 22, 170–171 in Foster 2005:85–88.
15 According to Peter Corrigan (2008: 155),

> Dress appears to have two major dimensions: it can be understood as an appearing surface that leads itself to interpretation (a phenomenon) and it can also be considered as an object in the world to which things may happen (a substance).

16 The linguistic turn is a rather broad term. It refers to philosophical and linguistic approaches of the twentieth century that stress the importance of language in human world-making. In the case of Barthes, it refers especially to the structuralism of Ferdinand de Saussure, which Barthes developed and used on objects of material culture.
17 Regarding the relationship between clothes and the self, the results of two older empirical psychological studies were inconclusive: "Preliminary evidence suggests that people differ in the extent to which they perceive clothing as the second skin and visible self" (Sontag and Schlater 1982: 7; see also Sontag and Lee 2004). However, with the more restricted wardrobe of the monastics, it is reasonable to believe that their clothes were tightly integrated with their *persona*. Adam and Galinsky experimented with people wearing lab coats and detected how it influenced their attentiveness and carefulness (2012, 2019). Some replica studies have criticized the stronger claim of Adam and Galinsky that "enclothed cognition has demonstrated effect on *how* we think rather than just what we think" (Burns et al. 2019: 155). Other articles support that clothing also can influence how we think (Adam and Galinsky 2019: 158). Adam and Galinsky conclude in a recent article that "the key tenet of enclothed cognition—clothing can have effect on how the wearer thinks, feels, and acts—appears to hold merit in at least some circumstances, and the question arises what these circumstances are?" (Adam and Galinsky 2019: 159).
18 A recent study of clothes along these lines concerns how hidden design features in sixteenth-century Ottoman court clothing most likely influenced the cognition of the wearer (Orakçıoğlu, Orakçıoğlu, and Fletcher 2016).
19 An early example of the idea that objects have a social life is found in *The Social Life of Things*, edited by Arjun Appadurai. Cambridge: Cambridge University Press, 1986.
20 Influential early examples of research on clothes are the contributions of Thorstein Veblen, "Dress as an Expression of Pecuniary Culture," in *The Theory of the Leisure Class* (1899) and J. C. Flügel, *The Psychology of Clothes* (1930).
21 Compared to earlier anthropological literature, recent literature is more interested in the materiality of clothes and in how they work on the body (Andrewes 2004; Hermkens 2010; Kloss 2016).
22 In addition to the specialized research on monastic and ascetic clothes, there is an extensive literature on Christian asceticism and monasticism. A new boost in the field began with Peter Brown's article, "The Rise and Function of the Holy Man in Late Antiquity" (1971) and resulted in a growing interest in the 1980s in ancient ascetic and monastic cultures and milieus. See Brown 1988; Bianchi 1985; Pearson and Goehring 1986; Rousseau 1985.

23 While the transition from secular clothes to the monastic habit is sometimes expressed as a dramatic moment with almost no going back, the sources also point to a difference between what monastics wore on festival days and their daily wear. This point will be discussed in Chapter 3.
24 See also Virginia Burrus 2000.
25 Some examples that include or focus on ascetic women are Brown 1988; Clark 1999; Elm 1994; Undheim 2018.

2 Heroes in the wilderness
The mythical background

Gilgamesh and the clothing code

The chapter adopts a longtime perspective on clothing codes and vestimentary imaginations, going back to ancient Near Eastern mythology, as found in the Epic of Gilgamesh, Genesis 2–3, and the *Books of Kings*. The Mesopotamian *Epic of Gilgamesh* belongs to the ancient Near Eastern culture, of which Genesis is a later offshoot. The point of departure and end of the epic is the ancient city of Uruk, a Sumerian city state and a driving force in the earliest urbanization of Mesopotamia with a flourishing textile industry of flax and wool. The epic reveals general meanings, structures, and functions of clothes, which are precursors of clothing codes and ideas discovered later. Genesis 2–3 and its interpretations offer insight into the Jewish and Christian understanding of humans as dressed beings. The prophets Elijah and Elisha in *Books of Kings* came to represent a monastic ideal, and their mantle was regarded as a mythological prototype for the monastic habit. What are the functions and meanings of clothes in ancient Near Eastern mythology as reflected in these texts? In what ways are the functions and meanings of clothes in the texts relevant to ascetic and monastic conceptions of clothes?

The *Epic of Gilgamesh* presents several outfits.[1] The standard version of the oldest epic in the world dates from *c.* 1200 BC, but parts of it go back to the early second millennium BC and include stories loosely based on older Sumerian traditions—the oldest published fragment of a Sumerian Gilgamesh poem is from the last part of the third millennium BC, the Ur III period (George 2003: 4–70). The latest copies of the epic found so far date from 100 BC. The epic is about close friendship, the terror of death, and the unfulfilled wish for immortality. It is also a heroic tale and a manual for kings. Status and psychological states are expressed through clothes, and the protagonists are clad in accordance with their moods and circumstances. Even the serpent, which plays a small but crucial part in the epic, changes its skin, thus symbolizing regeneration and the extension of life.

The narrative introduces us to the wild man Enkidu, who becomes Gilgamesh's bosom friend, and to the prostitute Shamhat, who treats him to his first sexual experience and initiates him to civilization, including the wearing of clothes. Similar to Genesis, nakedness, sexuality, and the distinctiveness from animals are part of the narrative. But unlike Genesis, clothes are described as an already established part of a developed civilization. However, in another Mesopotamian myth, and similar to Genesis, the first humans did not know about the wearing of clothes: "The humans of those far-off days did not know the eating of bread, did not know the wearing of clothes. The people were naked-limbed, eating grass with their mouths like sheep, drinking water from ditches."[2]

Clothes in the epic range between two extremes. One extreme is the hairy nakedness of Enkidu. His hairiness is connected to his original coexistence with animals in the wilderness. In his pre-civilized state, Enkidu is "clad in a garment like Shakkan's" (George 2003: 545). In Mesopotamian mythology, Shakkan was the lord of animals and as hairy as his subjects (George 2003: 790). This means that Enkidu bears similarities to the animals among which he lived, which are "clad" in their fur. A faint echo of this way of living in the wilderness, being hairy and without clothes, is later heard in the stories about some of the desert ascetics (Mobley 1997: 217).

The other extreme in the epic's range of clothes are the festive garments of civilized city life. In the cities, people wash themselves, drink beer, wear clothes, and, in short, live life to its full. In their most elaborate dress, humans attract gods. This attraction is either deliberate, as when the mother of Gilgamesh, Ninsun, dresses herself in a fine dress and jewelry to call on Shamash, the sun god (*Gilgamesh*, III 39–42), or is unintended, as when Gilgamesh, after having slain the monster Humbaba, cleanses himself, dresses in kingly robes with his crown, and attracts Ishtar, the goddess of love and war (*Gilgamesh*, VI 1–5).

In the episode of the wild man Enkidu and the prostitute Shamhat, clothes have both a sexual dimension and a civilizing function. When Shamhat is encouraged to sleep with Enkidu as a means of removing him from the animal world and transferring him to the world of humans, she is urged: "Spread your clothing, so he may lie on you, treat the man to the work of a woman!" (*Gilgamesh*, I 184–185). Undressing is part of having sex. Her clothing is used as a blanket to lie on (George 2003: 796), and "Shamhat let loose her shirts, she bared her sex and he took in her charms. She showed no fear, she took in his scent: she spread her clothing and he lay upon her" (*Gilgamesh*, I 188–191). The result of their intercourse is that the animals flee away from Enkidu, because his mating with a woman made him a stranger to the animal world. His joining the human world is described as a series of steps in the process of being clothed. As a "first aid," Shamhat shares her clothes with Enkidu: "She stripped off her clothing, dressed him in one part, the other part she put on herself" (*Gilgamesh*, P 70–71). Later, a new stage in the civilizing process of Enkidu takes place when "the barber treated his body so hairy" (*Gilgamesh*, P 106). His hairiness, and thus his similarity to animals, is removed. The final part of the civilizing process is when his garments are brought in line with his new role, and he "put on a garment, becoming like a warrior, he took up his weapon to do battle with the lions" (*Gilgamesh*, P 110–111). Clothes are a demand of civilized life and have a civilizing function. In the case of Enkidu, the clothes are those of a warrior hero, one who is destined to become the friend of King Gilgamesh and do heroic deeds together with him.

Much of the *Epic of Gilgamesh* is about travels and expeditions between worlds. Laura Feldt and Ulla Susanne Koch have recently described the epic in relation to three worlds—the world of wild animals (Nature), the human world (Culture), and the world of the gods (Supernature)—arguing that the epic's concern is to maintain the proper boundaries between these worlds (2011). They characterize the boundaries between the worlds as spaces and mediating zones where exchanges and encounters take place (Feldt and Koch 2011: 113).

When clothes are part of these exchanges and encounters, they are harmonized with the actions of the heroes and their state of mind.[3] This makes it fruitful to see clothing as one of the codes of the epic. The clothing code is developed in the tension between the two extremes, the festive dress of the city and the hairiness of the wilderness, and mainly displayed in the encounters that take place in the intermediate zones between the three worlds.

The main plot-driving element in the epic is the death of Enkidu, which prompts Gilgamesh to embark on a quest for immortality. He discards his festive dress (*Gilgamesh*, VII 46–49) and goes into the wilderness where he wears pelt or hides and is fearful to look at (*Gilgamesh*, X 5–6). His "body is tousled with matted hair; the beauty of whose flesh the hides have ruined" (*Gilgamesh*, XI 251–252). Animal skins make a suitable garment for a royal hero roaming the space between civilization and wilderness. It is a wilderness garb befitting an existence betwixt and between worlds.

The clothing code in the epic expresses the aristocratic civilized life in the cities as opposed to wanderings in the wilderness and as a contrast between clothes that are new and fresh and clothes that are dirty or worn out. When Gilgamesh heads for the alehouse at the end of the world and says, "I had not reached as far as the ale-wife, my clothing was worn out" (*Gilgamesh*, X 258), the keeper of the alehouse, Shiduri, describes his clothes: "He is clad in a *mashhandu*-garment, instead of. . . , instead of a belt, a cord of . . ." (*Gilgamesh*, X 274–275). According to George, this is a garment worn for warmth, "evidently in this context it is a rude item of no sophistication" (George 2003: 874). Shiduri wishes for him: "Let your clothes be clean! Let your head be washed, may you be bathed in water!" (*Gilgamesh*, Si III 10–11).

Since clothes are social markers, to reduce a person's status is, among other things, to mess with his or her clothes. When Enkidu is dying, he curses Shamhat for the destiny she has brought unto him and includes her clothes in his curse: "May the ground defile your fine-looking garment! May the drunkard smear with dust your festive gown!" (Gilgamesh, Ur 16–17).

In the *Epic of Gilgamesh*, clothes are markers of status, mood, and space. The contrast between clean and unclean clothes, linen and wool versus animal hides, and between torn and untorn clothes is part of the expressive repertoire of the clothing code.[4] Such characteristics are, in the main, universal aspects of clothing codes. Of special interest in relation to the later monastic garments are the versions of wilderness clothing in the epic. These garments include the nakedness and hairiness of Enkidu, closely connected to the world of animals, and Gilgamesh's garb of pelt, which he wears when he roams the intermediate zones between the worlds of animals, humans, and gods.

Before we turn to Genesis and to how clothes affected the first humans, and from there to the mantles of prophets and monastics, we will pose a final question regarding the *Epic of Gilgamesh*, a question, which points forward to ideas about clothes of salvation in later times (see Chapter 8): in what ways does clothing refer to immortality?

The skin-sloughing serpent and its dust-eating descendant

The wish for immortality is implied in the unchangeable garments that Uta-napishti, the survivor of the great flood, gives Gilgamesh on his way back to his kingdom, the city state of Uruk:

> Let him cast off his hides, and the sea carry (them away)!
> Soak his body so fair!
> Let the kerchief of his head be renewed!
> Let him be clad in a royal robe, the attire befitting his dignity!
>
> Until he goes (home) to his city,
> until he arrives at (the end of) his road,
> let the robe show no stain but stay brand new!
>
> (*Gilgamesh*, XI 255–261)

According to Andrew R. George, Uta-napishti contrasts the lot of kings with the lot of fools, using clothes as markers. Gilgamesh has behaved like a fool in his quest for immortality, dressed in ragged skin and eating raw meat, but he is now dressed in royal robes (George 1999: xliii). The clothes that Uta-napishti bestows on Gilgamesh are made to resist the natural processes of clothes, that is, dirt and tear. In other words, they have a sort of inalterability, the very quality that Gilgamesh unsuccessfully seeks for himself. While "his robes" seem to have been given the quality of permanence, the epic's conclusion is that for humans, permanence and immortality are unattainable. The only attainable goal is to live one's life to the full and gain a hero's reputation after death. The monumental city walls of Uruk, which were discovered by archaeologists in the twentieth century, were allegedly built by Gilgamesh. They gave him, according to the epic, such posthumous fame that it compensates in a way for his mortality. In line with this message, the epic begins and ends with a description of these walls.

However, almost as an afterthought, and before Gilgamesh leaves the realm of Uta-napishti, the latter is gently urged by his wife to reveal to Gilgamesh the existence of a certain plant that has the power to rejuvenate. Uta-napishti has, along with his wife, achieved immortality, so he might be regarded as an expert in these matters. Gilgamesh picks the plant from the bottom of the sea, but, unfortunately, his rejuvenation is not meant to be: while he is bathing in a pool, he leaves the plant on the shore, only for a serpent to appear on the scene and bear the plant off, and "as it turned away it sloughed a skin" (*Gilgamesh*, XI 307). The plant works as promised, but it is the serpent, not Gilgamesh, who benefits from its effects. The serpent gains a new skin, which symbolizes regeneration. Like Gilgamesh's unchanging garment hints vaguely to the theme of permanent life, a second, perhaps inferior, form of permanence—rejuvenation—is revealed when the serpent sloughs its skin.[5]

It has frequently been pointed out that the *Epic of Gilgamesh* influenced Genesis 2–3, which is regarded as a reinterpretation of several motifs present in the epic (Römer 2012). A comparison between the two reveals both similarities and differences. The two texts belong roughly to the same cultural sphere and work with similar protagonists and themes, but in different ways and with different intentions. Duane E. Smith has particularly pointed out the roles of the serpent and of an immortality plant, the Tree of Life (2015: 47). Adam, initially alone with the animals and afterwards joined by Eve, is seen as a parallel to Enkidu and Shamhat.[6] As in the *Epic of Gilgamesh*, Shamhat clothes Enkidu, in Genesis, Yahweh clothes the two humans (*Gilgamesh*, P 70–71 and Genesis 3:2).[7] As part of the process of their integration into the world of humans, both Enkidu and Adam are dressed, and for both the dressing takes place in two stages. Enkidu is first dressed in the garments of Shamhat and then in the garments of a warrior/hunter/hero. The primordial couple eats the fruit that the serpent offers: "Then the eyes of both were opened, and they knew that they were naked; and they sewed fig leaves together and made loincloths for themselves" (Genesis 3:7). Adam and Eve first cover themselves with fig leaves and are then dressed by God in tunics of skin: when God walks in the garden in the evening, they hide from him and reveal that they realize their nakedness. God understands that they have eaten the forbidden fruit and punishes them: from now on, woman shall bring forth children in pain and man in toil shall eat of the earth (Genesis 3:16–19). Then "the Lord God made garments of skins for the man and for his wife and clothed them" (Genesis 3:21) and expelled them from the garden (Genesis 3:22–24).

A difference between Genesis and the *Epic of Gilgamesh* is that in the *Epic of Gilgamesh*, clothing is a part of the civilizing process and regarded as something positive, while in Genesis, humans are equipped with clothes as a result of their transgression and fall. Nevertheless, the result is the same: a gradual integration into the world of humans.

In a way similar to that in the *Epic of Gilgamesh*, in Genesis humans are denied immortality, for before they can proceed to the next level and eat from the Tree of Life and live forever, they are hindered by Yahweh, who drives them out of Eden (Genesis 3:22–24). Both stories feature a serpent, but the serpents' fates differ. In the *Epic of Gilgamesh*, the serpent gets away with stealing the plant and receives a reward from what it has done: a new skin. In Genesis, after the serpent gets Eve to eat from the Tree of Knowledge of Good and Evil, it is punished and transformed in an explicitly negative way:

The Lord God said to the serpent:

> Because you have done this, cursed are you among all animals and among all the wild creatures; upon your belly you shall go, and dust you shall eat all the days of your life.
>
> (Genesis 3:14)

Although the origin and mythological context of the bold serpent are unknown, we do know that serpents in Mesopotamia frequently had metaphysical qualities. In contrast, the serpent in Genesis is explicitly said to be one of God's creatures (Genesis 3:1; see also Mikaelsson 1980: 89).

The *Epic of Gilgamesh* and Genesis 2–3 feature similar themes: the place of humans in the world, their relation to animals, the meaning of gender, the cycle of sexuality and death, and—not least—immortality denied. The function and meaning of clothes are part of these scenarios of cultural origins. Both texts afford a wide range of possible interpretations, reflected in a vast literature of ancient commentaries on Genesis and modern research. Scholars have probed the different interpretative possibilities, including making comparisons between the two texts. Ancient Christian interpreters of Genesis reshuffled the themes and turned immortality into an attainable goal. As part of these exegetical processes, new interpretations of the clothing of Genesis were developed: the fig leaves and the tunics of skin were given new meanings.

Interpreting fig leaves and tunics of skin

Clothes are at the heart of the biblical story of creation and include both the fig leaves and the garments of skin. Ancient theologians offered various interpretations of these garments, and the variety of their interpretations spanned from literal to metaphorical understandings. Clothes were intertwined with human origin, fall, and even salvation, because some exegetes identified the tunic of skin with the human body, a view, which was contested by others. Clothes in Jewish and Christian interpretation were intimately connected to the human condition, and these interpretations informed ascetic and monastic life and practices.

The fig leaves and tunics of skin represent the two main types of materials for cloth production: plants and animal hides. Garments made from fig leaves are described as the most primitive type of clothes, though they too have been worked on by being sewn together. That this is the only biblical reference for people completely clad in garments made from skins (Zwickel 2019: 193) shows that these garments are rather special.

How do the fig leaves and the tunics of skin relate to each other? How did God make the tunics of skin, and why did he dress his two human creatures? Did animals have to pay with their lives to keep humans clothed? Or did "garments of skin," like the Hellenistic-Jewish philosopher, Philo from Alexandria, thought, symbolize the fleshly body of humans? Philo was roughly contemporary of Jesus, writing several hundred years after the Genesis narratives were created.[8] He interpreted the story of creation in line with contemporary Platonic philosophy and saw humans as layered beings. In his view, the two accounts of human creation, Genesis 1:27 and Genesis 2:7, are narratives of the creation of the human spirit and of the soul, respectively. Philo sees the tunic of skin as the corruptible outer layer of human beings, "for it was fitting that the intellect and the outward sense should be clothed in a body as in a garment of skins," and he shows how vestmental metaphors help to think about human constitution (*Questions and Answers on Genesis* 1.53).[9]

Were humans in Philo's interpretation still naked after the body of flesh had been added to their original constitution? Did the two humans put on the same fig leaves that they had earlier sewn into loincloths, or did they skip underwear? Did their clothes, whatever they were, elude Philo's description because he did not find them important enough to mention, or did he think that Adam's and Eve's new fleshly nakedness was to be taken care of later as part of their living outside Eden? Why did he interpret "the tunics of skin" as something other than clothes? Philo comments on the last matter: "Perhaps someone may laugh at the expressions here used, considering the small value of the garments thus made, as if they were not at all worthy of the labour of a Creator of such dignity and greatness." But when one understands the "real" meaning of "the garments made of skin," they deserve "to be looked upon as a more noble possession than a purple robe embroidered with various colours" (Philo, *Questions and Answers on Genesis* 1.53). The Alexandrian exegete introduces the purple robe to better explain the meaning of the simple tunics of skin. Actual garments were apparently of so little significance to Philo that their literal meaning could not really be what the Genesis passage described.

The tunics of skin continued to challenge ancient exegetes in the centuries to come (Reuling 2006: 17).[10] Since the Hebrew words *kotnôt 'ôr*, which means "tunics of skin" sound similar to *kotnôt 'ôr*, meaning "tunics of light", some rabbis made a distinction between the garments of light, which

Adam and Eve had worn before their expulsion from Eden, and the garments of skin that they wore afterwards (*Genesis Rabbah* 20.12.1). Obviously, those learned men did not want to think of the first couple as having been stark naked.[11] What sort of skin were the tunics made of? The ancient rabbis made a list of suggestions: for instance, that they were made of goat's skin; hare's skin; "skin with its wool"; "Circassian wool, and these were used [later] by first-born children"; camel's wool; or wool of hares (*Genesis Rabbah* 20.12.3–4). Others claimed that they were made from the skin of the scheming serpent. At a later time, these tunics were sometimes made from the skin of the terrifying sea monster Leviathan, which, according to Jewish lore, had been slaughtered and preserved by God.

According to Robert A. Oden, "both the verb for the act of clothing and the garment mentioned in Genesis 3:21 are words used in significant contexts. These contexts are those of status marking" (Oden 1987: 100–101). Oden objects to the traditional theological explanation that sees God's equipping humans with clothes as a generous act (Oden 1987: 97). "Yahweh's act in presenting clothing to the man and the woman is not a gracious concession. It is an authoritative marking of the pair as beings who belong to a sphere distinct from that of the divine" (Oden 1987: 104). The dividing function of clothes, which serve not only to mark status but also to separate humans from worlds in which they do not belong, is part of what happens to clothes in this myth. That the first humans' clothes divided them from the divine is a reasonable interpretation. At the same time, clothes obviously also divided humans from animals. However, there were exegetes who saw clothes as something that widened the gap between the divine and the human and, in fact, reconnected humans to animals. Augustine is the most prominent example, as we will see later.

Christian authors were as puzzled by these divinely made clothes as were their Jewish contemporaries. Some, like Philo, leaned toward allegorical interpretations, and some of these Christian exegetes had read Philo. In his treatise *On the Apparel of Women*, Tertullian asks rhetorically, "And do you think about adorning yourself over and above your tunics of skin?" (1.1). Origen is usually seen as the most prominent advocate of the tunics-of-skins-are-bodies interpretation:

> And the statement that the man who was cast out of the garden with the woman was clothed with 'coats of skins,' which God made for those who had sinned on account of the transgression of mankind, has a certain secret and mysterious meaning, superior to the Platonic doctrine of the descent of the soul which loses its wings and is carried downwards to earth.
>
> (*Contra Celsum* 4.40)[12]

The words are cryptic, but Origen seems to share Plato's view of an original superior state of the soul. However, he trades the Platonic image of the soul, which has lost its wings, for the biblical concept of the "tunics of skins" (Reuling 2006: 75). Origen reads the skin tunics in *Leviticus* as hide taken from animals and as symbols of human mortality (*Homilies on Leviticus* 6.2. 7). In what is preserved of his writings, it is not entirely clear that he favored any one solution to the question of what these tunics were, but later critics read him as saying that the tunics of skin referred to bodies (see Layton 2013: 260; Reuling 2006: 75–76).

More than a hundred years after Origen, Epiphanius, bishop of Salamis, speaks in his florid and polemic way against Origen's views on the tunics of skin:

> I pass over his idle explanations of the coats of skins, and say nothing of the efforts and arguments he has used to induce us to believe that these coats of skin represent human bodies. Among many other things, he says this: 'Was God a tanner or a saddler, that He should prepare the hides of animals, and should stitch from them coats of skin for Adam and Eve?' 'It is clear', he [Origen] goes on, 'that he is speaking of human bodies.'[13]

Epiphanius opposes allegorical interpretations of Scripture on a general basis, and, in line with this attitude, he interprets the tunics literally.

Christian writers in Alexandria read both Philo and Origen and followed their lead. According to Didymus the Blind, "the body is the skin tunics," and the tunic *cum* body is related to sin (Layton 2013: 162; Reuling 2006: 73). For Ambrose of Milan, the tunics refer to "the post-lapsarian human condition and the loss of the primordial glory" (Reuling 2006: 109). Didymus and Ambrose share a spiritual approach to Scripture and hunt for hidden meanings (see Reuling 2006: 112–114). Two texts in the Nag Hammadi Codices, which were probably part of a fourth- or fifth-century monastic library (Lundhaug and Jenott 2015), reflect similar interpretations of the garments of skins. The *Apocryphon of John* describes how the creator God cast Adam and Eve out of the garden and "clothed them in gloomy darkness" (NHC II,1 24:6–8). The *Interpretation of Knowledge* refers to the tunic that Adam got from the beast and bluntly calls it "a garment of condemnation" (NHC XI,1 11:27–28). In both texts, the tunics are disastrous signs of the fallen bodily existence.

Several Christian authors rejected the view that the tunics were bodies. Clement of Alexandria (*c.* 200), referring to Julius Cassianus, an encratite, says that "Cassian thinks the 'tunics of skin' are our bodies." (*Stromata* 3.14). Clement distances himself from this view. Methodius (*c.* 300) stresses that "the question has already been raised and answered, that the 'coats of skin' are not bodies" (*Discourse on the Resurrection* 1.2). Irenaeus saw God's making of tunics as an act of compassion (*Against the Heresies* 3.23.5).[14] Similarly, John Chrysostom (350–407) pointed out that the garments were made by God to protect Adam and Eve (*Homilies* 18).[15]

But among the Christian thinkers who opposed the idea that the tunics of skins were bodies, there was a tendency to interpret them as a physical sign of bodily existence and fall at the same time. Origen and, later, Augustine return repeatedly to the tunics and make them part of their evolving thinking about the human predicament.

Augustine mentions the "coats of skins" on several occasions, associating them to the consequence of Adam's sin, which is human mortality (*Confessiones* 7.24; 13.16). To him, they are part of the downward movement of humans to the realm of animals:

> so the slippery motion of falling away takes possession of the negligent only gradually, and beginning from a perverse desire for the likeness of God, arrives in the end at the likeness of beasts. Hence it is that being naked of their first garment, they earned by mortality coats of skins.
>
> (*On the Trinity* 12.11)[16]

Augustine asks rhetorically: "What more effective indication, after all, can be given of the death, which we are aware of in the body, than skins which are flayed as a rule from dead cattle?" He ends this passage concluding that the punishment for going against God was that man "was cast down into the mortal condition of monstrous beasts" (*On Genesis: A Refutation of the Manichees* 2.32). Augustine uses the tunics of skin, which, together with the fig leaves, separate humans from animals, to draw humans closer to the life and state of animals.

In *The Literal Meaning of Genesis*, Augustine's elaboration on the new bestial state of humans takes another turn when he says that

> their bodies contracted that liability to disease and death which is present in the flesh of animals—and thus also that motion of the genitals which stirs in animals the desire to mate, and so ensures the birth of young to take the place of those which die.
>
> (*The Literal Meaning of Genesis* 11.42; see also 11.52)

Augustine, who set the pace for Christian thinking for centuries to come, made a point of showing that human beings, because of the fall and through their garments of skins, share the sexual urge with animals and partake in the vicious circle of procreation and death.

The Genesis narrative is an authoritative account of the human predicament, including the relationship with animals, gender differences, and female subordination. When the Christian interpreters of Genesis identified the tunics of skins with bodies or used them metaphorically to describe the human condition, they did it as part of a master narrative of origin, fall, and salvation. For many of the ancient exegetes, the first humans' clothes were overshadowed by their allegorical and metaphorical meanings, but it is exactly the extensive metaphorical use of clothes that indicates their general significance in human life.

The mantle of Elijah and Elisha

Both the *Epic of Gilgamesh* and Genesis associate clothes with the human condition and present persistent meaning structures and functions of these clothes. The Genesis narrative and its interpreters associate clothes particularly with human origin and fall and the narrative has a general relevance for ascetic monastic life and practices and for how they try to reverse the fall. In comparison, the narratives about the mantle of Elijah in *Books of Kings* have a more direct relevance for monastic garments, as the mantle works as a prototype for one of the items in the monastic habit, the *melote*, a garment made of fleece.

Most striking is that the narratives of Elijah and Elisha in the *Books of Kings* are filled with miraculous events (1 Kings 17–19 and 2 Kings 4–7). Elijah is first fed by ravens and then from the magical jar belonging to the widow in Zarpath, resurrects the widow's son from the dead, gets rain to return after drought, has fire from heaven set fire to his sacrifice, and is finally taken up to heaven in a chariot of fire and leaves his sheepskin/mantle (*melote*) behind for Elisha to pick up (2 Kings 2:13–14). Elisha inherits the mantle:

> He picked up the mantle of Elijah that had fallen from him and went back and stood on the bank of the Jordan. He took the mantle of Elijah that had fallen from him, and struck the water, saying, "Where is the Lord, the God of Elijah?" When he had struck the water, the water was parted to the one side and to the other, and Elisha went over.
>
> (2 Kings 2:13–14)

Elisha continues the wonder-working activity of his predecessor. He divides the water of the Jordan; curses children who have mocked him, which results in two bears immediately coming out of the woods and killing forty-two boys; cleanses water; makes a tiny amount of oil multiply; and heals people.[17]

The mantle of Elijah is mentioned five times.[18] The first is when Yahweh is about to reveal himself in the form of an extreme meteorological phenomena (1 Kings 19:11–12), and Elijah hid in a cave and wrapped his face in his mantle (1 Kings 19:13). The next time is when Elijah finds Elisha ploughing and casts his mantle over him without saying anything (1 Kings 19:19). The mantle is the sign of a prophet, and, in casting it, Elijah declares Elisha a prophet. Elisha immediately decides to follow Elijah. Later in the narrative, Elijah takes his mantle, folds it, and divides the waters of Jordan with a strike (2 Kings 2:8). When Elijah invites Elisha to request something from him, Elisha asks him to "please, let a double portion of your spirit be to me" (2 Kings 2:9). When Elijah is taken up to heaven and leaves his mantle behind, it is now Elisha's turn to use the mantle: he strikes the Jordan river with it—apparently, he has to strike twice and call on Yahweh before the waters part, as they did for Elijah, and Elisha walks over. No more is said about the mantle in Kings.

Elijah's mantle is endowed with authority and functions as a sign of the prophetic office (see also Zech. 13:4).[19] The mantle is a physical link between the two prophets, which Elisha wears as Elijah's successor. Elijah's casting of the mantle over Elisha has sometimes been seen as an initiation as well as an imitation of the act of adopting a child. Since Elisha asks to receive a double share of Elijah's spirit, it is easy to interpret the mantle as a symbol or even as a physical expression of the presence of this spirit. The mantle directly reveals its power in two instances, which mirror each other. The first is when Elijah uses it to part the waters of Jordan; the second is when Elisha does the same, which shows that the transfer of power from the former to the latter has been successful. The mantle makes things happen and is a physical expression of the power of the two prophets—or even its source. It transforms Elisha twice, first into Elijah's apprentice and then into his successor. It is a garment of transformation and power.

Centuries later, Christian evangelists had the clothing of John the Baptist recall and refer to Elijah's mantle in 2 Kings 1:8. According to Mark, John "was clothed (*endedumenos*) with camel's hair" (1:6a). Matthew says that he wore "clothing (*endyma*) of camel's hair" (3:4a); likewise, Matthew has Jesus connecting him directly to Elijah: "He is the Elijah who was to come" (Matt. 11:14; see also Luke 1:17).[20] Elijah's prominent position is further reflected during the transfiguration of Jesus, when he appears alongside Moses (Matt. 17:11–12). When the monastic literature saw Elijah and his mantle as a significant model in monastic life, it was continuing a tradition already present in the gospels and in ancient Judaism more broadly.[21] The narratives about Elijah and Elisha constitute a canonical prototype for the monastic world—a world, which, in a way similar to the world of the two prophets, is filled with miracles, according to the anecdotic sources.

The monastic literature makes a general connection between Elijah and the monastics, as well as particular connections with specific monks. Examples of general connections between the monastics and Elijah, either alone or together with other Old Testament heroes, are found throughout the monastic literature.[22]

After the monks Paesios and Isaiah had died, they were both deemed to be perfect: "The one demonstrated the work of Abraham, the other of Elijah" (Palladius, *Lausiac History* 14.4). According to the *Historia Monachorum*, people "said that the spirit of Elijah rested on" an old man in the desert of Antinoe, called Elijah (*HM* 7.1). Paphnutius compares the relationship between the monastics Aaron and Isaac with that between Elisha and Elijah (*Paphnutius* 26, see Siegal 2013: 156). Elijah is cast as an incarnation of the eremitical life as opposed to the communal model of asceticism (Siegal 2013: 157). In *Vita Antonii*, the mountain of Antony is mentioned several times, which alludes to 2 Kings 1:9b and Elijah "who was sitting on the top of a hill."[23] In the *Life of Paul the First Hermit*, when Antony sees Paul, he says, "I have seen Elijah, I have seen John in the desert, I have really seen Paul in Paradise" (13). In the Bohairic *Life of Pachomius*, the beginning of monasticism and the "virtuous life of our holy father Apa Antony" is likened to the life "of the great Elijah, of Elisha, and of John the Baptist" (2).[24]

Monastics are connected to specific episodes in the narrative of Elijah, especially to his miraculous feeding by God who commands wild animals in the form of ravens to bring him bread and meat in the desert (1 Kings 17: 1–6) and provides him with bread in the wilderness (1 Kings 19: 5–9). In the *Lausiac History*, the monk Elijah lives in a cave alone, and when he needs bread, he finds loaves in his cell (51; see also *HM* 7). John of Lycopolis gets a loaf of bread on his table at a prescribed time every 2 or 3 days (*HM* 1.47). Another desert father, Apollo, is compared with Elijah when he multiplies loaves of bread to feed the hungry (*HM* 8.47; see also Siegal 2013: 157). In Jerome's description of Paul, he is fed by ravens. The competition between the Baal prophets and Elijah is probably alluded to when an elder, called Copres, is in a competition with a Manichaean and endures an ordeal with fire, which he wins (*HM* 10.30–32; 1 Kings 18: 20–40; see also Ward 1980: 40).

The identification between Elijah and the monastics was so well established in the literature that it was sometimes mentioned as a matter of fact—for instance, in a description of how Satan and his demons continually attempt to mislead the monastics: when Apollo's community of monks are fed in a miraculous way, Satan appears to him and asks whether he is Elijah or one of the other prophets; Apollo states that it is God who works miracles through him (*HM* 8.46–47). When demons try to tempt Abba Or to try to aspire to the greatness of Elijah and show him a host of angels and a chariot of fire in an imitation of the ascension of Elijah, thus trying to make him exalt himself, Or realizes what the demons try to do and rejects them (*HM* 2.9–10).

The Elijah/Elisha stories are the only example in the Old Testament of a prophet who appoints his successor (Carroll 1969: 403). According to Gene Rice (2006–2007), "Elijah's 'spirit' is the vital energy and source of Elijah's gifts and authority and is the point of contact between him and God." Keith Bodner (2013) sees Elisha as a "doubling" of Elijah and the more important character of the two, arguing that he accomplishes much more than his predecessor. In monastic literature, however, Elijah is the more popular one. The idea of prophetic succession, expressed through the transfer of a mantle, is used when someone inherits the mantle of his predecessor or monastic "father" and, with it, his authority. In Athanasius's influential account, the dying Antony donates his clothes to his followers. His two mantles (*melote*) are given to two bishops, Athanasius and Serapion. In Jerome's account, Paul donates his mantle to Antony before he dies. Both episodes are clear references to Elijah (see Chapters 4 and 6; see also Rollason 2016: 149–156). Most spectacular, however, is Shenoute of Atripe who as a boy, according to his biography, received the real mantle of Elijah from an angel. Apa Pjol is told by the angel,

> when you get up in the morning, put the mantle which you will find before you upon the young boy Shenoute, for it is the mantle of Elijah the Tishbite which the Lord Jesus has sent to you to put upon him.
>
> (Besa, *Vita Shenoute* 8)

The mantle is an important part of the Elijah–Elisha narrative. In Kings, it is a link between the two prophets. In the monastic literature, it connects them to the monastics. Even more poignant than stories about inheriting mantles, however, is how the term designating Elijah's mantle in the Septuagint is used for a standard item of the monastic habit. *Melote* was a rare word meaning "sheepskin." In the monastic literature, it became the *terminus technicus* for fleece, which was part of the monastic habit, either from sheep or, in the Pachomian monasteries, from goat.

Because it refers to an actual monastic garment, the *melote* was a permanent connecting link between the monastics and the two miracle-workers of Kings. According to monastic literature, the monastic mantle was in special cases equipped with the same type of supernatural power as the prototypical mantle of the two prophets; for instance, Palladius mentions a brother in the remotest desert, who "found three warm loaves in his sheepskin" (*LH* 71.3). The fact that the term *melote* connotes the prophetic garment probably contributed to assigning some sort of superhuman status to it. We will return to the question of what sorts of garments the mantle/*melote* referred to in Chapter 3.

The relevance of wilderness clothing

In the introduction to the chapter, we asked how the conceptions of clothes in the *Epic of Gilgamesh*, Genesis 2–3, and the *Books of Kings* were relevant for the conceptions of clothes in the monastic literature.

First, there is the relevance of specific themes, which are discussed in Gilgamesh and in the biblical books and by their interpreters. These texts discuss clothes in relation to the place of humans in relation to animals, sexuality, mortality, and immortality (and rejuvenation). Although such themes are universal and have a general significance in human culture, they have a special relevance in Christian and monastic interpretations because of the development of the idea that it is possible to conquer death and live forever in a higher state of being.

Second, while the ancient Mesopotamian and Biblical texts say something general about the clothing code—in other words, about clothes as specific symbols of the human condition connected to status, group, and gender—and about how clothes intensify belonging and mood, they also say something special about wilderness clothing and garments of skin. Different versions of hairiness as well as garments of skin are connected to the marginal—the existence between worlds—and to the wilderness. Examples are the hairiness of Enkidu and the pelt of Gilgamesh as well as the hairiness and mantle of Elijah. Further, when Adam and Eve are clothed in their garments of skin and wear them on their way out of Eden, it can be argued that these garments in a similar way reflect an intermediary state between their original existence as the first humans in Eden and their new existence as farmers and breeders.

Varieties of wilderness garments are present in the canonical and monastic texts as well. In them, animal fleeces are worn by people who live in the wilderness and in intermediate zones or, rather, are associated with or want to be associated with these zones. These garments are not identical with the royal version of the wilderness garbs, like Gilgamesh's torn fleece, but are made of the skin of domestic beasts, like camels, sheep, and goat. The mantle of Elijah and Elisha and the mantle of John the Baptist draw the world of the ascetic close to the ancient models (Feldt 2013: 342–347; Krueger 1997: 412; Mobley 1997: 228). The hairiness of life in the wilderness is reflected not only in Enkidu, Elijah, and John, but also in the literary *topos* of Egyptian ascetics living among wild animals, only dressed, so to speak, in their long hair (see Chapter 7).

The world of the text sometimes merges with the world in which the readers live (Petersen 2016: 508). The monastic literary sources refer to the biblical world, with its echoes of the larger Near Eastern mythological cosmos, and project this world onto the Egyptian landscape with its desert, monasteries, and ascetic dwellings.[25] As Anders Klostergaard Petersen has pointed out, narratives are accorded religious character when elements of a story are projected onto actual landscapes, include agents with counter-intuitive abilities, and "invite readers to view their own lives in continuity with the recounted world" (2016: 500). The readers are in turn invited to convey these story worlds to their own lives and identify their own worlds with those of the heroic past. Religious texts have, in the words of Laura Feldt, a tendency to strive "to merge with the audience's world and elicit the appropriate actions, attitudes, and lifestyle on the part of the audience" (Feldt 2015: 185). This means that Elijah, Elisha, and John are reflected in the lives of monastic heroes like Pachomius, Theodore, and Shenoute, and that the monastic readers try to emulate these heroes in their own lives. One of the connecting links between the world of the prophets and the world of the monastics is the specific wilderness garment, the *melote*, which in various versions became part of the monastic and ascetic habit. In the following chapters, we will see how this item of wilderness clothing is combined with other monastic garments with other functions and connotations.

Notes

1 The quotations from the *Epic of Gilgamesh* are from Andrew George's translation (2003), and the citations not marked by a letter indicate the so-called standard version of the Babylonian epic. The references to other versions are marked by a capital letter: *P* refers to the Pennsylvania tablet, *U* to the Ur tablet, and *Si* to the Sippar Tablet.

2 *Lahar and Ashnan* 20–25, quoted from George 2003: 450.

3 Feldt and Koch see clothes as a positive marker of culture (Feldt and Koch 2011: 120, 124). Andrew George remarks that new clothes symbolize Gilgamesh's new state of mind (George 1999: xlviii).

4 Even though the clothing code is used in relation to aristocratic heroes, especially Gilgamesh, and not to people in general, it still offers a glimpse into the general working of the code.

5 In the Netherworld, the dead are stripped of their clothes (*Descent of Ishtar* 10). Sometimes, as in the dream of the dying Enkidu, "they are clad like birds in coats of feathers" (*Gilgamesh*, VII 189).

6 Gregory Mobley sees much of the wild man in the portrait of Adam in Genesis 2–3 (1997: 227).

7 See also Oden 1987: 102.

8 Philo and Christian authors comment not only on a Greek translation of the Hebrew Bible, usually the Septuagint, but also on other Greek versions.

9 Philo elaborates on the allegorical meanings of nakedness in *Allegorical Interpretations* 3.69 and speaks about "that leathern mass which covers us, namely, the body." The quote leaves no doubt that Philo saw the body as evil (see also *On the Posterity of Cain and His Exile* 137).

10 Hanneke Reuling (2006) has made an insightful and significant analysis of interpretations of Gen. 3: 16–21. She focuses on four Christian authors, Didymus the Blind, Ambrose of Milan, John Chrysostom, and Augustine, as well as two rabbinic works, *Genesis Rabbah* and *Abot de-Rabbi Nathan*. Her approach has been particularly helpful in the analysis of the various interpretations of the tunics of skin in this chapter.

11 James L. Kugel points out that the "idea that humanity's first parents were somehow clothed, albeit only by 'glory,' seems to reflect Jewish modesty and, as well, opposition to Hellenistic culture's celebration of the naked body" (Kugel 1998: 115; see also 132–133).

12 See also Plato, *Phaedrus* 246B, C; Porphyry, *On Abstinence* 1.31.

13 The quotation is from Jerome, who renders a letter from "Epiphanius, bishop of Salamis, to John, bishop of Jerusalem" (Jerome, *Letter* 51.5).

14 See also Layton 2013: 259; Presley 2015: 121.

15 Ambrose of Milan muses on how the fallen were cut out from all their enjoyments so that they might do penance, and at once, "God clothed them with garments of skins, not silk" (*On Repentance*, 2.11).

16 See also *Exposition of the Psalms* 103.1.8.

17 Laura Feldt has made an illuminating analysis of these narratives as loci for fantastic events such as metamorphosis, impossible tasks, exaggerations, and coincidences that sway between the unlikely and the impossible (2012: 198–226, see also Feldt 2013). She stresses that these fantastic events are directly related to the personas of Elijah and Elisha in a way that makes them superhuman agents almost in their own right. It is difficult for readers to fully approve of the two prophets and what they do, which, according to her analysis, opens up for reflection, doubt, and ambiguity in the interpretation of them (Feldt 2012: 206). According to Feldt, in relation to the fantastic stories of Exodus, the stories about Elijah and Elisha in *Books of Kings* "introduce many new phantasms, a

new site of a fantastic effect (the person), they have a more individual focus, and spend their attention on problems of everyday life" (Feldt 2012: 222).

18 To those may be added an ambiguous reference in 2 Kings 1:8, where Elijah is described as a hairy man. Commentators' opinions differ as to whether this is a reference to the mantle (see Schott 2019: 477–478). A further reference to the active use of clothes is when Elisha tears his clothes in two pieces (v. 12b). According to Rice, not only does he tear them, but also he tears them in two pieces, "tangibly expressing the depth of his pain" (2006–2007: 7).

19 Brian Britt discusses the possible connections of the mantle both to the garment of the prophetic office and to a heavenly garment. In his view, the mantle both hides and reveals. He compares the veiling of Elijah with the veiling of Moses (Exod. 34) and speaks of "prophetic concealment" (Britt 2002). Christina M. Fetherolf argues that "the mantle symbolizes Elijah's decline and decommissioning; it becomes the sign of prophecy gone awry" (2017: 200).

20 The connection between Elijah and John the Baptist is mentioned several times in the gospels (e.g., Mark 6: 14–16 and 8: 28; John 1: 19–23). Cf. also Schott 2019: 485–486.

21 Laura Feldt pointed out Mal 3: 23, and the eschatological Elijah in Sir 48: 1–11 and 1 Enoch 89: 52 (personal communication). Elijah is understood as a precursor of Christ (Mark 6: 14 and 9: 2–8; Matt 14: 1 and 17: 1–13; Luc 9: 7–8 and 9: 28–36). According to Martin Schott, the "Markan prologue presents a composite quotation of Exod. 23: 20; Mal. 3: 12 and Isa 40: 3, which the author strangely enough assigns to the prophet Isiah (Mk: 1: 2–3)" (Schott 2019: 485). The use of Elijah in Egyptian Christianity includes him as a pseudonymous author of apocalypses, an "archetypal speaker of magic words," as well as linking him to prominent monastics (Frankfurter 1990: 78–107).

22 According to the *Instructions of Pachomius*, "either listen, or submit to one who listens; either be strong and be called Elijah or obey the strong and be called Elisha. For obeying Elijah, Elisha received a double share of Elijah's spirit" (17). The Alphabetical Collection of the *Apophthegmata* presents Elijah together with Abraham and David, saying that he "loved inner peace and God was with him" (Nisterus 2). In the *Lausiac History*, Elijah is one of the exemplary past figures, along with Abraham, Moses, and John (*Prologue* 7). See also Frankfurter 1990: 91–93.

23 *Vita Antonii* 59.2; 60.9; 66.1; 84.2; 93.5; see also Bartelink 1994: 50–51.

24 According to *The First Greek Life of Pachomius*, the comparison of Antony with Elijah, Elisha, and John the Baptist was made by Athanasius (G^1 2). In addition to the Greek Lives, there are also Lives in Coptic, in Sahidic and Bohairic (see Pachomius, *S. Pachomii vitae sahidice scriptae* and Pachomius, *S. Pachomii vita Bohairice scripta*). The Pachomian sources are translated by Armand Veilleux in *Pachomian Koinonia* (1980–1982).

25 This was not the only cultural and spatial projection on the Egyptian landscape. Various ideas and interpretations were at work, and Dag Øistein Endsjø has pointed out how Athanasius understood Antony's desert dwellings and wilderness in line with Greek mythological views (Endsjø 2008, 2012).

3 Clothes and the construction of the monastic world

The first monastic garments

In the *Historia Monachorum in Aegypto* (*HM*), there is a story of Pater-muthius, where he is presented as the one who invented the first monastic habit: "For example, there was a father who lived before us called Pater-muthius. He was the first of the monks in his place and was also the first to devise the monastic habit (*monadikon enduma*)" (*HM* 10.3). It is told by 90-year-old Copres to a party of pilgrims traveling from Palestine to visit monasteries in Egypt at the end of the fourth century. The unnamed author, one of the travelers, describes the journey and transmits monastic values in a highly entertaining form. The travelogue is filled with stories of monastics with supernatural powers and is peppered with miraculous deeds—not least the story of Patermuthius. Several miraculous healings are attributed to him, including raising the dead and stopping the sun in its course. According to Andrew Cain, Patermuthius is "perhaps the most thaumaturgically gifted monk profiled in the *HM*" (2016: 173). One suspects that by ascribing the story of Patermuthius to Copres, the author was somewhat skeptical of all the miracles and did not want to identify fully with the story.[1]

According to the *Historia Monachorum*, Patermuthius was a former pagan and robber who converted to Christianity and spent long periods of his life in the desert. Every Sunday, he found a loaf of bread beside his head, an allusion to the miraculous feeding of Elijah (see Chapter 2). When he looked for apprentices, a nameless young man joined him. Patermuthius dressed him in the monastic habit, which, according to the quotation above, he is said to have been "the first to devise" (*HM* 10.3). The garments are listed from the innermost to the outermost and then from the top to the middle of the body—from the head to the shoulder and then down to the waist:

> A certain young man went to him, wishing to become his disciple. He dressed him at once in a sleeveless tunic (*lebiton*) and having put a hood (*koukoullion*) on his head, a sheepskin cloak (*melote*) on his shoulders, and a linen cloth (*lention*) round his waist, he introduced him to the ascetic life.
>
> (Historia Monachorum 10.9)

The habit, then, consists of only four items. These are typical of the monastic habit as we know it from other sources. Even though unlike the miracle stories that precede and follow it, the description of the habit and the dressing of the young man is presented in a matter-of-fact way, so one needs to be cautious. It is unlikely that this is the true origin of the habit; more likely, it is what the author of the *HM* imagined that the first monastic looked like based on a minimal version of what seems to have been the established or rather the model habit at his time, especially its signature garments. Actual habits varied according to the type of monastic settlement, the degree of organization, and the place. According to Mariachiara Giorda, "there were at least four variations on the monastic habit, two in the desert around Nitria, one in the zone between Nitria and the Thebaid and the fourth in the Pachomian desert" (2011: 183).

The sources reveal that ascetic attires varied from the extreme of being completely naked, which may have been more of a literary *topos*, to being clothed in whatever a hermit had managed to scrape together and to the full habit, presented in its ideal version in the story of Patermuthius, as well as in the Pachomian Rules.

In Patermuthius's dressing of his disciple, one can discern a faint echo of the story of Elijah, who dresses Elisha by casting his mantle (*melote*) over him. But in the story of Patermuthius, it is the disciple who chooses the master and not the other way around, as in the Old Testament story, where Elijah chooses Elisha (see Chapter 1). A similar dressing of monastic apprentices is also found in the *Bohairic Life of Pachomius*, where Palamon clothes Pachomius "in a monk's habit with a belt," and Pachomius later clothes his first disciples in "the monastics' habit" (SBo 10 and 23). In the case of Pachomius, the belt is the only garment or accessory that is specifically mentioned.

Monastic clothes changed from place to place and over time, and a variety of garments were used in Egypt in the fourth and fifth centuries (Bagnall 1993: 32–34). Mariachiara Giorda notes that it

> is most probable that the components of the habit were elements of traditional dress, worn by average men and women; once these components became obsolete in normal use, the monks, thanks to their conservatism, did not follow the fashion of the times, and these elements then became the characteristic parts of the monks' habit, the *schema*.
>
> (2011: 183)

Though this is a useful observation, it is also likely that the habit and its various parts were especially chosen and designed to characterize the monastic. The clothes should help the monastics to maintain the ascetic way of life in accordance with the Pachomian Rules, distinguish them from other social groups, and show other people that they belonged to a monastery.

Evagrius comments on the difference between the monastic garb and laypeople's clothes as follows: "For you have considered that it is not by chance or superfluously that it is so different from the clothing of other people" (*Praktikos*, Prologue 1). While understanding that an outfit is more like solving a puzzle than interpreting a language (McCracken 1985; see also Introduction), unlike jigsaw puzzles, not all the pieces in an outfit are equally important. What sort of garments helped people to recognize a monastic? Which ones were the signature garments? The hood (*koukoullion*) and the mantle (*melote*) are obvious candidates and therefore part of the habit, which the author of *HM* claims that Patermuthius devised. The belt (*zone*) was also significant due to its biblical references, its instrumental role in shaping and giving character to the habit, and the frequently mentioned function of fencing the body against interaction with the world (see Chapter 4).

This chapter provides a brief overview of the varieties of ascetic and monastic life and of the different types of ascetic living that affected the choice of clothes. We will present the categories of sources and analyze what kind of information they offer and how garments appear in them. We will then turn to the Pachomian Rules (*Praecepta*) and their clothing inventories, consider how much space clothes are afforded in the Rules, discuss the origin of the habit, and survey the contexts in which clothes appear. While clothes in this chapter are mostly conceived as more static, the next chapters will also include clothes in interaction with their wearers.

Varieties of ascetic and monastic life

Terms used to characterize the celibate way of life were *monachos* (alone, solitary), *anachoretes* (withdrawn), and *apotaktikos* (renouncer) (see Sheridan 2015: 13). Sources distinguish between different categories of monastics, and it is reasonable to assume that different clothing codes applied to the various types of ascetic living at the same time as there was a pronounced fluidity in what those groups were wearing. In addition to the better-known categories of anchorites and cenobites, a third category is frequently mentioned: the wandering ascetics (Caner 2002: 7–9).[2] Jerome calls the third group *remnuoth*—an Egyptian word for a "solitary man," corresponding to the Greek *monachos* (Jerome, *Letter* 22.34; see also Goodrich 2007: 94), while Cassian calls monastics who did not observe cenobitic discipline the *sarabaites*, another Egyptian word (John Cassian, *Conferences* 18.4. 2 and 18.7. 2).[3] Monica Blanchard (2007: 60) suggests that these terms went "from names associated with some recognized type of monastics to terms of abuse." Ascetic wanderers are usually unfavorably treated in the sources and accused of sponging on society. Jerome, for instance, describes the clothes of the *remnuoth* in a hostile way: "Everything with them is done for effect, loose sleeves, big boots, clumsy dress, constant sighing, visiting virgins, disparaging the clergy, and when a feast day comes, they eat so much that they make themselves ill" (*Letter* 22.34). In his interpretation, wandering ascetics' clothes reflect their sloppy living and self-assertive style. These people were obviously a reality in late antiquity, though here they are presented in a consistently negative way. Though their garments likely varied, it is conceivable that they were usually simple and worn.

The term *hermit* is derived from the Greek word *eremos*, which means "wilderness" or "desert." Hermits lived in the desert, for instance, in man-made cells, caves, or even tombs from pharaonic times. They usually lived in groups consisting of a master and his disciples, for instance, in the monastic sites of Scetis, Nitria, and Kellia in the desert valley of Wadi Natrun, west of the Nile Delta. Some hermits lived in cells connected to monasteries (Choat 2017: 28–29; Layton 2014: 13). Shenoute lived outside his monasteries even if he was the abbot of these monasteries.

Antony (250–356) has traditionally been regarded as the first and prime example of a hermit (Bremmer 2019; Endsjø 2008). This is owed to his biography, *Life of Antony*, written by Bishop Athanasius of Alexandria and in a short time translated from Greek into several other languages. Through this biography, Antony and his way of living were immortalized and became "the definitive hagiographical model" (Brennan 1985: 209). According to his biography, Antony always wore "a garment of hair (*trichinon*) on the inside, while the outside was skin, which he kept until his end" (47: 2). When Antony is about to die, he donates his clothes to Bishops Athanasius and Serapion and to two nameless monks. Two sheepskins (*melote*), one cloak (*himation*), and the garments of hair (*trichinon enduma*) are specifically mentioned (91:8–9).[4] The garment of hair points to extreme asceticism (see Chapter 7, Wolves in sheep's clothing), the sheepskin is the prophetic/ascetic garment *par excellence*, while the cloak is usually mentioned as one of the belongings of an ascetic.

Semi-eremitical communities did not necessarily have a uniform dress. However, when the sources describe the origin of such communities, they sometimes present them as in a stage leading to established monasteries. The narratives about Patermuthius and Pachomius supposedly describe a phase in the development of monasticism supposedly before habits and monasteries existed and make a point of their dressing in a traditional monastic garb.[5] Monasteries obviously went through foundation processes. Although such processes are sometimes reflected in the sources, they are difficult to reconstruct because they tend to be overwritten by events and ideals of later times (see Schroeder 2015). Clusters of ascetics living together in small semi-eremitical communities were common, as were monasteries with adjacent semi-eremitical cells. Some monasteries were joined in federations. Variations clearly existed in ascetic and monastic living in Egypt (see Mossakowska-Gaubert 2015: 25–27).

Cenobitic monasticism implies a shared way of life (*koinos bios* in Greek) and refers to monastics who lived together in communities. The term used by the Pachomians for this type of life was *koinonia* ("community"), which referred to the assembly of monastics from all the Pachomian monasteries (Sheridan 2015: 17–21). Their inmates were organized in a hierarchical structure with leaders, ranks, and defined positions, and their life was governed by the Rules. Some monasteries were small with few inhabitants, others had many, and some developed into confederations. The more developed form of monasticism has traditionally been thought to originate in Upper Egypt and is attributed to Pachomius; hence, Egyptian monasticism is sometimes labeled "Pachomian" (see Layton 2014: 5–9). The history of the monasteries of Shenoute, which were established in Upper Egypt some decennia after the Pachomian ones, was long overshadowed. One reason for this is that the Pachomian sources are more easily accessible, having been written in Greek and Latin, in addition to Coptic. The Shenoudian monasteries and sources were more of a Coptic enterprise.[6]

The fully developed monasteries consisted of several buildings. Some were living quarters with cells, and others were communal buildings used for eating, working, and carrying out divine services. Large monasteries had a kitchen, a bakery, an infirmary, several storage buildings, and sometimes a church. They were surrounded by a wall with an entrance hall, which was the contact point between the monastery and the surroundings (Layton 2007; Hedstrom 2017: 221–273; Rousseau 1999: 147–153).

The rulebound and strictly organized life in the cenobium was reflected in a uniform way of dressing. The monastic dress contributed to a way of living in accordance with the Rules. Because the monastic habit expressed a norm, it is explicitly described in the sources. A list of the items of the standard habit is found in the Pachomian Rules from the monastery of Metanoia in the Nile Delta, while Evagrius and Cassian mention a standardized monastic garment, worn at the semi-eremitical settlements of Scetis, Kellia, and Nitria (see Krawiec 2014). Evagrius and Cassian interpret these garments in ways that connect them to biblical models and ideals (see Chapter 5). It is worth noting that four descriptions of the monastic habit—the short version in Palladius's *Historia Lausiaca* (*HL*), connected to Patermuthius, the description of the Pachomian habit in Jerome's translation of the Rules, the description of Evagrius, and the description of Cassian—were all written between AD 395 and 420. It is reasonable to assume that the uniform and standardized monastic outfit was at the time a recent development, though monastic life had been developing from the latter part of the third century through the fourth century. Although a certain conformity in dress among ascetic and monastic groups had existed earlier, the introduction of more uniform monastic garments probably took place in the fourth century as part of the institutionalization of asceticism and the process of establishing monasteries. This was also the period that witnessed the final victory of Christianity in the Roman Empire and the closure of the pagan temples.

While the Rules of Pachomius give the clear impression that they were written for male monastics, the Pachomian monasteries included females as well, as did Shenoute's monasteries (Layton 2014: 12; Krawiec 2008).[7]

However, the sources pay less attention to the female than the male monastics. For instance, female monastics are mentioned only in the penultimate of Pachomius's Precepts (P 143) and, even then, more like an afterthought. The Precept refers to them as "the virgins" ("Let us also speak about the virgins' monastery [*virginum monasterio*]" and contains strict regulations on the contact between the male monastics and inmates of the female monastery. We can assume that the latter's habit was similar to that of the male monastics (Martinez 2008; Muc 2009: 188), but this is by no means certain. The Rules do not mention what the female monastics wore, but Palladius makes the important point that the female monastics did not wear the *melote*, the sheepskin or goatskin, which thus became a distinctive mark of maleness and succession, connecting exclusively male monastics to the Old Testament prophetic tradition (*HL* 33.1). That it was only used by male monastics means that the *melote* was an example of a "heavily gendered coded garment" (Entwistle 2015: 52). The presence, active role, gender-exclusiveness, and supernatural qualities of the mantle of Elijah/Elisha made it into a monastic signature garment.

The garments of ascetic females of groups other than monastics must have varied as did those of male ascetics. There were also virgins living with their parents or other relatives who committed themselves to an ascetic life. According to the Canons of Pseudo-Athanasius, such virgins took a vow and were "appointed to the habit (*schema*)."[8] Although we cannot be certain that the various groups of ascetic females dressed in ways that clearly showed that they were females, it is likely that they did. We know from the literature that in some cases, women wore male ascetic or monastic clothes and that their sex was only revealed in transitional situations, such as when their bodies were prepared for burials (Upson-Saia 2011: 94–96; see also Chapter 7).[9] Such cross-dressing was controversial: "Other women, under the pretext of religion, cut off their hair, and behaved otherwise than is fitting for woman, by arraying themselves in men's apparel" (Sozomen, *Church History* 3.14). Sozomen refers to Armenia, but the point would have been the same in Egypt.

Egyptian monasticism was mainly characterized by a communal way of living where each and every monastic worked on his or her salvation. At the same time, the inmates also worked on the self-sufficiency of the monasteries. Solitary ascetics were similarly working both on their salvation and for self-sufficiency (see Caner 2002: 12, 19–49; Brown 2016). Large monasteries were religious institutions and at the same time economic enterprises comprising farming units and craftspeople. The Egyptian ideal life combined an ascetic life with working for a living, unlike other types of Christian ascetics, who were intent on working on their own salvation without the disruptions of work. The latter category included especially ascetics connected to Syria but also ascetic groups within Egyptian society, such as the elite Manichaeans (Brown 2016). Those who lived at the expense of society without contributing economically, such as the wandering monks who begged for alms, were usually objects of scorn. If, on the other hand, monks who refrained from manual labor remained in the wilderness, they were not considered a problem (Caner 2002: 14).

Large monasteries and monastic federations owned fields and animals, including beasts of burden, sheep, goats, and sometimes pigs (Wipszycka 2011: 212–213). They interacted with society at large, as well as with its religious institutions on various levels. This cooperation was previously underestimated; the monasteries clearly had a much livelier interaction with the surrounding world than hitherto acknowledged. According to Samuel Rubenson, "we now see the rise of monasticism in Egypt as less detached from its surrounding society, less uniform and orthodox, and more closely related to ecclesiastical, theological, educational and cultural developments in the late Roman society" (2017: 178).

Monastic material reality consisted of the spaces where the monastics lived and the material objects that were part of monastic life. In human societies, there is a ceaseless traffic of material objects, and the Pachomian and Shenoudian monasteries were no exception. Things were moving in and out of the monasteries, as well as circulating within them. Foodstuffs and other products from farming, ropes, mats, baskets, papyri, and books were some of the things that were part of this traffic. The ingredients and products of the different stages of cloth-making, such as wool, linen, thread, spinning wheels, looms, textiles, and garments, took part in the locomotion of things; the same is true of the clothes that were worn by the monastics themselves and moved along with them. Boats on the Nile, donkeys, camels, and people made this movement of things possible.

The items of clothing that comprised the monastic habit were usually made of linen and wool, usually homegrown. The *melote* was made of sheep- or goatskin. Monastic clothes were part of Egypt's thriving textile industry. The epicenter of the linen fabric production was in Akhmim/Panopolis, close to the Shenoudian monasteries (Fluck 2008). The documentary literature reveals that textiles and clothing were made not only in the homes, but also on a larger scale in professional workshops. The textile and garment production in the monasteries lay somewhere between the family business and the professional workshop. The monasteries usually had several looms, as seen in the monastery of Epiphanius from the seventh century, but the monastics also did handiwork in their cells on a daily basis (see Chapter 5).

After the raw materials had been processed, garments were woven from linen or wool or made from skin. The textiles were sometimes dyed and then cut, sometimes sewed, and made into garments. They wore with time and were mended, and they were frequently reused before they were finally reduced to rags (Morgan 2018: 80–97). In Shenoute's monastery, the female monastics were responsible for making textiles and clothes (Krawiec 2008: 17, 184, note 66). This responsibility gave women a certain power and sometimes led to conflict. Shenoute's letters offer a unique insight into conflicts over clothes in his monastery, especially in a conflict concerning his cloak, and into the subversive power of textile-producing female monastics (Krawiec 2008: 150–154).

Access to wool and linen as well as to materials for making baskets and mats made weaving, binding, and plaiting daily tasks in the monasteries. In addition to generating profit and providing the monasteries with objects for barter, this type of work also helped the monastics to maintain a meditative state of mind and to keep their focus on the religious universe of Christian heroes and narratives, as handicraft was combined with praying and listening to biblical texts being read out (Gilhus 2020). Sometimes, however, the two economies—the spiritual economy, aiming at salvation, and the economy of this world, aiming at material self-sufficiency—came into conflict with each other. Clothes were sometimes part of this conflict, as we will see in Chapter 6.

Sources

As already noted, in his exposition of French fashion, Roland Barthes discerns between image clothing, which is a garment that is photographed or drawn, a written garment, which is described and transformed into language, and real clothing—what is actually worn (2010: 3–7). According to his analysis, these garments are characterized by three different structures: iconic, verbal, and technological. The circulation of fashion is dependent on a transformation of the technological structure—the real garment—into a narrative structure and an image structure. Barthes's distinction creates an acute awareness of the various aspects of clothes and of wearing clothes reflected in various types of sources. A picture of a monk in a monastic garb (iconic), list of the items in the Rules that constitute the habit (verbal), and the garments found on a monastic mummy (technological) imply different things and address different levels of understanding.

In Barthes's material, the three types are parallel presentations of the same clothes. In the monastic sources, they are not. A monastic garment is never accompanied by a picture of exactly that garment or by a description of it. This means that it is sometimes difficult to identify a type of garment across the textual, iconographic, and archaeological sources and to match garments depicted in pictures or found in burials with descriptions of similar clothing in the written sources. Another problem is related to terminology and translation between languages. The sources use several terms for what might be the same type of garment (Muc 2009: 183). The written sources are mainly in Greek, Coptic, Syriac, and Latin, but in other languages as well. Translating terms between these languages, as well as into modern languages, is notoriously difficult. According to Bolman, Davies, and Pyke, there is "considerable ambiguity in late ancient evidence related to the names and significance of monastic clothing" (2010: 457, note 10; see also Boud'hors 2009). In his book about the monastic rules of Shenoute,

Bentley Layton (2014) chooses not to translate some of the Coptic terms for monastic clothes. An additional problem is that over time, new terms are introduced to denote similar clothes, such as tunics, or that the same term is used to designate different garments. The latter seems to be the case with the term *melote*, which refers both to a mantle, with a special connection to the mantle of Elijah and Elisha, and to the peculiar apron-like garment characteristic of the Egyptian monastic dress for several centuries (Boud'hors 2009).

The clothing code of Egyptian monastics in late antiquity was more restricted than that among French women of fashion in the late 1950s, whom Barthes referred to, which makes it easier to survey. The monastic garments also had a much longer *durée* than French fashion, which means that burials dating to the seventh and eighth centuries still bear some relevance for the description of monastic clothes of the late fourth and fifth centuries. However, the age of the sources is also notoriously difficult to determine precisely. In many cases, oral narratives were written down much later than the things that they describe and were altered in line with new religious and political circumstances. The *Apophthegmata Patrum*, "the sayings of the fathers," is a case in point. Here as well, we must place some trust in the conservatism and long *durée* of monastic clothes and make use of sources outside the strict timeframe of the fourth and fifth centuries.

Barthes's theorization helps to realize that different categories of sources speak to different aspects and *modi* of a garment—for instance, a garment in a static position as opposed to a garment in motion. The various categories of sources further speak to different senses and manners of imagination. Many of the literary sources, such as sayings, travelogues, and *vitae*, refer to events that did not necessarily happen or did not happen as they are presented, and the clothes themselves or the scenarios where clothes play a part do not necessarily have exact real-life references. However, these sources are valuable for a more general understanding of the function, *modus*, and emotional repertoire of monastic and ascetic garments. Studying clothes in texts is different from handling clothes as artifacts, but textual descriptions are built on experiences with clothes and their interaction with humans in social and cultural settings. Texts refer to clothes as part of human life and as partakers in social situations, which makes them valuable sources for the study of the enclothed life of ascetics and monastics. These clothes are embodied, usually described in motion, and intimately connected to human beings and to the life of the monastics.

The various categories of sources reflect monastic clothes in different ways. These categories include monastic rules, literary sources (sayings, travelogues, *vitae*, and church history), documentary sources, pictures, and archaeological material. What follows is a brief introduction to the categories of sources and to the ways in which they construct and present ascetic and monastic clothes.

Monastic rules

Pachomius (292–346) is regarded as the founder of cenobitic monasticism in Egypt. His Rules, which were developed by him and his successors, include the *Praecepta* (*Precepts*) with 144 rules, the *Praecepta et instituta* (*Precepts and Institutes*), *Praecepta atque iudicia* (*Precepts and Judgements*), and the *Praecepta ac leges* (*Precepts and Laws*).[10] A standard list of items of monastic dress is found in the *Praecepta*. Another federation of monasteries in Upper Egypt was that of Shenoute. His Canons do not include a list of garments like the Pachomian Rules do but describe the demand of uniformity of monastic clothing in more general terms (Krawiec 2008: 187, note 99; Goehring 2020; Schroeder 2015). Both the Pachomian Rules and the Canons of Shenoute stipulate how the monastic garments should be worn on different occasions, such as during liturgy, work, or sleep, as well as when monastics were punished. They also indicate, and sometimes explicitly state, in what ways clothes can be instruments of sinful behavior.[11]

Rules are not sociological descriptions but monastic ideals, though what they explicitly forbid is obviously what happened sometimes. Thus, the value of rules as sources for the life in the monasteries is immense. Some of the rules concern washing, storing, and preserving clothes. Regulations of monastic life are also found in the writings of Evagrius of Pontus and in the *Institutions and Conferences* by John Cassian (*Institutes* 1, 3–8, 43–51). Both Evagrius and Cassian list clothing items that together constitute the monastic garb and offer theological interpretations of these items.

Literary sources

Literary sources are travelogues such as *Historia Monachorum in Aegypto* (*HM*) and Palladius's *Historia Lausiaca*; the *Apophthegmata Patrum*, various collections of sayings of the desert fathers (and a few desert mothers); *vitae*, which are pious biographies; church history, for instance that by Sozomen; and letters. These sources are generally not realistic descriptions of what happened but literature intended to reflect monastic and ascetic ideals in close relation with biblical texts on the one hand and the life of the monastics and other readers on the other.[12] Generally speaking, the literary sources heroize the monastic characters and present a variety of events that may have happened and others that may not. It is easy to accept, for instance, that Palladius and the anonymous author of *HM* traveled to Egypt, met monastics, heard their stories, and wrote about their experiences, but it is not necessary that all the details that these stories include, such as the many miracles, are true.

The *Apophthegmata Patrum* originated in a living, oral tradition. They were transmitted orally in the fourth and fifth centuries and written down from the end of the fifth century onward and exist in several collections and manuscripts (Rubenson 2017). They are usually referred to in three main collections, the Alphabetical Collection (A), the Anonymous Collection (N), and the Systematic Collection (S).[13] The apophthegms are basically about teachings or rather practical instructions of the desert fathers, and some desert mothers, to one or more disciples.

The most prominent of these fathers found their way into the biographical genre of *vitae*, narratives about the lives of saints.[14] Some *vitae* resemble novels, for instance Jerome's *The Life of Paul the First Hermetic* but also Athanasius's highly influential *Life of Antony*, a rather fictional account of Antony's life and more a biographical novel than an actual biography.[15]

In addition to these sources, the collection of thirteen papyrus codices written in Coptic, which was discovered at Nag Hammadi in Upper Egypt in 1945 and which probably belonged to the nearby Pachomian monasteries, is drawn into the discussion (Lundhaug and Jenott 2015). The Nag Hammadi texts are referred to especially in relation to metaphorization and mythologization of garments.

Documentary sources

Generally speaking, letters are in an intermediate position between everyday documents and literature. Some of them were transformed "from everyday documents to part of a burgeoning literary genre" (Choat 2015: 80), which also means that they are a rather fluid genre (Choat 2015: 87).[16] Shenoute's letters to his monasteries are of special importance because they reflect the life and issues in those monasteries, offering more revealing insights than most of the Pachomian sources, which are hagiographic to a higher degree (Krawiec 2002: 52, 91), except the letters of Pachomius, Theodore, and Horsiesios.

Documentary sources such as letters reflect monastic communication networks in Egypt in the fourth and fifth centuries. According to Susanna Elm, "the papyri contain largely accidental information, generally as a by-product of other everyday activities" (1994: 234). They refer extensively to clothing—garments made, sold, bought, given away, or inherited. The term *schema*, designating the monastic habit, appears for the first time in the documentary sources around 350–360 AD (Mossakowska-Gaubert 2015: 48). However, in a letter dating to the late third or early fourth century, a man named Isaios writes to Herakleios that a transaction must be settled so that "it benefits the cloak (*proschema*) we wear" (*Groningen Papyrus* 17, quoted in Choat 2017: 23).[17] Malcolm Choat contends that the association of moral standards with a garment suggests a monastic context and a monastic cloak in this case, adding, however, that it could also be a reference to other types of uniforms (2017: 23). If it is a reference to a monastic cloak, it is interesting, as it is so early into the fourth century.

Iconographic sources

Most of the mural pictures and graffiti depict monastics from the sixth
to eighth centuries and only a few from the fifth century (Mossakowska-
Gaubert 2015: 34–35, 55).[18] They usually depict the monastics in an idealized way. The depicted clothes are generally recognizable and consistent
with archaeological finds and with descriptions of monastic clothes in the
written sources, though at the same time they are usually idealized, presenting the depicted as a mediator between the human and the divine. One
example is a depiction in a tomb chapel at the White Monastery, probably
dating to the end of the fifth century, and arguably of Shenoute. It shows
a man in a tunic with a belt and a mantle, who is wearing a leather apron
and has a long scarf or stole with four crosses over his shoulder (Bolman,
Davis, and Pyke 2010). The man is barefoot, his arms are raised toward a
crown or wreath, and he has a square red halo around his head. Bolman,
Davis, and Pyke suggest that the square halo of Shenoute indicates that he
is in a transitional stage to sainthood (Bolman, Davis, and Pyke 2010: 461;
see also Chapter 8).

It is striking that the depicted monastics in this and similar pictures are
decked in textiles, except for their head, hands, and feet. Because of the
generous use of textiles, their outfits signal spiritual status rather than material poverty. These men are usually shown without the hood (*koukoúllion*)
that, judging by the Pachomian Rules, seems to have been mandatory, at
least on "official" occasions and when among laypeople. Instead, they have
a halo, like the man in the aforementioned depiction in the tomb chapel.
One theory is that the monastics are depicted without hoods because their
faces, which should be visible in the pictures, would otherwise be obscured
(Innemée 1992; Giorda 2011: 185).[19] Another possibility is that a halo was
chosen over the hood to symbolize an ideal state of salvation and holiness.
This means that the hood, which symbolized humility and contributed to
keeping the monastics focused by restricting their gaze, is no longer necessary for them to wear. The hood is a tool for living in the world, but it
is not needed when the monastic has reached a higher state of being (see
Chapter 4).

Archaeology

Monastic burials mainly date to later times than the fourth and fifth
centuries—most of them no earlier than the end of the eighth century
(Mossakowska-Gaubert 2015: 31).[20] They sometimes contain mummified
bodies, dressed in clothes and shrouded. One example is a monk's mummy
found in St. Mark's monastery in Gurnet Marei. He was buried in a sleeveless tunic, reaching down to the ankles, a hip-length shirt, a cap with two
crosses on the back, and a leather apron (Muc 2009: 185; Castel 1979;
see also Chapter 8).[21] Examples of well-documented monastic burials are

the Monastery of Epiphanius near Luxor, the Monastery of Apa Apollo in Bawit, opposite Antinoopolis, the Monastery of Abu Fanah in the Western desert, and the monastery in Deir-el-Bachit (Apa Paul) at Thebes.

One question in this context is how to interpret clothes in the literary texts. When the literary sources—travelogues, sayings, and *vitae*—present monastic clothes and similar garments, what are their functions and meanings, and how can these sources be used? One way to tackle these problems and to understand how the various sources function, when it comes to monastic garments, is to make a distinction between normative and formative texts. Rules are normative texts that teach what to do, while formative texts create identity (cf. Assmann 2006: 38). For a text to create identity, it must be possible to relate to it, which implies that the readers should be able to identify the garments described and make associations to them. Faith Pennick Morgan also stresses the dichotomy between "the reality, as represented by the archaeological sources and the intention and purpose, as indicated in the literary and artistic sources" (2018: 13). The purpose of clothes is very visible in literary sources. However, I argue that what Morgan fittingly describes as "vestimentary markers" in literary sources also points to reality, but in a different way than the archaeological sources. The latter include clothes found in tombs, either on a dead body or disconnected from a body, sometimes in fragments. These clothes are no longer part of "an embodied activity" (Entwistle 2015: 10). In contrast, literary sources refer to clothes as part of lived life. They present a variety of garments, show how they interact with their wearers, explore their potential use, and tend to have a dynamic approach to these clothes.

There are certain discrepancies between what the literary sources say about ascetic and monastic life and how this life was practiced. The literary sources are usually more extreme. There was an ongoing discourse about varieties of ascetic practices and ideals (Freiberger 2019: 167–197; see also Chapter 7).

The different categories of sources reflect several contrasts, which are discussed in this book. One is the contrast between ideal clothes and clothes in actual use. Another is between clothes in an immobile state as seen in lists of garments, for instance in the monastic rules, and clothes in motion, as presented in the literary sources. A similar contrast is between the clothes found in graves, which are "frozen" in time, and clothes that are embodied and moving. Another contrast is between clothes as a norm and clothes as deviations from the norm, an opposition that is always implied in the genre of rules and explicitly stated in the literary sources. The rules and the literary sources are helpful in illuminating these oppositions and are the categories of sources most frequently referred to in this book. First, however, we need to establish what a norm was by consulting the main list of monastic clothing, found in the Pachomian Rules, the *Praecepta*. This was, of course, not the only norm, but one connected to a particular place and a specific time, presented in Latin by the learned Jerome. The Pachomian Rules provide an indication of what constituted the ideal habit of male monastics in Egypt in late antiquity. It is important to note that developments from these habits have more or less continued to be the norm for Christian monastics to the present day; hence, the first monastic habit, devised by the Pachomians, became a sort of "fossilized fashion," for some of its elements are the ancestors of monastic clothes today.

The Pachomian Rules and items of the monastic habit

When Jerome translated the Pachomian Rules into Latin in AD 404, he translated them from a Greek text, which might have been a translation from a Coptic original. He translated them some two generations after Pachomius had died. The narratives about Pachomius' life attribute the Rules to him (G[1] 25; SBo 23),[22] but it has been debated to what extent the rules really go back to him (Rousseau 1999: 53; Harmless 2004: 117, 123; Joest 2009, 2012), not least because later descriptions of Pachomian monasticism presuppose that there were no written rules to begin with (see G[1] 24; SBo 23). However, when we take Pachomius' military background into consideration, it makes sense that he established rules early. The rules, which have survived, were used in the Pachomian monastery *Metanoia* in the Delta *c.* AD 400 and describe how monastic clothes were regulated in that place at that time. Even if the exact same clothes were not used everywhere, the list gives an idea of what was considered standard and ideal. The space dedicated to the items of the monastic habit in these rules is also indicative of the importance of clothes in the shaping of monastics, similar to how other kinds of uniforms shape those who wear them.

Jerome begins his presentation of the *Praecepta* with a personal introduction about his own circumstances and the reason that he translated the rules. He devotes about 12 per cent of the Introduction to the monastic habit. In his translation of the actual rules, which immediately follows the Introduction, 16 out of 144 Precepts concern monastic clothing, which are about 11 per cent of the total and account for approximately 10 per cent of the text. The space that this type of rules is allotted suggests that regulations of clothes were regarded as important. Clothes make the man, and the habit made the monastic and reflected the principle that the clothes and the wearer, male or female, should be in consonance with each other.

The Pachomian Rules standardize the monastic habit, which means that it is presented as a uniform habit (Krawiec 2009, 2014: 53). The habit is mandatory and worn by everyone. It is intended to reflect dignity, command respect, and show where its wearer belongs. The Pachomian Rules include more items of clothing than the short list in *Historia Monachorum*, but the impression of the basic garments that constituted the monastic habits is the same:

> This is their equipment (*armatura*): two linen tunics (*lebitonarium*) plus the one already worn, a long scarf (*sabanum*) for the neck and shoulders,

a small skin (*pellicula*) hanging from the shoulder, shoes (*gallicula*), two cowls (*cucullus*), a belt (*zona*) and a staff (*bacillus*). If you find anything more than this, you shall take it away without contradiction.

(Praecepta 81)

The term *armatura* that describes the assembled items means "equipment" and has military connotations (see later in this chapter). Four garments (tunic, scarf, sheepskin/goatskin, and cowl/hood) and three accessories (belt, shoes, and staff) are listed. The materials are linen, wool, and skin. The colors seem to have been whitish or other light colors (*AP A Cronius 5; HM* 1.12,39; 10.9,79). The following paragraphs present the various garments mentioned in the Pachomian Rules (Latin text in Jerome, "La Règle de S. Pachome", translated in Veilleux 1981).[23]

Tunic

The basic garment of the monastic habit was the tunic, *lebiton*, made of linen. *Lebiton* was a Greek term for a sleeveless tunic and a simple garment worn by laborers. In contrast to other types of tunics, some of which were abundantly decorated, the *lebiton* symbolizes simplicity and moderation, in line with the ideals of the monastic life. According to Maria Mossakowska-Gaubert, the term is used in the literature in the latter part of the fourth and in the fifth centuries. In the documentary sources, it is mainly attested in Coptic and in monastic milieus (Mossakowska-Gaubert 2017: 330–331; see also Mossakowska-Gaubert 2004). Mossakowska-Gaubert sees it as a term specifically used in monastic environments and for a specific garment, after it had fallen out of use elsewhere.[24] A Coptic term for the tunic was *štên*. There are also examples of tunics with sleeves; there are, for instance, indications that the Shenoutean habit included a tunic with sleeves (Muc 2009: 187).

Scarf

The rules particularly stress that the scarf or stole (*sabanum*) should be long so that it covers neck and shoulders. It was made of linen and seems to have been fastened around the neck. According to Anne Boud'hors, though uncertain, the Greek term for this item could be *análabos*, while the Coptic one might be *moursknah/marcknah* (2009: 2–6, 13).

Sheepskin/Goatskin

The Greek word for sheepskin or goatskin was *melote*, while the Coptic term was probably *ballot* (Boud'hors 2009: 8–9). The word indicates unshorn sheepskin. The Latin term used by Jerome for this garment is *pellicula*, which means a small skin or hide. As already noted, the term *melote* refers to the prophetic mantle of Elijah in the Septuagint and embodied charismatic prophetic authority, which was transferred to monastic garments (see Chapter 2). In the Pachomian sources, this item is described as the skin of a goat.[25] In burials and pictures, the *melote* seems later to be a leather apron (Patrich 1995: 214; Boud'hors 2009; Muc 2009).[26] While *melote* could have been a label for different items of clothing, in the form of a leather apron, it is a peculiar garment, which was multifunctional and usually utilized as a tool (see Chapter 4).

Cowl or hood

Like the sheepskin or goatskin, the cowl or hood was a signature garment, and its importance is confirmed by the documentary sources (Giorda 2011). It was originally a garment for children, and in a monastic context it was associated with innocence and childhood, associations that are sometimes explicitly stated in the sources. Sozomen says that the Pachomians "wore a covering on their heads called a cowl to show that they ought to live with the same innocence and purity as infants who are nourished with milk, and wear a covering of the same form" (*Church History*, 3.14). A Coptic term for the cowl was *kleft* or *klaft*. The cowl or hood (*koukoullion*) was made of a rectangular piece of fabric, folded, and sewn together, sometimes fastened below the chin. According to Giorda (2011: 183), it "was a little cap, which should cover the head finishing on the shoulders." Cowls found in burials were made of linen or wool and sometimes they bore small decorations, such as crosses (Muc 2009: 187–188). The literary sources mention that they sometimes had signs indicating the house and the monastery to which the wearer belonged. Several authors note that the cowl limited the wearer's view. In that case, it seems to have been a hood rather than a cap, since it could mold the monastic's perception (Giorda 2011: 185). It is also a question whether the hood was sometimes attached to another garment (Tovar 2007: 222). Another variety of headdress was called *tiara* or *para*, which was a scarf wound around the head (Sozomen, *Church History* III 14, 7 and 13, see Giorda 2011: 185). According to the *Historia Monachorum* (7, 6), Apollo, the founder of the monastery Bawit in Thebaid, wore a linen cloth around his head (*lentinon*) in addition to a tunic (*kolobion*).

Belt/Girdle

The term used for this accessory is *zone* (Greek) or *cingulum* (Latin). It was made either of linen or of leather. The belt not only had a practical purpose, to keep the dress in place, but also had the symbolic meaning of being in control of one's body and self (Maguire 2003; see also Chapter 4). Generally speaking, among other things, the various items of a garment or an outfit serve to mark the different zones of the body in line with cultural and religious ideas about symbolic values and purity. The monastic belt was a strong symbolic marker of the monastic's body. Distinguishing the upper part of the body from its lower part, it made a distinction between what was regarded as the impure lower part from the purer upper part. Cassian introduces his *Institutes* with an entire chapter dedicated to the girdle, which is indicative of the importance that he attached to it (see Chapter 5).

Shoes

Sandals were not used on a daily basis but only when necessary. They were made of various materials, especially leather, palm leaves, and papyrus.

Staff

The staff (*baculum* in Latin, *rabdos* in Greek) was used to keep away dangers, such as stray dogs, when the monastic was traveling. It was an extension of the body and a sign of dignity.

Cloak

A cloak *himation* (Greek), or *pallium* and its diminutive *palliolum* (Latin), is also mentioned sometimes. According to the Rules, it was not part of the standard outfit in the Pachomian monasteries, where monastics had to make do with a scarf and a small mantle. However, the conflict over Shenoute's cloak shows that he owned a more substantial type of cloak, and there is also a reference to cloaks of other monastics in his monastery (see Chapter 4). Coptic terms for cloaks or coverings are in the case of Shenoute *prês*, which means "thing spread, mat or cloak" (Crum 1962: 270a), and *ršôn*, which means "cloak, covering" (Crum 1962: 310a). A difference between a *prês* and a *ršôn* seems to be that the latter is a cloak or covering that is bigger and heavier than the former.

In a perceptive article, Thelma K. Thomas has shown how important the *himation* was in monastic paintings, and that the corpus of these paintings "includes alternative figurations of monastic fathers to those emphasized in texts" (Thomas 2019: 10).

Dressing systems

Each of the aforementioned garments is part of the monastic dressing system, which was related to and was part of the general dressing system of the Roman Empire in late antiquity. According to Mary Harlow, "the ancient Greco-Roman wardrobe was, by modern standards, rather limited. Across several centuries it consisted of some form of tunic worn with a mantle, cloak or wrap" (2017: 1). Monastic clothing included similar garments, but the monastic versions of these items were usually simpler. The Pachomian

Rules concerned not only what garments the monastics should wear but also on what occasion they should wear them, as well as what they should *not* wear: "no woolen tunic (*non tunicam laneam*), no mantle (*pallium*), no soft sheepskin with unshorn wool (*non pellem intones arietum lanis molliorem*)" should be worn (P 81; see also P 98). Compared to the general clothing system in antiquity, the monastic garments were less colorful. They were probably usually undyed, as that was the cheapest and less pretentious kind of textile. Monastic clothes from burials reveal that they sometimes had simple patterns and small decorative details; when they were decorated, they only had small and unobtrusive decorative elements. In burials, a difference between the colorful and embroidered clothes of laypeople and the simple, everyday clothes of monastics is noticeable (Muc 2009: 184).

The various items of the monastic habit are further on the conservative side in relation to the total system of clothes. One example is the tunic in the form of the old-fashioned *lebiton*, as noted earlier. In relation to ancient clothes in general, the monastic habit was meant to reflect modesty. The contrast between the luxurious garments of some of his readers and the simple clothes of the ascetic Paul is stressed in Jerome's epilogue to the *Life of Paul the First Hermit*: "Your tunics are of wrought gold; he had not the raiment of the meanest of your slaves" (17; see also Chapter 6). At the same time, the habit gave status to its wearer, and its simplicity contained considerable symbolic capital.

The monastic dress can be seen in relation to other versions of religious garments in antiquity, such as the ritual dresses of the mystery religions. The color of the monastic habit has already been discussed. Sometimes it is mentioned as white or undyed, which is an expression of its simplicity and refers to a general conception of ritual purity in antiquity. Dress was a dynamic part of Christian life and acquired more significance than the traditional religious robes had until then, especially because it was a way for Christians to express their strong ideology. Carly Daniel-Hughes puts it eloquently:

> Christians did not develop totally unique clothing, but endowed dress with symbolism more intensely than the other communities. . . . Christians relied on notions about the body drawn not from ancient cultic religion, but from moral philosophy—namely, that outer appearance revealed inner dispositions, even divine truths. Extending this view to their entire community, they made clothing a critical marker of Christian identity.
>
> (2017: 80)

Dress "began to take on moral and theological character" (Daniel-Hughes 2017: 85). The increased significance of clothes in Christianity was due to the all-encompassing character of this religion, which was intended to cover all aspects of life. How and why did the specific monastic dress originate? What were its models?

It does not seem that at first clothing distinguished Christians so much from their neighbors. What was important was that Christians should be modestly dressed and that their clothes should be gendered. In his treatises on clothes titled *On the Pallium*, *On the Apparel of Women*, and *On the Veiling of Virgins*, Tertullian expresses his clear preference for the pallium at the expense of the toga and for Christian virgins to be veiled, a wish that he shared with Paul. Tertullian also refers to the ability of clothes such as those connected to pagan worship to render their wearers unclean: "In things unclean, none can appear clean. If you put on a tunic defiled in itself, it perhaps may not be defiled through you; but you, through it, will be unclean" (*On Idolatry* 18). In his treatise *On the Spectacles*, Tertullian condemns a man who dresses like a woman, citing the condemnation of cross-dressing in the *Book of Deuteronomy* (*De Spectaculis* 23; Deut. 22).

Basil of Caesarea presents general considerations of how Christians should be dressed. His point of departure is that clothes have a double purpose, to keep the wearer warm and to cover him or her for decency and that these purposes are fulfilled by garments governed by the principle of poverty. He stresses that no more than one garment is needed, and that it "can serve for all occasions: for suitable wear during the day and for necessary covering at night" (*The Long Rules* 22). In his view, Christians should be identified by the way they dress, and he makes an interesting comparison with other groups that can be identified by what they wear:

> As one style of dress bespeaks the soldier, another, a senator, a third, some other high position, so that the rank of these dignitaries can generally be inferred, so also it is right and proper that there be some mark of identity for the Christian which would bear out even as to his garments the good order spoken of by the Apostle.
>
> (*The Long Rules* 22)

Women, he adds, referring to 1 Timothy 2:9, should be decently clad. It is worth noting that not only does Basil want Christians to be identified by their clothes, which should reflect their religious ideals, but also that he compares them with soldiers, another large and easily identifiable group.

Ascetic life was regarded as the closest to a perfect life and the highest version of Christian life. It is obvious that when people started to live full-time ascetic lives, this had some consequences for how they dressed, as their dress should reflect an ideal of modesty and even poverty, as seen in the literary sources (see Chapter 6). The development of monasteries implied a uniform way of living and a totalitarian system that encompassed all aspects of life. The introduction of the monastic dress is a natural outcome of this development. It was born of the wish to show that its wearers were part of a well-defined group, distinct from others, and it was intended to display the status and symbolic capital of the monastics and the monasteries. In the fourth and fifth centuries, the dress of Christian bishops was still not fixed.

Bernhard Jussen notes that some bishops in southern Gaul "were accused of emulating the ascetics and the laboring population by tying a belt around their hips" and explains that since "the occupants of episcopal office at this time did not have official vestments but rather wore their usual clothing, their social origins were easily recognizable" (2001: 157). The monastic habit seems to have been developed before the ecclesiastical dressing code was firmly established.

When the ascetic dress evolved into a monastic habit, its design represented a middle ground between poverty and solidity (see Chapter 6). This dress did not necessarily represent a linear development from pre-monastic ascetic dressing; it might well be the case that the monastic habit had other models as well. One of them could have been the military uniform. The monastic habit is frequently associated metaphorically with military uniforms, as in Basil's view. When Jerome characterizes the full Pachomian habit as "armour," *armatura*, an allusion to Paul's Letter to the Ephesians (6: 10–20), where Christians are encouraged to put on "the whole armour of God" (Eph. 6:11a), is obvious. In the Vulgate, Jerome uses the term *armatura* in his translation from the Greek *panoplía*. Battle metaphors regarding the habit are found in Athanasius' *Life of Antony* and in other texts, such as those by Evagrius, which refer to the fight against passions and demons, the internal and external enemies that often fused in monastic life.

References to military uniforms were also made when the Pachomian monastics were punished and made to ungird their habits. Shenoute speaks of expelling monastics and breaking their girdles, just as is the case with soldiers (see Chapter 4). In a similar way, the military uniform, like the monastic habit, was characterized as *schema* (Morgan 2018: 10, note 101). Pachomius had a military background, having been a conscript before he became a monastic, and Christian Barthel argues that "the military has been severely underrated as a source of inspiration in the study of Pachomian monasticism" (2019: 35). He reassesses and contextualizes the conversion narrative of Pachomius and the way in which the literary tradition was shaped. It could also be argued that there was a certain military-like structure in the Pachomian monasteries pertaining to living quarters, daily schedule, and possibly the development of a monastic habit. One hypothesis is that the inspiration of a monastic garment among the Pachomians came from the dress of soldiers. Pachomius' military background makes it rather likely that he was the one who established a monastic habit.

There are structural similarities between some of the items of the military uniform and the monastic habit. A distinct mark of the soldier was the military belt (*cingulum*), made of leather and frequently bearing heavy and shiny attachments (Hoss 2012: 30), similar to the way in which the belt was a distinctive part of the monastic dress. The soldiers also had a leather band called a baldrick (*balteus*), worn over the right shoulder down to the left hip and holding a sword (Hoss 2012: 30). It can be likened to the monastic scarf, which evolved into a scapular. Similar to how "the weapon, the *balteus* and the ring-buckle belt were taken for distinctive markers of soldiers" (Schiek 2012: 106), the belt, the scarf, and the *melote*, as well as the hood, were distinctive markers of the monastics. Structural similarities between the two uniforms are combined with differences in function and look, which made both the soldier's uniform and the monastic habit characteristic and recognizable. Soldiers and monastics seem to have worn clothing with the respective characteristics that distinguished them but were not necessarily uniformly identical. Both types of dress changed over time. And even when some of the items of the monastic habit were used continuously, their meanings changed over time and in new circumstances. Cassian's description of the Egyptian habit shows how the monastic dress partly changed and partly remained the same (see Chapter 5).

Recent research tends to see the full monastic habit more like a ritual dress that was not used in everyday activities but on more formal occasions (Mossakowska-Gaubert 2015). This bears another similarity to soldiers, who were not dressed in full battle gear in their daily life but only in battles and parades, and perhaps during some forms of training. The full monastic dress reflected and spoke about the social status of the monastics. They received it when they entered the monastery and used it on Sundays in church. A formal dress marked the monastic as special and commanded respect. Joanne Entwistle discerns between unreflective dressing and situations where "the act of dressing is brought to consciousness and reflected upon" (2015: 31). Among her examples are dressing for the weekly shopping contrasted with dressing for formal occasions such as weddings or job interviews. In a similar vein, to put on the daily wear of a monastic did not demand much thought, but when the monastic dressed for a more formal occasion it probably invited a higher level of attention about the meaning and values of the various items of clothing. In other words, if the full monastic habit was limited to ritual and extraordinary occasions, it must have kept its power to invite reflection. Evagrius and Cassian make this type of theological reflection explicit (see Chapter 5).

Spaces for clothes

The crocodile that mistook a habit for a monastic and ate the naked bathing monk because he acted like a layperson illustrates that clothes appear not only closely integrated with people but also sometimes separated from them, and in case of the crocodile, with disastrous consequences (see Introduction). In the Pachomian Rules, monastic garments are disconnected from their wearers when they appear in a list or inventory (P 81), mentioned as lying on the ground to dry after having been washed or are described as being kept in the storeroom (P 47). The last piece of information alludes to the fact that the Pachomian and Shenoutean monasteries had dedicated common storerooms for keeping spare clothes (P 81, *Leges* 15; *HM* 12.39).

When clothes are not worn, they have meanings different from when they participate in bodily movements and are part of social situations (Entwistle 2015: 10). Separated from their wearers, they are not embodied, which means that life and movement have left them, and they resemble empty shells. At the same time, they have functions other than when they take part in the movements of their owners. When Jerome lists the items that the monks have in their cells in his preface to the Pachomian Rules, he describes clothes disconnected from their wearers. At the same time, these clothes are in proximity to them:

> They have nothing in their cells except a mat and what is listed here below, two *lebitonaria* (which is a kind of Egyptian garment without sleeves), and a third one, already worn, for sleeping and working, a linen mantle, two hoods, a goat skin which they call *melote*, a linen belt, and finally shoes and staff to go on journeys.
>
> (Jerome's Preface to the Rules, 4)

Based on Jerome's description, the Pachomian monastic cells were furnished with a mat (used to sleep on) and their inmates' garments.[27] In the way they are presented by Jerome, clothes kept in the cell retained the connection to their wearer. The clothes and the sleeping mat mediate between the monastic and his surroundings and leave a personal stamp on the cell. They incarnate the various aspects of monastic life—sleeping, working, eating, and journeying, and, not least, participating in the ritual life of the monastery. In this way, the clothes in the cells function as an external memory field in the form of a vestimentary autobiography of the monastic.

Another monastic ideal was *not* to have any extra clothes, as illustrated by this apophthegm: "You do not have a spare garment hanging in your cell because it is death to you since you, a sinner, have a superfluity and other more righteous than you are shivering with cold" (*AP* N 592.3). The bare cell reflected in this case the monastic ideal of absolute poverty and compassion for others. In a similar vein, another apophthegm notes that the things in the cell should be in such a condition that nobody would want to steal them. The apophthegm particularly mentions "your bed, your vessels, your footwear and your belt," which is another way of describing the ideal of owning no more clothes than those that the monastic was wearing (*AP* N 592.15).

After reviewing the various items of the ascetic and monastic dress and their background and contexts, we will turn to the interaction between monastics, their clothes, and the surroundings.

Notes

1   In a similar manner, the anonymous author of *HM* tells the story of John through the words of Apelles and ends the narrative in a rather ambiguous way, saying that there are even more marvelous stories about this saint, but they are so very extraordinary that we have not written them all down—not because they are not true, but because some people will be skeptical. As for us, we were fully

convinced because many great fathers told us these things and had seen them themselves with their own eyes.

(*HM* 13.12)

2 According to Daniel Caner, "the near uniformity of this *genera monachorum* tradition might suggest there was agreement in late antiquity over what constituted good and bad ascetic practices and monastic types" (2002: 10).

3 See also Caner 2002: 8–9; Dietz 2005: 69–106; Goodrich 2007: 95. Later, they were also called *gyrovagi*, "circle wanderers" in the anonymous collection of monastic rules *Rule of the Master* (Caner 2002: 9–10).

4 The fact that Antony owned as many as two sheepskins has been discussed. Most likely it has to do with the textual necessity to have enough items of clothes to donate in such a way that served the author Athanasius's agenda (see Chapter 6).

5 Apollo, the founder of the monastery in Bawit, wore a tunic (*lebiton*), which is also identified with a *colobium* and a small linen cloth wrapped around his head (*lentinon mikron*) (*HM* 8.6, 49; cf. *HM* 19.54).

6 The sources have been divided and fragmented between many collections and university libraries around the world. There is a boost in the research on Shenoudian monasticism. See, for instance, Orlandi (1985) and *Shenoute's Literary Corpus* by Stephen Emmel (2004).

7 For the relationship between the Pachomian tradition and the monasteries of Shenoute, see Goehring (2008, 2020).

8 Canon 98 quoted in Riedel and Crum (1904: 63); see also Canon 66 (103).

9 Jennifer Ball has written an interesting article about the habit of the Byzantine nuns, combining literary and pictorial sources. While it includes some references to the earliest period of monasticism, most of her material dates to later periods (Ball 2009–2010).

10 The Rules were transmitted by Jerome in a Latin translation from Greek but were originally written in Coptic (see Jerome, *La Règle de Pachome*). There are Coptic and Greek excerpts from the four collections. Parts of the *Praecepta*, for instance, exist in Sahidic Coptic (Rules 88–130). Rules are also attributed to Pachomius's successor, Horsiesios (*Regula Horsiesii* [*Regulations of Horsiesius*]), see also Joest (2012).

11 There is also some information about clothes in the Canons of Hippolytus, Pseudo-Basil, and Pseudo-Athanasius (see Elm 1994: 227–234).

12 The interpretation of the literary sources has traditionally been conservative, in the sense that this literature has tended to be regarded as realistic descriptions of events, even when what they narrate is unlikely. The years of Shenoute's birth and death are routinely given as 347 AD and 465 AD, respectively, and those of Antony as 250 AD and 356 AD, respectively, which means that they reached the mature age of 118 and 116 years, respectively. In the research literature, these dates are frequently accepted uncritically. For a discussion of the age and chronology of Shenoute, see Krawiec (2002): 175, note 2; Krawiec (2014): 66, note 37; and Emmel (2016).

13 See also the digital platform for research on the *Apophthegmata Patrum*, Monastica (Centre for theology and religious studies, Lund University): https://monastica.ht.lu.se.

14 On the value of hagiography as historical source, see Rubenson (2013b).

15 Samuel Rubenson has written a seminal work where he makes a strong case for the authenticity of the letters of Antony (1995). It indicates that the "real" Antony was an educated man, and that Athanasius' Antony is more of a monastic ideal than a historical person.

16 The monastic letters are divided into papyrological archives and literary collections. Samuel Rubenson identifies three types of letter collections: "the archival

collections related to specific monasteries, the collections of letters of monastic founders and of leaders of monastic communities created by their disciples and successors, and finally the collections of scattered letters attributed to monastic authors" (2015: 69).

17 Like *schema*, *proschema* is a term denoting the monastic habit.

18 Maria Mossakowska-Gaubert (2015: 35) mentions a painting of Shenoute, his stele, and two ostraca from the monastery of St. Phoibammôn as the only examples of fifth-century pictures of monastics.

19 In contrast, according to Ball, Byzantine nuns are always depicted with headgears (Ball 2009–2010).

20 For an overview, see Mossakowska-Gaubert (2015): 31–32.

21 By extension, and generally speaking, the production and wearing of replica clothes can also be a source of useful information about ancient clothes. Faith Pennick Morgan recently reconstructed ancient tunics and cloaks, and her research offers valuable experimental knowledge about the behavior of ancient garments (2018: 98–142).

22 G¹ (*First Greek Life*) and SBo (*Bohairic Life*) refer to the two main recensions of the *Life of Pachomius*. In Veilleux' reconstruction of the *Bohairic Life*, he has also incorporated pieces of the *Sahidic Life* where he felt that it was necessary (Veilleux 1980).

23 The research on the garments of ancient Egyptian monasticism has shifted focus from literary sources to documentary and archaeological materials. The terminological problems are also discussed in the relevant literature (Boud'hors 2009; Giorda 2011; Mossakowska-Gaubert 2005: 63–83, 2015, 2017; Muc 2009; Patrich 1995: 210–218; Tovar 2007).

24 According to Maria-Mossakowska-Gaubert, the most important element of the vestment was the tunic, which could be either short- or long-sleeved. Three different words were used, *kolobion*, *lebiton*, and *chiton*. According to her, *lebiton* is the most characteristic term in the monastic vocabulary for tunics (Mossakowska-Gaubert 2004).

25 Egypt witnessed an increase in sheep rearing in the Ptolemaic period. Goats were usually kept together with sheep and often functioned as lead animals (Clarysse and Thompson 2006: 222–223).

26 *Rahtou* is also used as a term for "a monkish garment," which Crum suggests was a leather apron (1962: 312b).

27 Mats and clothes have sometimes overlapping functions: mantles function as mats, for instance, in Athanasius's narrative of Antony's death, when Antony lies on his mantle, and monastics sometimes wear odd garments, such as mats and baskets, intended to create an impression of extreme frugality (see also Thomas 2019).

4   Interacting with the habit

Wearing the habit, shaping the monastics

Clothes affect their wearers, and being dressed is to interact with clothes. Different sorts of fabric act on the body in different ways. Palladius describes how the monk Piôr comes out of the great desert: "just at the sixth hour, in the burning heat, an old man wearing his sheepskin cloak (*melote*)" (*HL* 39.4). As he appears from the desert in the midday heat wearing a sheepskin, the skin and the desert define the old man as an ascetic. It is implied that the sheepskin makes him hot and thus inflicts discomfort on him, which he endures. This chapter moves from the techniques of wearing the habit to the ways in which it interacted with the body and contributed to making the wearer a monastic. How intimately were monastic clothes connected to the body? How did they act on their wearers? In what ways were clothes extensions of the body, and how did they enable and restrict the monastics?

For monks, the full monastic garb includes layers of textiles—tunic, scarf, and goat- or sheepskin (*melote*). It makes the wearer a monastic and a male. One function of the habit is to give status to and reflect the position of the wearer. This is especially seen in depictions of monastics covered in textiles, except for their feet, hands, and head.[1] When dressed in the full garb, the monastic was expected to carry himself with a certain dignity and had to learn how to do so. This is not unusual, either for monastics or for other social groups. Joanne Entwistle reminds us that at one time young ladies of the elite were sent to finishing schools for training in "how to walk tall and graceful, get in and out of a car, eat at a formal dinner party and so on" (2015: 135). In a similar way, and in line with the monastic rules, it is reasonable to assume that the novices had to learn how to wear the habit so that it functioned according to the monastic ideals and made the wearer an asset to the monastery. According to the Pachomian Rules, "all the hoods shall bear the sign of the community and the sign of the house" (P 99). The monastic dress commanded respect from others and was intended to work on its wearer so that she or he internalized what the dress represented.

Ancient clothes were not cut, shaped, or tailored, but woven into shape or draped, and it was sometimes a challenge to keep them in place.[2] A chief example of draped clothes is precisely the old-fashioned Roman upper-class garment, the toga, about which Tertullian asked rhetorically: "Do you feel yourself clad, or laded? Wearing a garment, or carrying it?" (*On the Pallium* 5). In addition to being critical of the wearing of this typical elite male gown, Tertullian's rhetoric also reflects the fact that it feels differently to wear different sorts of garments. It was not so difficult to wear the habit. Unlike the toga, it was not burdensome and did not demand much attention. The Pachomian loose-fitting and short-sleeved tunic was easy to manage. It was belted and equipped with a scarf, or *scapula*, and knitted around the upper part of the body, so the habit did not need much care to be kept in place. Generally, "persons whose tunics were girded were more fit for action" (Olson 2017: 18).

With some practice, the monastics could move comfortably wearing their habit. Cassian says that the belt was worn so that the monastic "may always go without being hindered by the dress" (*Institutes* 1.11), which is a comment on its direct and physical function.[3] Still there were challenges, such as sitting in a proper way in the assembly, where the habit seems to have required some adjustments. The second rule of the *Praecepta* sets the standard for handling the dress when the monastics sat down in the assembly:

> He shall sit with all modesty and meekness, tucking under his buttocks the lower edge of the goat skin which hangs over his shoulder down his side, and carefully girding up his garment (*vestimentum*)—that is the linen tunic (*tunicam lineam*) without sleeves called *lebitonarium*—in such a way that it covers his knees.
>
> (Praecepta 2)

The goal was to sit "with all modesty and meekness" (*cum omni decore et mansuetudine*), and the state of the dress was to be in line with this goal. This also means that all monastics had to wear the dress in the same way so that no one drew attention to themselves. In the *Regulations of Horsiesios*, it is stipulated that "our garments be gathered about us so as to cover our legs" (20); and in the *Praecepta*, it is stated that the monastic shall be "carefully girding up his garment (*vestimentum*)" (P 2). The girdle or belt was key. It kept the tunic in place. In a similar way, the goatskin was not allowed to live its own life; it is explicitly stated that its wearer must take command over it by sitting on its lower edge. Armand Veilleux notes that sitting on the goatskin protected the tunic from becoming dirty or worn out. He also stresses that the command to keep the tunic over the knees is easily understood when one knows that the monastics wore nothing underneath their *lebiton* (1981: 185; see also Cassian, *Institutes* 1.10). The lack of underwear could make a wayward tunic indecent either unintendedly or as part of a conscious flirtatious move, as we will discuss later. The Coptic version of Precept 99 insists that the goatskins should be belted up as well (*eunahokou*), while the Latin translation of Jerome states that "all the goat-skin should be bound and hang from the shoulders."[4] In both versions, the point is that the skin should be kept firmly in place.

Likewise, Shenoute's canons include rules for covering the body in a proper way. Here it is stipulated that "except for dire necessity when they [the monastics] are working with mud or some other job, the border (*top*) of their *hoeite*-garment shall be covering their arms down to their elbows" (FM 188 in Layton 2014: 290–291). Shenoute shows a certain degree of tolerance in this regulation "because of the measure of the poor, cheap *hoeite*-garments, it does not matter so long as they cover their elbows" (FM 188 in Layton 2014: 290–291).[5] In the Coptic versions of the Bible, the Coptic term *hoeite* is used for several types of garments, such as *khiton* and *himation* (Crum 1962: 720b; Mossakowska-Gaubert 2017: 334–336). In Shenoute's case, the garment might have been a girded tunic where superfluous textiles on the shoulders ended in a hem or border and were used to cover the upper arms.[6] The main point, however, is that the interaction between the body and clothing should be controlled and decent.

The habit was part of what it meant to be a monastic. In a way, it materialized her or him, and it was an ambition to be in consonance with the ideals that it expressed. Like the sari referred to by Miller, the monastic habit wears the monastic (Miller 2010: 23, see Introduction), and it has an emotional repertoire according to how it is manipulated and perceived by its wearer (Miller 2010: 28). An ethnographic fieldwork about contemporary Greek Orthodox nuns sheds some light on the actual workings of monastic garments. Eleni Sotiriou (2015) uses the habit as a lens in her examination of the process of socialization of these nuns. In her view, clothing, body, and identity are closely interconnected in the making of the nun (Sotiriou 2015: 158). When putting on the habit, the nuns reproduce the monastic structure, take on the monastic values, and map them on their bodies. Sotiriou argues that "the habit had a profound socializing effect" (2015: 161). The clothing of the nuns is a strategy for educating them, as well as for realizing and exteriorizing their new identity (Sotiriou 2015: 163). She shows convincingly that "the habit *does* make the nun" (Sotiriou 2015: 164).

This was most likely also a point when the first monastic habits were developed and used in Egypt in late antiquity. The monastic is or becomes what she or he wears. At one level, the habit *is* the monastic—an opinion clearly shared by the talkative crocodile mentioned in the Introduction. The habit is frequently used synecdochically to refer to the ideals of the monastic life. According to the *Instruction of Theodore*, "he (i.e. God) causes our consciousness to burn us at every moment when we do not walk as benefits the dignity of the holy vocation of the habit we wear" (3, 1), and further that "we have all sought to put on the acts of the habit we wear, of the name spoken over us, and of the law that we have promised before God and the faithful to keep" (3, 3). In the first part of this quotation, a special way of dignified walking is connected to the habit, which is used figuratively, refer-ring to the right way to live as a monastic. In the second, the habit is con-nected to specific acts. This monastic way of life should be in line with "the laws of the habit."[7]

When the monastics do not live up to the ideals of the habit, for instance by craving food and overeating, they dishonor it. Shenoute forbids the monastics to receive alms from people outside the monastery, "lest they become like beggars on occasions of this kind, and many laugh at them and they scorn the great and glorious habit (*schema*) because of their bellies."[8] The belly is used as a metaphor for greed. The phrasing reveals a dissonance between the ascetic connotations of the habit and a fat monastic and implies that the habit and its wearer's body were expected to be in consonance with each other.

Shenoute refers to those who have been expelled from the monastery as "those who have been expelled from the habit (*schema*) of monasticism" (BZ 24 in Layton 2014: 138–139). According to Rebecca Krawiec, for "both male and female monks in the White Monastery, clothing does not just signify monastic identity but also the spiritual status of that self, either pure or polluted" (2009: 146). She notes that the dress was an immediate marker of monastic identity, and that "the properly dressed monk (male or female) instituted a monastic outfit that defined and communicated the values and social status of that figure" (Krawiec 2014: 55). The habit is fre-quently mentioned as a contrast to transgressions of the norm, for instance when the *Instructions of Horsiesios* refers to "those in no way conformable to our habit (*schema*)" and ascertains that we "must therefore allow no pleasure now to revile our holy habit (*penschema etouaab*)" (1.2). Here as well, the implication is that the habit should be worn in accordance with a certain way of living and acting. When the habit is characterized as holy, it indicates that this type of dress is not only a uniform, which distinguishes a monastery's inhabitants from outsiders, but also that their manner of dress-ing has a higher significance. Krawiec labels these habits "the garments of salvation" (2009: 125).[9] However, the habit was also regarded as a dress of transition from a sinful life on the earth to a heavenly life. When a monas-tic complains that he has worn the habit for 8 years and not found peace, Theodore of Pherme replies that he has worn the habit for 70 years and "on no day have I found peace" (*AP* A Theodore of Pherme 2). The ideal of the habit was something to strive for.

At the same time, the habit acted on the monastic. According to Pierre Bourdieu (2000: 244), when entering a group and at the same time incarnat-ing it,

> the nominee enters into possession of his function only if he consents to be possessed bodily by it, as is asked of him in the rite of investiture, which, by imposing the adoption of particular clothing—often a uniform—a particular language, itself standardized and stylized, like

a uniform, and an appropriate body *hexis*, aims to fasten him durably to an impersonal manner of being and to manifest by this quasi-anonymization that he accepts the—sometimes exorbitant—sacrifice of his private person.

By *hexis*, Bourdieu means using one's body in a certain way. The habit was part of this bodily performance and of how one carried oneself. It acted on the monastics by its shape and by the traditions and meanings that it incorporated. At the same time, the rules of the monastery and ritual life, which more or less filled the day of the monastics and included work as well as religious activities, molded and changed them. It was a continuous interplay between external and internal influences, which together shaped the monastic.

Ritualization of dress

Ritualization of dress implies both that a dress is put in a ritual setting and that it promotes a ritual attitude and behavior. According to Catherine Bell, "basic to ritualization is the inherent significance it derives from its interplay and contrast with other practices" (1992: 90). She sees ritualization at a basic level as differentiating from other ways of acting and at a more complex level as "a way of acting that specifically establishes a privileged contrast, differentiating itself as more important or powerful" (Bell 1992: 90). Wearing the habit means differing from all non-monastics in the way of dressing, belonging to a spiritual elite, and acting in line with this belonging. The ritualized dress is an integral part of the ritual body of the monastic.

Wearing the habit was part of both the *rites de passage* and of daily and weekly rituals. Rites of passage included the initiation to the monastery, in some cases expelling monastics from the monastery, and, finally, burying them (see Chapter 8). These rites implied a fundamental shift in status and always involved the habit. Leaving his or her former clothes behind when a person became a monastic was a strong marker of changing from one type of life to another and a standard reference of literary accounts to becoming a monastic.

According to the *Praecepta*, when someone first comes to the monastery, he is not allowed in for several days. His personal situation is closely examined, and he is taught the Lord's prayer and as many psalms as he can learn (P 49). When he is ready to join the brothers, "they shall strip him of his secular clothes (*vestimentis saecularibus*) and garb him in the monastic habit (*habitu monachorum*)" (P 49). The change of identity is absolute and expressed by the change of clothes. However, the Precept goes on to say that "the clothes he brought with him shall be given to those in charge of this matter and brought to the storeroom; they will be in the keeping of the superior of the monastery" (P 49). It does not say what happens to the clothes—whether they are sold or given away, or whether they are returned if the monastic later chooses to quit or is expelled from the monastery. According to John Cassian, however, the novice's clothes were kept until it was ascertained that he was not guilty of fault and disobedience and would be allowed to stay on a permanent basis. If found guilty, he would be re-clothed in his old garments and expelled (*Institutes* 4.6).

A colorful description of the monastic initiation is offered in one of the apophthegms (*AP* N 51). The story reflects the close association between clothes and their wearer. In this narrative, a man wants to join a monas-tery but repeatedly fails because of his own remonstrances, characterized as *logismoi* (evil thoughts). Suddenly, one day he takes off and throws away all his clothes and runs stark naked to the monasteries. There, one of the elders has a revelation from God: "Get up and receive my athlete." The elder lis-tens to his story and puts the monastic habit on the naked runner. This ini-tiation marks a dramatic break between living in the world and joining the monastery. The two stages are represented and contrasted by the worldly clothes on the one hand and the monastic habit on the other, while the limi-nal phase is represented by the initiand being naked and running from his life in the world to his new monastic dwelling. The metaphor of the athlete, which is so frequently used for successful monastics and ascetics, takes on a new and strong meaning in this narrative, which is realized in a literal way by the prospective ascetic's running toward the monastery.

The process was reversed when monastics were expelled from the mon-astery and stripped of their monastic clothes. A Pachomian monastic, Sil-vanus, who had been an actor in his former life, gradually drifted away from the monastic life and "even fearlessly declaimed among the brothers improper quips from the theatre" (*Paralipomena* 2). Pachomius decided to expel him. The procedure was as follows: In the presence of the brothers, Pachomius ordered him "to be stripped of the monastic habit, to be given secular clothes, and to be expelled from the monastery by the brothers" (*Paralipomena* 2). The stripping was a collective action, which signaled Sil-vanus's return from monastic to secular life. The story indicates that when a monastic was to be expelled, all his clothes were to be removed. In the end, Silvanus was not expelled because he begged and repented, and later he came to be considered a model for the other monastics. Shenoute, who actually expelled many monastics, is more specific:

> Just as we tore the cloaks (*štên*), having broken off the girdles (*zone*) of those who had sinned among us, as if they were soldiers, for they sinned against their king, Jesus, so we pursued them and sent them away from us.
> (XO 71: ii.29–72, translated in Krawiec 2002: 233, note 101)

It is noteworthy that cloaks and girdles are seen here as the defining ele-ments of the habit and are used metonymically for the habit *in toto* and fur-ther that there is a reference and a connection to the uniform of soldiers (see

Chapter 3). Most important, however, is how the destruction of garments is conceived as a destruction of the monastic identity.

While the rites of passage effectuated the transfer from one religious and social state to another, daily or weekly ritualized behavior involved one or some of the garments. Such ritualized behavior was part of the general religious script of the monastery. The basic principle of uniform clothes is, of course, that they must be worn by everyone. At the same time, it is also a question of when and how to wear the various items of the habit. For instance, P 91 states, "No one shall walk in the community without his goat skin or his hood, either to synaxis or to refectory."[10] Such reminders not to leave out one or more of the garments indicate that these items were not always worn.

There are at times discrepancies between the Precepts regarding when and on what occasions the various garments should be worn. According to P 61, "no one shall take his linen mantle (*lineum palliolum*) with him when going to work, except with the superior's permission. And in the monastery no one shall walk around wearing the same mantle (*palliolum*) after the *synaxis*" (P 61). However, P 102 says something slightly different: "No one shall go to the synaxis or to the refectory with shoes on his feet or clad in his linen mantle (*lineum palliolum*)" (P 102). P 61 presupposes that the monastics wore a mantle at the synaxis; in contrast, P 102 indicates that the mantle should *not* be used in the *synaxis*. Veilleux has offered a solution to the discrepancy by suggesting that the mantle (*palliolum*) was used during the night and morning synaxes but probably not at the evening one (1981: 188).[11] This might have been the case, or perhaps the discrepancy is due to Jerome's translation of the Precepts. Sometimes Latin and Coptic terms have a slightly different range of meanings. While *lineum palliolum* in the Latin text denotes a small linen mantle, the term used in the Coptic text is *prêš*, which means "thing spread, mat or cloak" (Crum 1962: 270a). It may also have been used by the monastics during the night (Draguet 1944: 104–105), as it was a fluid transition between some items of clothes and spreads or coverings. The point remains, however, that the intention of the Precepts is to ensure uniformity in clothing.

The habit was also part of an orchestrated play where the presence or absence of its various items produced meanings. One example is the hood, a monastic signature garment, to which the Pachomian regulations give a more direct religious meaning and significance. According to the Precepts, the monastics must always wear the hood and the goatskin when they are among the community (P 91). When they come to eat, "they shall sit in order in appointed places, and cover their heads" (P 29; see also Cassian, *Institutes* 4.17). However, when they leave the assembly (*synaxis*) and go to their cells or to the refectory, the monastics must recite something from Scripture and "no one shall have his head covered" (P 28). It appears that walking and reciting Scripture is an exception to the general rule of having the head covered. This could be due to not only a reverence toward the holy

Scripture, but also the need to open up to the spiritual world. One of the hood's functions was to hinder communication with other people and with the world in general, as we will discuss later. When the communication is vertical, with the world above, the monastics do not need the hood. Removing the hood in this specific situation is part of the ritual language of clothing, where the hood's state speaks to the relationship between the monastics and the world on one hand (covering the head) and between the monastics and the world above on the other (revealing the head). In the iconography, the holy fathers of the past tend to be depicted without a hood but with a halo, which signifies their state of salvation.

Flirty fringes

The habit should be worn in a prescribed manner, but prescriptions always imply that things can be done differently—and often are. Otherwise, there would have been no need for them in the first place. Instead of signaling dignity and posture, the habit could reflect sloppiness. Instead of decency and chastity, it might send out sexual signals.

Similar to the second precept, which stresses that the habit should be kept in place below the knees when the monastics were sitting and attending the synaxis, the *Praecepta* also stipulate that "no one should do the laundry with his clothes drawn up higher than is established" (P 69). In Shenoute's canons, things are said more bluntly: those who inadvertently uncover themselves are cursed (YA 257–58 in Layton 2014: 108–109; see also Chapter 6). Transgressions of the dress code could happen both unintentionally and intentionally, and the standard items of the habit could be consciously manipulated to become flirtatious. The signals that clothes sent out had to be monitored by their wearers, and they were also closely scrutinized by the superiors of the monastery. The formidable Shenoute and his successor Besa are cases in point.

Besa suggests that clothing could be a site for attack of demons and for stirring up lust (Krawiec 2014: 71). The Coptic term used by Besa is *ōlm*, which, according to Crum, means "embroidery" or "to entwine" (Crum 1962: 522). The offending garments were either condemned by Besa because they were embroidered—even with heathen motifs—or entwined, which was also intended to make them more attractive, but in an improper way— at least in Besa's opinion (Krawiec 2014: 71–73).

Generally, monastic clothes should not be made of expensive textiles, and they should be simple, without fringes and elaborate patterns. Decorations such as fringes, cords, entwines, and borders changed the look of the garments and gave them new meanings, not necessarily in line with the ideology of asceticism. Such extras are condemned in Shenoute's canons.[12] However, Shenoute's own cloak was equipped with fringes, and we will also see later that he had very specific ideas of how these fringes should be and how they should move. Fringes were obviously an intricate topic. In Shenoute's case, it is also a point that, unlike Pachomius, he saw wealth as a sign of the grace of God, as Kimberley A. Fowler notes (2018: 444; cf. López 2013: 67–95, see chapter 6).

Clothing details like fringes and cords might seem insignificant. In real life, however, they tend to draw attention and can be powerful tools in altering the meaning of a garment. All the same, at first glance it is difficult to understand why Shenoute made such fuss about these details, but less so when we look closer at how he interpreted their meanings and functions:

> No person among us shall attach a fringe/border (*tōte*) spun down in/ from the cord (*hos*) of his hood (*koukoullion*). If someone is found to have attached more than two digits spun down after the sewing with which the cord is attached to its fellows, he shall be censured like a person who has sinned against his soul in the desire of his heart. And he shall be treated according to his iniquity.
>
> No person among us shall wear a hood (*koukoullion*) without sewing its cord into its fellows, according to the ordinance that we mentioned previously—not on account of what we said, namely, that this is the custom of filthy heresy; but also because of another matter, which it is unseemly to set in writing.
>
> No person among us shall permit the border (*top*) of his *štên*-garment to cover the palms of his hands as he is going up for the Eucharist, again because of the same thing that we said before, for it is unseemly to set in writing.
>
> (XL 260 in Layton 2014: 216–217)

These rules focus on two garments, the hood and the *štên*-garment, which seems to have been a tunic. Regarding the hood, the rule refers to cords that either hang loose or are attached to each other but with fringes hanging loose from them. As for the *štên*-garment/tunic, it is constructed so that it is possible to make part of it into sleeves, similar to the belted tunic mentioned earlier. What is important is that the tunic's borders must not cover the palms.

As already mentioned, in the Pachomian monasteries, marks on the hood indicated the monastery and the house from which the wearer came. Some hoods and cowls found in burials have discrete patterns and crosses, but they date to a later time. Shenoute's repugnance is related to two aspects. One is heresy, while the other repugnance is, according to Shenoute, "unseemly to set in writing" (XL 260 in Layton 2014: 217). The heresy part could be because cords and fringes were associated with certain non-Christian religious groups or even pagan priests. It could also be that such clothing details on hoods and headgear were believed to have apotropaic functions. Because they were associated with pagan practices, they were condemned.

Another reason for Shenoute's repugnance could be that fringes and cords were more generally associated with female dress and were thought to make clothing effeminate. We can further surmise that the reason the *štên*-garment was not allowed to cover the palms was because it indicated effeminacy, just like the loose fringes and the cords. There are parallels in Roman literature. At the end of the second century, Aulus Gellius writes that "for a man to wear tunics coming below the arms and as far as the wrists, and almost to the fingers, was considered unbecoming in Rome and in all Latium" (6.12.1–2). For women, however, they were *not* unbecoming (6.12.3). In other words, long sleeves indicated effeminacy (see also Olson 2017: 142). Aulus Gellius even quotes Virgil about men who wear effeminate and shameful tunics and ribbons in their headgear: "Sleeves have their tunics, and their turbans, ribbons" (6.12.6, see also Virgil, *Aeneid* IX, 616). This means that, like loose fringes, the covering of the palms suggested an effeminate behavior.

Fringes and dangling cords appear as extras that circumvent the monastic dress code and violate basic functions of the hood, which were to close off the monastic from the world and to send out messages of innocence and childhood, as noted earlier (see also Carter 2012: 352). Commenting on the contemporary fashion system, Prudence Black contends that the "fringe as a detail has its own energy" (2009: 507). In her view, the "insight that details might speak more loudly than the whole, will be, in the first instance, a theoretical demonstration that semiotic systems are not self-contained, but open out onto other systems" (Black 2009: 500). This is not only an argument against Barthes and the systematic character of fashion, but it also shows how clothing details can contribute to circumventing the monastic clothing system. At the same time as the hood signals that the wearer belongs to a monastery and to a Christian world of ascetic values, the loose cords or fringes and the covering of the palms send signals in the opposite direction, indicating playfulness and sexual invites. Beware of loose fringes! They have the power to undermine the established and normative meanings of a garment and, by extension, of its wearer.

How do fringes affect their wearers? The fringes indicate a lack of restraint, an attempt at worldly engagement, playfulness, and even erotic advances.[13] This is in stark contrast to the original intention of the normative monastic hood. Shenoute's words imply that inappropriate clothing not only reflects but also encourages deviant behavior. This observation stresses the embodied character of clothes and points to the interplay between clothes and their wearers, as well as with their surroundings. While Shenoute wanted the textile of the dress to cover the elbows when the monastics took part in the Eucharist, it should not be covering their arms completely. These are indications of the significance of the subtle language of dress and dressing details. Although specific punishments for transgressions involving fringes, cords, and long sleeves are not mentioned in the quotation above, they were most clearly implied. The hood was an ascetic piece of clothing. When it was converted into something else with cords and fringes, it contributed to setting in motion a series of events that were not part of the normative wearing of the garment and the range of allowed actions. The decorated hood is an example of a deviant item of clothing, which might tempt its wearer and his surroundings to engage in deviant behavior, that is, behavior not in line with an ascetic way of life.

Bodily extensions and emotional repertoire

Monastics should never have more items of clothing than what is prescribed. Superfluous clothes should be brought to the storeroom and disposed of by the housemaster and the second (*Precepts and Laws* 15). Some of the curse formulas in Shenoute's canons were aimed at monastics who were involved in stealing garments, selling garments made stealthily, or giving garments to relatives.[14] The canons also mention those who fix their hearts upon having specific garments or shoes that are made beautiful and are not equal to what others have.[15] It is for this reason that monastics were not allowed to keep garments that they owned before they joined the monastery. All should be equally clothed, and no one should keep anything different from what everyone else had.[16]

In the Pachomian corpus, and in a similar vein, he who is lazy and does not work but is fed and clothed through the work of his monastic brothers will be punished in the next world. Then "he lies in the shame of begging, with the disgrace upon his shoulders of a beggar's habit (*schema*) and shame, soaking him and being wrapped around him" (*Regulations of Horsiesios* 18). Lack of participation in the production of food and clothes in the monastery has direct consequences for the freeloader in the world to come, where his true nature will be reflected in the habit he gets. While in this world he has gotten everything for free, in the next world his monastic habit will be replaced with the shameful habit of a beggar. The beggar's habit is intertwined with shame, and it both envelops and bothers him. This means that in a way similar to how the monastic habit is expected to work on the lazy monastic by being part of him, the postmortem garment of shame will become an integral and active part of the deceased.

Transgressions pertain not only to how clothes are worn but also to how they are treated. The interaction between garments and their wearer demands that the latter takes control over what he or she wears. Sometimes, however, the control loosens, and the clothes become unruly and might even be lost, such as garments that are left to dry in the sun and are not fetched by the owner. If a garment (*štên*) has been left for 3 days, the owner is punished (*Precepts and Institutes* 6). A person who loses anything is rebuked before the altar, and "if what he has lost is from his own clothing, he shall not receive it for three weeks; in the fourth week, once he has done penance, he shall be given what he has lost" (P 131). "Whoever finds a thing shall hang it up for three days in front of the *synaxis* of the brothers, so that the one who recognizes it may take it" (P 132).

Clothes sometimes participated in the infliction of punishments. According to the Pachomian Precepts, if a monastic speaks or laughs during a prayer, song, or reading,

> he shall unfasten his belt immediately and with neck bowed down and hands hanging down he shall stand before the altar and be rebuked by the superior of the monastery. He shall do the same also in the assembly of the brothers, when they assemble to eat.
>
> (P 8)

Eunice Dauterman Maguire points out that his "loose self-discipline and its negative effect on his spiritual status becomes visible in the slack and defenseless, humiliated posture of the body, and in the loosening of his dress" (2003: 45). The punishment of ungirding the tunics is not restricted to the Pachomian monastics. An ungirded tunic was regarded as degrading; it indicated an effeminate nature or some moral failing (Olson 2017: 16). Roman soldiers, for instance, were made to stand in unbelted tunics as a punishment for cowardice. (Speidel 2012: 9; see also Olson 2017: 16). Unfastening the belt deprived the habit of its structure and left its wearer humiliated. Honor and shame, which were so important in the Roman army, also played a role in a monastery. Shenoute refers to a military punishment, likening the expelling of a monastic and breaking his girdle to what happened to a soldier.

Another offence and consequent punishment involving clothes was theft. If someone takes "any object not his own it shall be put on his shoulders in the synaxis during one of the prayers and he shall bow down to the ground; and he shall stand in the refectory" (*Precepts and Institutes* 8). It is reasonable to interpret the stolen object as an item of clothing, and that the punishment is devised as a direct response to taking a garment not one's own and then being made an example of with the superfluous garment sitting on one's shoulders. The surplus garment created an awkward impression and shamed the culprit in an effective way. This is an example of a nonintegrated extension of the body, opposite to integrated extensions. Integrated extensions are made part of the *persona*, virtually merging with the person—with the totality of body, clothes, and accessories, which together constitute the person. Nonintegrated extensions stand out as awkward and, as such, make awkward impressions.

When extensions are integrated, they are not normally seen as extras but as part of the person, which means that they are embodied. A fable about Macarius, who healed the cubs of a hyena, illustrates this point. The hyena takes Macarius "gently by the hem of his tunic" and leads him to her blind cubs (*HM* 21.15). Hyenas leading a monastic by the hem of his tunic were hardly something that happened in real life, but the story points to the fact that people can be led by means of their garments, for they are part of and positive extensions of their wearers.

While clothes in general can be regarded as extensions of the body, some garments have specialized functions as tools in addition to clothing the body. When belted, it was possible to make a fold in the tunic, which thus functioned as a sort of pocket. Such use of the tunic as a tool for carrying things was widespread. Abba Helle "often carried fire to his neighboring brothers in the fold of his tunic" (*HM* 12.1). In the *Historia Monachorum*, performing miracles is presented as an advanced state of asceticism, and the story about Abba Helle not only is about a miracle, but it is also about the function and extended use of clothes. An apophthegm presents a priest who uses a cloak (*himation*) more prosaically to measure grain (*AP* N 282, S 13.16).

More specialized, however, was the use of the sheep- or goatskin. An elder who went to Egypt "took his sheepskin with some dried loaves in it" (*AP* N 348, S 17.21, 3; see also S 7.20, 4). In other words, he used his sheepskin as a sack. On one occasion when Bessarion was in the desert with his disciples, he became thirsty. He took his sheepskin, went "about a stone's throw away," prayed, and brought the sheepskin back, full of water (*AP* A Bessarion 4). A brother who for 9 years was tempted to leave his *cenobium* and every day had his sheepskin (*melotarion*) ready for his departure, but each day he postponed it to the next day (*AP* S 7.48).[17] After 9 years, the temptation ceased, and he no longer wanted to leave (see also *AP* S 7.57, N 207, N 215).[18] Also in this case, the sheepskin seems to function as a sack. Usually monastics would put on their sheepskin when they went away.[19] According to the code of monastic manners, when monastics arrived at the place of other ascetics and monastics, the sheepskin should be removed and put away by the host. John the Cenobite is rebuked for not taking the sheepskin from traveling brothers who have come to see him (*AP* A John the Cenobite 1; see also Draguet 1944: 99). Monastic politeness and social custom demanded that this was done. So, in addition to function as a sack and a travel garment, the sheepskin definitely had a role in the social protocol.

Theoretically, the hood could also make an effective container, but it should *not* be used for that purpose.[20] A curious reference in the Pachomian Precepts makes this clear. Here we learn that when the brothers leave the refectory after a meal, they receive something called *tragemata* at the refectory's door (P 37). The one "who receives the things that are handed out shall receive them not in his hood but in his goat skin; and he shall not taste what he has received until he reaches his house" (P 38). The last part is in line with the general order of the monastery, where all activities and things have their established place. What are the *tragemata*, and why should the monastics only receive this foodstuff in the goatskin and not in the hood?

Tragemata is originally a Greek word, which was adopted in Latin. It indicates something eaten as a second course in a meal, perhaps sweetmeats. The Rules stipulate that the portion of this foodstuff that a monastic receives shall be enough for 3 days: "What they receive shall be enough for three days. And if anyone has anything left over, he shall bring it back to the housemaster who shall put it back in the storeroom to be mixed with the rest and given out to all the brothers" (P 38). Whatever it is, it obviously does not rot or otherwise degenerate because if any is left, the brothers can bring it back, and the housemaster can mix it with what is in the storeroom and then give it out again. The *tragematia* were probably not fruits, for in Precept 53, which is about special food for the sick, fruit is mentioned as an alternative to *tragematia* (*tragematia uel poma*; 28.17). The mysterious substance might have been dried fruits, nuts, or seeds, or even something less luxurious, for instance some dried pastry. Whatever it was, why should it not be received in the hood? A main reason was probably that in accordance with the Precepts, the head should be covered when the monastics were walking in the monastery, for instance, walking to the *refectorium* (P 91). Another reason may have been that the hood could become sticky and smell of the foodstuff. If this happened, the hood would function as a reminder of the experience of tasting the *tragematia*, and thus potentially as a temptation, acting on the monastic in a negative way.

What the *Praecepta* say about the *tragematia* reveals the same as was pointed out above, that the sheep- or goatskin was regarded as the piece of clothing that was normally used to carry things. There might also have been other ways to use the *melote* as a tool. Dauterman Maguire (2003: 44) proposes the perceptive hypothesis that it functioned as an apron for palm-weaving monastics:

> It may have served to rub off excess fibers shredding from the palm strips; it would protect the underlying tunics from the strips' sharp edges; and it would provide a speeding glide-path to support the hands for hours of frictionless work, as the monk looked down to avoid distraction.

If she is right, the garment was used to protect both the wearer's skin and his clothes.

The literary texts present this garment, the *melote*, as a truly multifunctional as well as expressive garment. The skin clearly had an emotional repertoire and marked changes of mood and feelings. Theodore, the fourth leader of the Pachomian monasteries, repeatedly played on this repertoire, according to the anecdotic literature. One example is when a man who has stolen bread during the fast confesses. He falls at Theodore's feet, reproaching himself. "Theodore covered his face with his goat skin and did not let him be manifested to the crowd saying: Who is weak, and I am not weak?" (*A Letter to Bishop Amon* 21).[21] Theodore seems to relate to the sinner, and, in doing so, he shows his humility. The covering with the goatskin is not only a gesture of humility but also a spontaneous and instinctive reaction to grief and shamefulness (Davies and Llewellyn-Jones 2017: 63). Generally, hiding in one's clothes is a reaction to shamefulness when being exposed to the gaze of others, sometimes extended to a wish to hide the face so as to disappear behind the protective shield of one's clothes.

On another occasion, when Theodore first speaks in his capacity as the new leader of the monastery, he urges the brothers to repent and uses his goatskin as a pedagogical tool. The brothers weep; Theodore himself also weeps very loudly. "When finally, he paused from weeping with them, he suddenly wiped away his tears to restrain his weeping. Then he struck them with the goatskin he wore, saying, 'Control yourselves and pay attention to my words'" (SBo 141). The intention of striking with the goatskin is to get the audience to change their mood and make them alert and pay attention. The skin is used as a pedagogical tool not only to illustrate a point but also doing so with a physical effect. It can be compared with the stick used to strike Buddhist monks to make them alert. Its functions were both physical and mental. Another example of a pedagogical use of a garment is when an old ascetic named Zacharias "drew his hood off his head, put it under his feet and trampled on it, saying, 'The man who does not let himself be treated thus cannot become a monk'" (*AP* A Zacharias 3). The hood is used synecdochically as a metaphor for the monastic (Giorda 2011); however, in this case, the garment has no direct and physical effect on the audience.

Yet another use of the emotionally rich *melote* is in exorcism. In the *Historia Lausiaca*, Paul the Simple strikes a man on the back with his sheepskin in an attempt to drive out a demon (*HL* 22.11). His attempt is unsuccessful, and he resorts to invoking Christ to get the demon out. It is evident, however, that striking with the *melote* was a way to expel demons. Like the miraculous mantle of Elisha and Elijah, the sheepskin sometimes functioned as a medium between the monastic and the supernatural world. An example is again from the *Historia Lausiaca*, when Palladius speaks of "the brother who has been my companion from my youth until today," which is often interpreted as referring to himself (*HL* 71.1). According to the story, "when he was in the remotest desert and did not even have a crumb, he found three warm loaves in his sheepskin. Another time too he found wine and loaves" (*HL* 71.3). In addition to having a rich emotional repertoire, the sheepskin functions here as a link to the supernatural, a medium for miracles, and as a horn of plenty.

Tearing garments

There are two recurring themes where clothes appear as functional extensions of the body, directly referring to biblical models. One is healing by means of the medium of clothes, which will be discussed in Chapter 5. The other is the tearing of garments as an expression of strong emotions.

The Bible contains more than thirty examples of tearing garments (Köhlmoos 2019: 304–306). Tearing was not only a way to materialize emotions, but it also had ritual connotations. In the monastic and ascetic literature, it can be mentioned to make a point, but with no tearing actually done. The warning against the evils of being praised in Pachomius's *Instructions* refers to a story in the Acts: "Behold, our fathers Barnabas and Paul, too, when praised, rent their garments and beat themselves out of scorn for human glory" (*The Instructions of Saint Pachomius* 22; see also Acts 14:14). Other times, the anecdotic literature refers to tearing garments among monastics. One example is from the Pachomian corpus, where a monastic is forced by barbarians to offer libations to pagan gods and eat meat sacrificed to them (*Paralipomena* 9). Afterwards, "he knew his iniquity, or rather the impiety which he had done. He rent his garments, struck his face repeatedly and came to his monastery" (*Paralipomena* 10; see also Isa. 37:1). His acts have been so shameful that his despair finds an outlet in tearing his garment. The story is anecdotic. Did fourth- and fifth-century monastics really tear their clothes? We know that ancient Romans and Greeks did; the "ripping or tearing of garments indicated great anxiety in both sexes" (Davies and Llewellyn-Jones 2017: 63), and in the case of Shenoute of Atripe, we know that he tore his garments—and he did it repeatedly, at least according to his letters and his spiritual testament. He was also one who most consciously tried to emulate biblical prophets. The example of Shenoute shows that it is difficult to understand exactly what the purpose or symbolism of the tearing of a garment was.

One episode of garment-tearing occurred when Shenoute visited the female monastery. According to his letter, the interpretation of the tearing took two opposite directions: one was Shenoute's own interpretation of the event, while an alternative interpretation was made by at least one of the female monastics (Krawiec 2002: 33). The background was a conflict between Shenoute and the women. In the Shenoutean federation, the monasteries were considered a unity, but with the two sexes segregated in a patriarchal structure, with Shenoute as their prophetic leader. The conflict seems to have been about whether he should personally visit the female monastery, as he wished, or not, in line with the women's wishes. In a heated argument, Shenoute tore his cloak—according to his account, not because of any sins but because "we were not able to tear our heart in place of our cloak (*hoeite*)" (XC 219: i. 3–9, quoted in Krawiec 2002: 33, 193, note 21). The cloak became a metaphor for his heart, which is, when all is said and done, impossible to tear in two. While, in line with a common use of the term, the heart can be conceived of as a metaphor for Shenoute's inner being, the cloak turned this inner life into a material object. The other interpretation of the tearing, which was made by one or more women, was an accusation of sexual misconduct. This accusation made Shenoute so angry that he wanted to "tear her garments in half on her body" (XC 219: i. 16–32, quoted in Krawiec 2002: 34, 193, note 24).[22]

In this text, tearing garments has at least three possible interpretations: frustration and grief, sexual approach, and frustration and anger. The cloak is acted upon and acts in all three interpretations as an extension of and sometimes a substitute for Shenoute, who tore it. His wish to tear female monastic's clothes suggests that they seem to personify her at the same time as the tearing would have rendered her partly naked. When Shenoute seems to refer to this episode again, he wants his torn garments to be preserved for posteriority:

> Therefore, not only shall I command the siblings who are of one mind with us to take care of all the words that we write in that book and the things written in all the epistles, but also I shall command them to preserve my *hoeite*-garments that I have torn many times and finally tore in two when I was greatly grieved even unto death.
>
> (ZC 301–302, in Layton 2014: 128–129)

Here, Shenoute commands the monastics to preserve his torn garments, along with all that he has written in books and epistles, so that future monastics will say, "What are these torn *hoeite*-garments and all these written words and all these curses?" (ZC 302, in Layton 2014: 128–129). According to this missive, he did not tear only one garment—probably a tunic—but several, and it was not only a symbolic gesture; the garments were actually torn in two. This shows not only a high degree of agitation but also a high degree of showboating. The torn garments were intended to be left as an emotional testament, which Shenoute wanted to be preserved. Like books and epistles, the garments were tangible things that could be read and interpreted in later times. In this manner, they functioned as part of an external and emotionally charged memory field. This is one function that clothes had, and perhaps even more so when they were limited, as was the case in monastic contexts, and each garment was invested with significance and meaning.

Restricting and enabling monastics

Clothes can be restrictive and influence the body in a troublesome manner. This influence is either intended or unintended, visible or invisible. Vestimentary extensions of the body can be associated with power. When clothes restrict the body's movements and when they act on the skin, they can be powerful actors. The monastic hood, the ascetic hair shirt (see Chapter 7), and Shenoute's ill-fitting garments are examples.

In what ways did garments affect their wearers? In one of the apophthegms, an old father, Silvanus, leaves his cell to water the garden with his face hidden in his cowl, looking at his feet, "so that my eyes should not see the trees, my son, in case my attention should be distracted by them" (Silvanus 4). Here, the general function of restricting the wearer's view is pushed to the extreme, at the same time illustrating very well how the hood could act upon its wearer. The point made in Silvanus's case is that he pushes the range of functions of the hood in a restrictive direction. At the same time, the story underlines what those who wrote about monastic life described as a main purpose of the hood: to restrict the sensory impressions of the monastic.

While a Pachomian Precept (29) stipulates that the monastics must cover their heads while eating without giving a reason, Palladius, Cassian, and the anonymous author of the *Historia Monachorum* explain why it should be so. According to the latter, the Pachomian monks "wear sheepskin cloaks (*melotas*), with their faces veiled (*kekalummeno prosopo*), and their heads bowed so that no one should see his neighbour" (3.1). Palladius specifies the hood's function further, associating it with eating:

> Let them cover their heads with their cowls (*koukoúllion*) when they are eating so no one brother can see another chewing. They are not to speak while eating or let their eyes wander anywhere beyond their plate or their table.
>
> (*HL* 32.6)

Cassian says roughly the same but is more eloquent regarding the experience of wearing the hood:

> And while they are eating, the rule of this silence is so strictly kept that with their hoods drawn down over their eyelids (to prevent their roving looks having the opportunity of wandering inquisitively) they can see nothing except the table, and the food that is put on it, and which they take from it; so that no one notices what another is eating.
>
> (Cassian, *Institutes* 4.17)

According to Cassian and the anonymous author of *Historia Monachorum*, the hood was designed to hinder a full view of the surroundings. It was especially effective when the monastics were eating. In these descriptions, the hood becomes an actor and an example of how clothes may possess agency, in this case by restricting sight. Another type of acting was mentioned earlier: if the monastics received their *tragemata* in the hood and this type of food had a delicious aroma and/or was sticky, the hood would affect their senses of smell and touch and might invite thoughts about food instead of more worthy matters, and even tempt them to try to get more of what they were reminded of.

In monasteries, time and space were controlled through ritualized activities associated with religion and labor. They had a strong disciplinary structure, which was gradually internalized and embodied. Shenoute's pastoral power can be seen as a version of the special Christian salvific power (Foucault 1982: 214; see also Krawiec 2002: 7–8). Generally speaking, and in line with Michel Foucault's thinking, power is relational and multidirectional. His words, "where there is power, there is resistance" are frequently quoted (Foucault 1984: 95). Networks of power include forms of resistance. The relation between Shenoute's authority, exercised by himself and his appointed leaders, and the resistance that was sometimes put up by the monastics reflects that power was distributed across the monasteries and that female monastics had their share of it as well.

In her analysis of the inner life of Shenoute's monastery, built on rich but not easily accessible resources, Rebecca Krawiec (2002) presents the women in the White Monastery and their relationship with their patriarchal leader. Since the women were in charge of the production of textiles and clothes for the monastics, they were also the ones who made Shenoute's garments. Krawiec provides two examples from Shenoute's letters about conflicts between him and the women concerning his clothes. These examples offer glimpses of power struggles in this ancient institution and clearly show how garments can become physical instruments in such situations. Since the women controlled the production of clothing, garments worked and were interpreted as their special instruments of power. In the first example, the women make a cloak (*hoeite*) for Shenoute that does not fit him; it is too narrow on his shoulders (Amélineau 1907: 153–158; Krawiec 2002: 46, 53, 153). When Shenoute complains, the women make a new cloak, but this time it is too wide on his shoulders, and he accuses them of not having taken his measure properly in the first place. He asks them to take his measure again and alter the cloak. It seems that, like in the monastery of Epiphanius, clothes were made in standard sizes in Shenoute's monasteries, which may have been part of the problem (Krawiec 2002: 19–20). The women did not want the men coming to their monastery to have their measures taken. The conflict seems to have escalated, and Shenoute claims that other monastics' cloaks did not fit them either, and that some brothers laughed at them. For that reason, he says, these unfortunate brothers with ill-fitting cloaks hid them and did not want to wear them. Eventually, Shenoute threatens to take the production of clothes away from the women and have someone in another monastery take it over. He adds that then the women will no longer have to plan "the colour, length, width and decoration of garments," which indicates that these garments were elaborate to a certain extent.

Krawiec shows that the conflict over these garments was also very much about proper female behavior in a monastery, which in several ways functioned as an extended patriarchal family (2002: 153). At the same time, however, as these garments and the conflict over them took on a metaphorical meaning of proper monastic behavior, they also functioned as instruments of resistance to power. The garments acted on the monastics by being either too tight, thus restricting the male bodies, or too wide and thus difficult to handle. In both cases, they had the potential to make their wearers into laughing stocks. Clothes tend to raise a laugh when a discrepancy arises between them and the wearer, and the wearer has to struggle with them instead of effortlessly embodying them.

In the second example, the women originally make a cloak for Shenoute according to his measure and with his requested colors and decorations (XO 66–68; see also Krawiec 2002: 47, 83–84, 153–154).[23] Shenoute claims that the cloak has been destroyed by moth and that he needs a new one. The women doubt him, thinking that the bad state of the cloak was due to his own neglect, and that he hid the offending garment because of that.[24] He then gets a new cloak, but he is dissatisfied with it and gives a fascinatingly detailed and rather technical description of the cloak and how he wanted it to be:

> First of all, it is heavy on me. For, instead of attaching a fringe (*toote*) to it, or [setting] its tassels (*loou*) so that they will be spread apart, or so that when they get twisted or untwisted over time they will be entwined with the fringe (*loou*),[25] you have braided upon it like a tunic (*štên*) or a cloak (*prêš*).
>
> (XO 66: i.1–30, translated in Krawiec 2002: 202, note 157)[26]

Shenoute further wants the cloak (*ršôn*) to be "completely fringed and totally decorated" (Krawiec 2002: 202, note 158).[27] In a similar way as in the last example, one of the things that were wrong with the cloak had to do with its material qualities, which included its power to act on its wearer. The cloak in this case acted on Shenoute not by being too narrow or too wide on his shoulders but by being too heavy, thus restricting his movements.[28]

That clothes did not quite fit was probably not uncommon. In the monastery of Epiphanius, founded toward the end of the sixth century, instructions on the walls provide measures for tunics and shirts. Tunics (*lebiton*) come in one size, while shirts (*thalis*) come in two, large and small (Winlock and Crum 1926: 9; Morgan 2018: 74, 101–102; Wipszycka 2011: 180).[29] This means that monastic clothes would not always have fitted very well, and either they had to be changed or the wearers had to live with them. An ill-fitting tunic would not have caused much trouble, as its square shape and the accompanying belt made it a versatile item of clothing. Cloaks that were ill-fitting or too heavy, as in Shenoute's case, seem to have been more troublesome.

Clothes are extensions of the body. The more seamless the transition between the body and its clothes is, the less obtrusive the clothes are. When clothes are worn, they are part of social situations and interact with the movements of their wearers, both enabling and restricting them. When monastics learned to wear the habit, it affected their movements in predicted and intended, ideal ways. Some of the items of the habit had extended functions as tools for carrying things, exorcising demons, and punishing culprits, and as media for contact with the supernatural world. Their emotional repertoire enabled their wearers to express feelings and sometimes also heightened those feelings, ranging from a basic feeling of safety and protection to the expression of anger or grief.

Clothes interact with their surroundings not only in a direct and physical way but also indirectly, by speaking to cognition and feelings. According to Davies and Llewellyn-Jones (2017: 63), "gesturing with clothes was vital to non-verbal communication throughout the ancient world and could elicit many 'readings.' Putting or throwing off elements of clothing, lifting, and hiding behind garments were all indications of a wide range of meanings." Clothes participate in and set in motion a series of events. These events are sometimes expected and desired, as when monastics are formally dressed for the synaxis; other times, they are unexpected, as when Shenoute tears his garments in frustration, or are unwanted and forbidden, as when monastics wear hoods with alluring and forbidden fringes. Monastic garments were part of ritualized and formal situations as well as of subversive and unruly behavior.

When the functions, effects, and meanings of clothes—in this case, monastic clothes—are seen together, a complex picture emerges. Clothes are worn; they interact with the wearer and the surroundings; they are extensions of the body, enabling and restricting their wearers; they are used as tools; and they have an emotional repertoire. These multidimensional applications of clothes suggest that they are conceived of and act as part of the person wearing them, that they work on a physical as well as a cognitive and emotional level, and that they are an interface between the wearer and the surroundings. One of their functions was only briefly touched upon in this chapter, related to Shenoute's wish that his torn garment be preserved as a memory of him and his struggles. In the next chapter, we will delve into healing garments, olfactory coding, and the ways in which garments were part of monastic memory fields. But first we will look closer into the ways in which producing garments and textiles acted on monastic minds.

Notes

1 A similar function of clothes can be seen in pictures of Jesus. Joan Taylor shows that in traditional pictures, Jesus is decked with textiles, while according to the traditional way of dressing in Palestine at his time, he probably wore a tunic reaching down to his knees (2018).
2 "The male and the female *himation*, the toga, the female *peplos* and *chiton*, as well as the Roman *stola* and *palla* were all made from long lengths of wide, unstitched cloth and demanded vigilance; slippage must have been commonplace." (Davies and Llewellyn-Jones 2017: 56).
3 In addition, referring to the models of Elijah, Elisha, and John, Cassian says that the girdle symbolizes the mortification of lust, signaling chastity and continence, and makes the monk into a "soldier of Christ" (*Institutes* 1.1; see also Chapter 5).
4 *Omnes pelles ligatae erunt et pendebunt ex umeris.*
5 Crum translates *hoeite* as "garment" (Crum 1962: 720b), while Layton leaves the word untranslated.
6 Faith Pennick Morgan gathered experimental knowledge from her reconstruction of ancient clothes and showed how belting square tunics created sleeves (2018: 100–104).
7 In the *Fragments from Horsiesios*, it is said,

> This is why we have all heard about this name of monk, we have all taken the habit, thinking that the habit would be our recommendation to God. But when we break the laws of the habit, we are all cowards, we desert.
> (Veilleux 1982: 169)

8 XL frg. 5r in Layton 2014: 314–315. I have chosen to translate *schema* as "habit," but Layton translates it as "uniform" (2014: 139 and 315).

9 According to Eleni Sotiriou (2015: 144–145), Greek Orthodox nuns never describe their habit as a uniform (*stoli*), but they understand it as Krawiec describes it.

10 In Jerome's Latin text, *cucullus* and *pellicula* is used for the hood and goatskin, respectively, while the Coptic version uses the rare Coptic word *rahtou* for the goatskin and the loanword *tolomon* from the Greek *telamon*, which means "shoulder sash" and could be the scarf/scapula.

11 Veilleux identifies the linen mantle in Jerome's preface to the Rules (*amictus lineus*) with the scarf in P 81 (*sabbanus longior*) (Veilleux 1981: 184, note 10). *Amictus* denotes a garment that is thrown around someone, so the term might be used both for a scarf and for a mantle. It seems that monastics sometimes wore a mantle or cloak, *pallium*, in addition to the garments listed in Jerome's preface and in the Rules (see Chapter 3). Shenoute's conflicts over cloaks support this view. According to Faith Pennick Morgan, *pallium* "appears to be an almost generic term for any straight edged outer wrap" (2018: 14).

12 Permitted and prohibited textiles continued to be a theme in monastic rules, seen, for instance, in Caesarius's revised Rule for a monastery of nuns in Arles from 534 (Caesarius of Arles, *Regula ad virgines in Oevres monastiques*; see also Tilley 2018; Miola 2018).

13 There were, of course, certain erotic patterns in monastic societies (Corrigan 2008: 160). This is commented upon in the Pachomian Rules, and especially in Shenoute's rules, which might be helpful in reconstructing such patterns in the White Monastery. Erotic patterns, however, fall outside the scope of this book.

14 XC 8 in Layton 2014: 96–97; YB 76 in Layton 2014: 106–107; YA 303–304, in Layton 2014: 116–117; YA 113 in Layton 2014: 124–125; Besa fragment 12K Layton also in 336–337.

15 YA 303–304 in Layton 2014: 116–117; FM 114 in Layton 2014: 256–257; 6M 246–247 in Layton 2014: 322–323.

16 FM 192 in Layton 2014: 294–295.

17 According to John Wortley, the sheepskin is a thing where an ascetic "packed up his [few] belongings" (2012: 115, note 1). See also *AP* S 7.57, N 207, and N 215.

18 However, another monastic "often changed location, carrying his sheepskin in a basket" (*AP* S 6.5,1). In the *Systematic Collection*, this apophthegm is listed under the heading of Poverty, which implies that the monastic owned nothing but the sheepskin. However, it is not immediately intelligible why he did not wear it (see also *AP* A Agathon 7).

19 *AP* A Macarius the Great 5 and Mark, disciple of Abba Silvanus 4, N 278, S 11.110, N 526.

20 A monastic who is carrying a small vessel of gold coins in his hood while crossing a river falls in and loses the coins (*AP* N 448). The moral is that monastics should not receive gold coins, with the additional point that a hood is not to be used as a carrier.

21 2 Co 11: 29.

22 Krawiec argues that the women did not know how to interpret Shenoute's visits. She contends that they "misinterpreted them," and that the "combination of a male leader visiting their community with frequency, staying all night, and tearing his clothes could certainly lead to confusion, especially since these visits were also an innovation" (Krawiec 2002: 114). However, perhaps their reaction should not be written off merely as the result of confusion but instead be considered one of several possible interpretations.

23 For the Coptic text of XO 66–68, I have relied on Rebecca Krawiec's quotations (and translations) from the microfilm.

24 It is arguably rather strange to place a moth-eaten cloak among other clothes, which Shenoute specifically says that he did, since moths so easily spread from one garment to another. Could the information about the new coat being linen mean that there he wanted to replace an original woolen cloak with a more moth-resistant linen one?

25 The translation of *loou* could instead be "tassels" or "tasseled fringe" (Crum 1962: 147).

26 The difference between a *prêš* and a *ršôn* seems to be that the latter is a cloak or covering that is bigger and heavier than the former.

27 According to Krawiec, the episode of the cloak was connected to a broader conflict in the monastery, leading Shenoute to expel several of the monastics (Krawiec 2002).

28 Complaints about the weight of a mantle are not limited to Shenoute. According to his *vita*, when Pachomius was dying, he asked "for a mantle (*prêš*) which has been worn thin and spread it over me, because this one is too heavy" (SBo 120; see also Veilleux 1980: 286). The mantle was sometimes used as a covering. According to Jerome and the *Praecepta*, *palliolum* (*prêš* in Coptic) is used during the night and especially by the sick (see P 42, 61, 81, 102, 105; see also Draguet 1944, 1945). G¹ uses the term *strôma*, "blanket or covering." Seneca and Quintillian say that the *palliolum* is worn by those who are unwell (Seneca, *Natural Questions* 4.13.10; Quintilian, *The Orator's Education* 11.3.144; see also Olson 2018: 430).

29 The instruction for the tunics: 10 handbreadths in width, 21 in length. The large shirts: 7 in width, 14 handbreadths and 2 fingers in length, and 10 fingers its neck-opening. The small shirts: 6 hand-breadth and 8 fingers in width, 13 handbreadth and 2 fingers in length and 9 fingers neck-opening.

(Winlock and Crum 1926: 9)

Ewa Wipszycka (2011: 180) notes that the inscription was made with such care that it must have been meant to be preserved for a long time.

5 Molding monastic minds and memories

Plaiting ropes, spinning thread, weaving cloth

A fragment in the National Library in Naples presents the story of a monastery's establishment. In the middle of the process, when one of the brothers, Martes, saw that the number of brothers

> had increased and were distressed by the need for clothing, he went to him [the anonymous leader] and urged him to set up for him a loom to weave cloth—for that was his craft—so that he might make some coarse linen garments for their use.
>
> (Layton 2014: 17)[1]

Martes needs help to set up the loom, and a monk from an "outside monastery" responds to the request for help. However, when the brothers ask the outsider to visit a second time to help them with the loom, the monastery's leader is reluctant to accept him. The reason that the leader does not want the outsider to return is revealed: he saw "an unclean spirit mounted upon his shoulders in the form of a large dog" (Layton 2014: 17). Later, when there are thirty or more brothers in the monastery, the leader gathers them and has them agree in writing "to be one single bond whether in food or in clothing, with no differences among them nor any separation in anything that they might do, whether matter of the soul or that of spirit" (Layton 2014: 18).

The description of the founding process in this text is not necessarily an accurate account of how things really happened. As Caroline Schroeder (2015: 6) remarks, the "evolution from anchoritic to coenobitic monasticism is a literary and historiographical trope, beginning with the *Life of Antony* and continuing with the *Life of Pachomius*."[2] That is not to say that such narratives do not contain valuable information. The point is not whether the story about the establishment of this monastery is an accurate description of the events, but rather that it reveals processes at work in the monasteries, such as how the borders between insiders and outsiders were patrolled—in this case, by demonizing outsiders. The story also reflects the importance of weaving and making clothes. It shows that monastics' clothes were ideally produced in the monastery, that by being made of "coarse linen," they were considered simple, and that uniformity in clothing and food was a requirement. A loom is the key requisite in the narrative, and the story also indicates that setting up looms required special skills. That monasteries had looms was clearly demonstrated at the excavation of the Epiphanius monastery of Thebes, dating to the sixth–seventh centuries, which took place at the beginning of the twentieth century. Several looms were found there, and archaeological research has brought to light more looms in other monasteries (Wipszycka 2011: 174). Describing the monastics at Nitria, Palladius says that "all these men work with their hands in the manufacturing of linen so that they are self-sufficient" (*Historia Lausiaca* 7.5).

In the Egyptian monasteries, several fibers were processed: halfa grasses, rushes, sedges, and palm leaves to make ropes, mats, baskets, and sandals, and flax and wool to make textiles and clothes. The processing of fibers started by picking wild plants, planting and harvesting flax, and breeding and shearing sheep. Ascetics and monastics plaited (*plékein*) ropes and spun thread; wove mats, baskets, cloths, and ribbons; and made garments. In addition to their clothes and sandals, a rush mat was part of the monastic gear, used as a bed or a seat.[3] These things were part of the necessary equipment in the monasteries, as well as of their economic life, used for barter and sale. Equally important, however, is a point that has not yet been sufficiently stressed: that the processes of twisting fibers and making fiber-based products interacted closely with the spiritual and meditative life in the monasteries (see also Gilhus 2020).

This chapter focuses on minds, memories, and meaning, and consists of three parts. It begins with a discussion of the effects of crafting and processing fibers on minds and bodies of monastics. How did crafting and toiling with their hands work on the minds and bodies of the monastics? In what ways did plaiting and weaving help monastics to become immersed in the biblical world or facilitate a meditative state and help them empty their minds? The second part focuses on not only how items of clothing constituted mediums for healing but also contributed to transmitting knowledge and memories by channeling the senses and feelings of the monastics. The third part discusses how meaning and memory were mentally inscribed on the items of the monastic habits.

Processing fibers, processing monastic bodies and minds

Imitation (*mimesis*) of the ascetic way of life and the sayings of the fathers is a main point in the prologues of both the Systematic and the Alphabetic Collection of the apophthegms:

> This book is an account of the virtuous asceticism and admirable way of life and also of the words of the holy and blessed fathers. They are

meant to inspire and instruct those who want to imitate their heavenly lives, so that they may make progress on the way that leads to the kingdom of heaven.

(*AP* A Prologue, *AP* S Prologue, see also Rubenson 2013c;
Larsen 2016)

This type of mimesis included imitating biblical heroes, using biblical language, and wearing clothes modeled on the garments of Old Testament and New Testament heroes, as well as those of the monastic fathers. The monastics immersed themselves in the biblical world, and sensory knowledge and experiences contributed to making this world real. Birgit Meyer introduced the concept of "aesthetic formation," which describes the formation of social entities and rendering imaginative formations "tangible by materializing in spaces and objects" (2009: 5). In her own words, "in order to become experienced as real, imagined communities need to materialize in the concrete lived environments and be felt in the bones" (Meyer 2009: 5). This implies that the things that circulated in the monasteries partook in the processes of forming monastics and monastic communities, and that reading texts and performing rituals, as well as twining, plaiting, and weaving, worked together in these processes.

When the Pachomian monastics listened to Scripture being read and when they prayed and recited together in the assembly (*synaxis*), their acts were reinforced by standardized body movements (*Regulations of Horsiesios* 7–13). These daily rituals took place in a special context. The Pachomian Rules clearly state that when a monastic came to the *synaxis*, "he should not tread upon the rushes which have been dipped in water in preparation for the plaiting of ropes, lest even a small loss should come to the monastery through someone's negligence" (*Praecepta* 4). In addition to the religious rituals in the synaxis and as a contextualization of them, the monastics plaited ropes. They also had to adjust their movements to avoid treading on the rushes, which were always laid on the floor in the assembly.

According to Armand Veilleux, there "was a very close unity between prayer and work in Pachomian monasteries; the monks constantly prayed during their work and they did weaving and plaiting during the *synaxis*" (1981: 185). This type of activity took place on a daily basis and was part of the process of internalizing Scripture and embodying the monastic and the scriptural world. Similarly, in the monasteries of Shenoute, soaked reeds were laid down in the assemblies of men: "When it is time to spread out the soaked reeds for the gathering in the early morning or at evening, they shall go in fives or sixes, or on occasion fours and even three."[4] Wool was laid down in the assemblies of women:

And just as it is done in our (men's) domain so too shall you (women) do: not to let girls go in pairs to light the lamp for the morning gathering or to make the arrangement for the gathering at the time of evening by laying out the wool that you (plur.) work on, unless the house leader is present—or the second or a great woman who is perfect in propriety and the fear of the Lord.[5]

Plaiting ropes and spinning wool, accompanied by reading and reciting passages from Scripture, created a collective sense of self and belonging in the monastic community (see Riley 2008: 63). Listening and reciting and body movements involved the person's body and mind alike. When religious rituals in the strict sense were combined with crafting, rushes, ropes, and yarn were part of them as well.

The monastics worked on fibers not only in the assembly (*synaxis*) but also in their cells (Layton 2007: 70–71). The cell was a battlefield where the monastic fought against evil thoughts and demons (Hedstrom 2009: 756–791; see also Graiver 2016: 220) but at the same time a solitary workshop too. Alexandra shut herself in a tomb and lived there for nearly 10 years (*AP* A 5). She said that to conquer spiritual sloth (*accidie*), she prayed "every hour from dawn to the ninth hour while spinning linen" (*AP* A 5, 3). Crafting was an effective weapon against evil thoughts and demonic attacks because making the hands work fended off boredom and helped the mind stay focused.

In the anecdotic literature, there are several examples of the positive effects of crafting and of how it assisted the monastics in becoming and staying absorbed in the world of biblical imagination and in meditation (Gilhus 2020). John the Little is a case in point. He was so preoccupied with his weaving that he resisted any and all distractions. When a camel driver came to buy his products, John had to be called back three times, as he did not remember what he went in for, "because his spirit was fixed on God" (*AP* A John the Little, 31). The third time, he returned to his cell while he was mumbling, "weave—camel, weave—camel." Two realities conflicted in his mind: his internal reality, which was created by absorption in crafting, and the external reality of economic transactions, represented by the camel and its driver. This intense concentration, which resulted in similar conflicts, is the topic of several anecdotes about John. In one instance, when he was weaving rope for a basket, he did not notice that it had reached the wall "because his spirit was occupied in contemplation" (*AP* A John the Little, 11). In another story, a guest who praises his weaving receives no response, and when he breaks the silence for a third time, John states bluntly, "since you came here, you have driven away God from me" (*AP* A John the Little, 32). The anecdotes illustrate the degree to which John was absorbed in his crafting and combined it with spiritual contemplation. The conflict between economic gains and detachment from this world is a topic in these and similar anecdotes, which shows a lack of interest in the result of one's work and an atelic state of mind. John's aloof manner of crafting and selling his products illustrates his other-worldly attitude and makes his economic activity seem an unimportant side effect of his religious activities (see Chapter 6). At the same time, the anecdotes presuppose that crafting with fibers helped to fence the world out and create a receptive and meditative mood both when the monastics listened to Scripture being recited in the assembly and when they worked in the solitude of their cells (Riley 2008: 69–70).

Working with the hands was sometimes accompanied by more lively mental experiences. In the *Life of Pachomius*, there is a story about visions that Pachomius had while he was working on a mat.[6] These extraordinary experiences indicate that he had reached a state of mind that transcended the ordinary flow of thoughts. The rhythmic and monotonous occupation promoted a psychological change and made ordinary reality fade away. In its stead, Pachomius's imagination was filled with a biblical superhuman reality. These stories make a firm connection between being absorbed in crafting and being immersed in biblical contemplations.

Recent studies have suggested a close connection between crafting and well-being: crafting has therapeutic effects (Riley 2008; Pöllänen 2015). Provided that the necessary skills have been properly learned, these activities require little conscious effort and at the same time contribute to creating and maintaining a positive and productive state of mind. It is an obvious hypothesis that in ancient Egyptian monasticism, the processing of plant fibers and wool contributed to redirecting the monastics' thoughts from secular concerns to spiritual ends, thus promoting the goals of monastic life and realizing the monastic community. It is also likely that the state of mind that this activity helped to promote went in two directions. One was a meditation on the scriptural world through reading and reciting biblical stories, and another was a more technically refined approach, seen for instance in the works of Evagrius and Cassian, which focus on meditative moods and on emptying the mind. Various mental strategies were prescribed to hinder distraction and the wandering of the mind (Graiver 2017: 273–277; Graiver 2016: 200–201).[7]

In this chapter, I argue that making mats and baskets and engaging in plaiting and weaving assisted monastics in keeping their attention focused. Practicing these crafting techniques prevented distractions, both external and mental, created a receptive mood, disciplined the body, trained the monastics in developing staying power, and facilitated biblical imagination and meditation, as well as the perfection of more specific meditative techniques, such as contemplative prayer.

How did crafting function on the mental and bodily levels? The ancient sources give a strong impression that there are affordances present in fiber crafting, which not only cooperate with the industrious fingers of the monastics but also facilitate the maintenance of a meditative mood and the cultivation of biblical imagination (Gilhus 2020).

Lambros Malafouris has proposed a fascinating theory, or rather launched a research program, about the interaction between humans and things.[8] One of his examples to illustrate the link between material form and body memory has direct relevance for monastic fiber-based crafting. A case in point is his observations of wheel-thrown pottery in Greek pottery shops, where handcrafting can be seen as a form of thinking with and through clay. In his view, there is an interaction between the potter, clay, artifacts, and actions, but there is no casual driver. Memory is immanent in the creative process:

> Body memory refers to the ways in which the potter's body remembers its skill of producing the form of a vase through actively engaging with clay. Material memory refers to the ways the affordances of clay, on their part, actively engage the potter's body to produce the form of a vase.
>
> (Malafouris and Koukouti 2018: 174)

If we substitute fiber for clay and the weaver's body instead for the potter's body, we can imagine that when the fingers of the Egyptian monastics were industriously preoccupied with plaiting and weaving, the interaction between them and what they were doing took place in a way that obviously did not demand much thinking about what they were doing. Their work did not require a conscious attention. This is in line with the assertion that the "body remembers not so much through a process of passive recollection as by the re-enaction of internal memory traces. Rather, the body remembers through the active identification or re-enaction of traces which are both internal and external" (Malafouris and Koukouti 2018: 175). Like the affordances in the clay, there were also affordances in the different kinds of fibers, which interacted with the monastics when they were processing them; accordingly, "weaving, basket-making and carpentry all have their own rhythms and consequent forms and again those rhythms derive from the interplay of skilled bodies and the materials that have enskilled them" (Gosden and Malafouris 2015: 707).

How did plaiting and weaving promote spiritual goals? If it is true that "fabrication lies at the heart of the human condition" and that "human beings are shaped and constituted by the stuff they make" (Ihde and Malafouris 2019: 209), does it also mean that, by extension, such activities as twisting ropes, plaiting baskets, and weaving cloth were particularly suited as catalysts for the processes of spiritual reflection and transformation that were taking place at the same time? If it is true that "automatically in the sense of effortless performance of a task is usually associated with a loss of agency or loss of self—a feeling of being immersed in, rather than causing, the act" (Malafouris 2013: 224), does this type of automaticity and immersion simultaneously facilitate meditative moods and Scripture-based imaginations?

A discrepancy in the ancient sources regarding the importance of crafting is evident. According to the documentary sources, farming was the monasteries' main source of income (Wipszycka 2009: 552–528; Brakke and Crislip 2018: 16), while in the literary and anecdotic sources, various types of crafting based on fibers are given more importance than farming and husbandry (Wipszycka 2011: 172–173; Brown 2016: 84). Since both farming and crafting took place in the monasteries, a main reason that making ropes, mats, baskets, and cloth are given more space in the literary sources than farming is probably because crafting was considered more consonant with the goals of monastic life and more helpful for personal transformation. This discrepancy points to the dual function of the activity: the actual production of textiles and other things and the creation of moods that facilitated meditation and active imagination. Accordingly, the rhythmic, monotonous, and sedentary work of fiber crafting was easy to combine with internalizing Scripture, reciting, praying, and meditating, and acted as a catalyst for such Scripture-based activities.

Healing garments, olfactory coding, and monastic memories

Processing fibers is an embodied process whereby the perceived separation between mind and body is transcended, and the material with which the craftsman engages becomes an extended part of the body. Wearing clothes can also be regarded as an embodied activity. One example, only sporadically brought into awareness, is that clothes contribute to bodily comfort and psychic stability and make being in the world more frictionless than it would otherwise be. Another example of how clothes are part of human embodiment is found in the form of "enclothed cognition," whereby clothes are seen as having a systematic influence on perception and interpretation (Adam and Galinsky 2012, 2019; see also Introduction). In addition, clothes incorporate traditions and memories in ways that are not necessarily made explicit or only partly made explicit. Specific items of clothing incorporate and transmit moods, memories, and knowledge, for instance, when they are connected to specific persons, events, spaces, or times. Sometimes there are attempts at controlled transmission of knowledge where clothes are ascribed meanings and where they are intended to function as part of an extended mind. Both when clothes transmit personal memories and when they are ascribed specific meanings, they signal a close connection with those who wear them. This is in line with the thesis of this book about clothes being part of embodied identity and actors in people's lives. What kind of knowledge and memories were incorporated and transmitted by means of ascetic and monastic garments, how did such incorporations and transmissions happen, and in what ways did they make clothes part of embodied identity and actors in monastic life?

One way of transmitting memories is by inheriting garments. Clothes can be handed down from generation to generation. Inheriting garments from deceased monastic fathers is a literary *topos*, usually associated with succession and transfer of authority. Succession was a powerful strategic weapon in the battle for monastic and ecclesiastic authority—a theme that will be discussed in more detail later in this chapter. However, inheriting clothes is also emotionally engaging and triggers feelings about and memories of the deceased in those who inherit their clothes. Some of these memories and feelings are explicit but obviously not the entire range of them. When garments are seen as extensions of their wearers, inheriting them means that the limitations of this life are overcome and that through his or her clothes, the dead person still has power of presence and of engaging the new wearer. Abba Daniel says about Arsenius, a monastic who was known for his holiness and silence: "He left me his leather tunic, his white hair-shirt and his palm-leaf sandals. Although unworthy, I wear them, in order to gain his blessing" (*AP* A Arsenius 42). This indicates that the presence of Arsenius was still a force to be reckoned with and that his clothes were seen as part of him. Monastic texts focus on the beneficial influence of inherited clothes. They convey the idea that through the clothes, the deceased is a moral example for and a positive force in the successor's life. This also means that the dead person has a sort of continuous emotional and moral presence in the life of the successor. This presence varies from being vague and in the background to sometimes being brought into awareness.

Garments and textiles were also conceived of as conveyors of knowledge through supernatural mechanisms such as sympathetic magic. According to James Frazer (1950: 43–44), the basis of sympathetic magic is that a sympathy exists between a person and objects that have been in contact with the person, and clothes are examples of objects that are closely connected to their wearers. Because they were seen as extensions of them, clothes were frequently used as mediums in sorcery, as well as in healings, as we will see later. In a similar way, things that someone had made, for instance textiles and other fabrics, can be conceived of as having a continuous connection to their maker. This last point is illustrated by a story in the *Historia Monachorum*, where a brother called John weaves harnesses of palm leaves for beasts of burden. When a cripple mounts an ass and his feet touch the strap that John made, he is immediately cured (*HM* 13.9).

Because clothes are extensions of their wearers, touching the garment that someone is wearing means touching the person. Generally, when two people who do not know each other very well touch each other, they actually touch each other's clothes. Touching clothes is not as intimate as touching somebody's skin. When a servant in one of the apophthegms touches the sheepskin of a monastic to come into contact with him, this is a gesture of respect and subordination (*AP* S 15.10, 19).

A special effect of touching is produced when clothes are used as mediums for healing. In the main Greek version of the *Life of Pachomius*, there is a story about a woman who, like the woman in Matthew 9:20–22,[9] was bleeding (*haimorroousa*). While Pachomius was sitting in the church, the woman came and touched his hood (*koukoullion*) and was immediately healed (G[1] 41). In The Bohairic version, "she touched him and his clothing," experiencing a similar healing effect (SBo 41). These are stories where the power of holy persons extended to their clothes and where clothes acted as mediums between them and those in need of healing. The stories reflect the close connection between clothes and their owners.[10]

Clothes could act as media in both directions, from the healer to the sick and from the sick to the healer. In another story from the *Life of Pacho-mius*, the garment belongs to the sick. In it, a demon has afflicted a woman with an illness, and her father brings her to Pachomius, begging him to heal her (SBo 43; see also G¹ 43). Pachomius does not speak with the daughter directly, but he asks the father to send him one of her garments, specifying that it should be washed and that she should not use it after having washed it. Pachomius returns the garment and informs the father that his daughter has not kept her monastic purity (*ptoubo ntmetmounache*), which implies that the daughter has vowed chastity. When she is questioned, the woman confesses and promises never to sin again. The holy man then sends her some oil over which he has prayed. After she anoints herself with this remedy—a frequently used medium in monastic miraculous healings, "she is healed in the name of the Lord" (SBo 43).[11] In this case, her garment gave Pachomius access to knowledge about her way of life and to things that perhaps she would have rather kept secret.

Why did the garment have to be washed before it was given to Pachomius? The story does not tell. One reason is probably that when unwashed, it was considered unclean; and obviously, the holy man should not be exposed to the perceived female lack of purity. Another reason is that when the garment no longer smells of the woman's body odors, nor has any stains, Pachomius's verdict becomes even more astonishing. How could he have known what she had been up to? The story is a testimony to the holy man's clairvoyance. A main point in this story is that clothes can reveal things about those who wear them to those who have the power to listen to what they silently tell.

Used clothes may have telltale stains, and they smell of what they have touched—of their wearers and sometimes of other things as well. The following apophthegm definitely points to "other things." The apophthegm is about a monastic who is hopelessly in love with a married woman. When the woman dies and the brother still cannot forget her, he fights his passion in a rather peculiar way:

> There was a brother fighting the good fight at Scete, and the enemy put him in mind of a certain most beautiful woman, cruelly afflicting him. Then, by providence of God, another brother came down from Egypt to Scete, and as they were speaking together, he said that the wife of so-and-so had died: the very woman on whose account the brother was embattled. On hearing this, he took his *lebitón*, and going up to Egypt by night, he opened her tomb. He mopped up her bodily fluids with the *lebitón* and returned to his cell with it. He would set the stench before him and do battle with the *logismos*, saying: "Look, the desire you are pursuing: you have it before you, take your fill!" In this way he tormented himself with the stench until the warfare ceased from him.
>
> (*AP* S 5.26)[12]

Two narrative patterns are at work in this text. One is an inversion of the familiar pattern of love and desire for the beloved. The monastic went to the dead woman's tomb and "mopped up her bodily fluids" with his tunic in the hope that by smelling the tunic, infested with her putrid remains, he would overcome his desire. Since the tunic was mixed with her bodily remains, it had become intimately connected to and reminded the monastic of her. Its purpose in this case was not to arouse lust but the opposite, to wipe out desire. This implies that the tunic was supposed to function as a sort of inverted necrophile fetish.[13] In this case, the fetishized object did not belong to the dead woman but to the one who was attracted to her, the monastic. In a similar way, the standard sexualized image of young women who are made alluring by their scent, which is usually caused by flowers, ointment, or make-up, is reversed here. By being dead, the woman, the original object of the monastic's desire, is even more devoid of agency than female objects of male desire in stories sometimes are. The narrative pattern of love and desire is thus inverted in multiple ways.

The other narrative pattern in the story is the battle scenario—so characteristic of monastic texts. Good fights evil, and God and his angels fight the devil and his demons. The apophthegm bristles with battle metaphors, using a common name for the devil, "the enemy" (*ekhthros*; 5.26, 2) as its point of departure. This designation for the devil is used a little under a hundred times in the Systematic Collection (Guy 2005: 334). In line with this term, the monastic in the story is a champion (*agonistes*; 5.26, 1) who goes to war (*polemos* 5.26, 13), "fighting (*polemein*; 5.26, 6 and 5.26, 11) the good fight." The infected *lebiton* has become a weapon in this never-ending fight against the devil. Susan Ashbroke Harvey comments on the narrative in a pertinent way:

> Penitence, punishment and discipline forged together in the monk's actions to become a form of spiritual combat. For having fought the demon of fornication within himself, the monk then used Satan's own weapon against him, subjecting himself to the 'intolerable stench' and to meditation on the corpse's 'infected' decay until he had conquered his inner turmoil. The very mark of Satan's domain, the stench of mortality, became the means of his defeat at the hand of a monk.
>
> (2006: 215)[14]

In addition, the story includes a touch of necromancy. Necromancy designates the calling forth of dead people from their tombs and from the underworld by ritual means to ask them questions (Bremmer 2002: 71 ff; Ogden 2004). In this case, the woman is made present by means of the infected tunic. She, or rather her mortal remains, are called upon by the monastic to tell the "truth" about herself. This can be seen as a more general "truth" propagated in male monastic circles about women: they stink.

The anecdote captures in a rather bizarre way a dimension of clothes that has not so far been commented upon, although it is universal. Because clothes smell of what they have been in contact with, they trigger memories and are thus effective vehicles of knowledge. In fact, there is a shortcut from scent to memory. By smelling a special scent, the brain can sometimes recall a memory of something that happened in the past. This means that the story about the tunic that was infected with the remains of a female corpse is built on a general mechanism of clothes that triggers feelings and memories. Because clothes are infused with the scent of their wearers, they embody them and sometimes directly bring them to others' memories.

Inscribing memories, making lists, and creating meaning

From the examples provided in this chapter, it becomes clear that clothes and their raw materials were staged in such a way as to trigger specific moods and emotions. Clothes have an emotional repertoire and some more than others (cf. Miller 2010: 28). The process of incorporating memories and traditions is to a great extent based on sensual and emotional mechanisms. Peter Stallybrass expounds as follows:

> In a cloth society, then, cloth is both a currency and a means of incorporation. As it exchanges hands, it binds people in networks of obligation. The particular power of cloth to affect these networks is closely associated with two almost contradictory aspects of its materiality: its ability to be permeated and transformed by makers and wearers alike; its ability to endure over time. Cloth thus tends to be powerfully associated with memory. Or, to put it more strongly, cloth is a kind of memory. When a person is absent or dies, cloth can absorb his or her absent presence.
>
> (Stallybrass 1993: 38).

John Sutton (2007: 23) expresses similar ideas when he says that clothes

> are not merely external triggers for forms of remembering which are always internal, but are rather themselves memories—enduring bearers of information and meaning and affect always standing in complex more-or-less coupled and tangled relations to different embodied human wearers.

He adds that "essentially incomplete creatures like us naturally parasitize, lean on, and incorporate 'external' tools for thinking" (Sutton 2007: 23).

Inscribing and fixing memories on clothes is a special way of transmitting knowledge, because inscribing memories and making them explicit rest more heavily on rationalization than when memories are vaguely incorporated in emotionally loaded clothes. It is a way of attempting to define and take control over tradition and memory by spelling them out. One example is an apophthegm that refers more generally to the elders: "The elders used to say that the cowl (*koukoullion*) is the symbol of innocence, the scapular (*analabos*) of the cross, the girdle (*zone*) of courage. Let us live a life that is consonant with our habit (*schema*)" (*AP* S 10.192; N 55).

Such inscribing on garments is found in more elaborate versions in the prologue to the work *Praktikos* by Evagrius of Pontus, concerning the praxis of the Egyptian monastics, and in his disciple John Cassian's *De institutis coenobiorum*. Both authors describe the Egyptian monastic habit based on their experiences of the ascetic communities in Nitria and Kellia, both ascribe symbolic meanings to the various items of the habit, and both address outsiders.[15] Evagrius wrote to Anatolios, who was staying in a monastery on the Mount of Olives, and Cassian wrote to monastic brothers in Gaul. Both transform the items of the habit into text with the intention to fix and transmit their symbolism and values to monastics outside Egypt.

Inspired by Paul Connerton's work, Rebecca Krawiec contends that the monastic habit transferred memory in two ways, either by incorporating it or by inscribing it on the habit (Krawiec 2014; cf. Connerton 1989: 72–73). She makes the salient point that just "as ancient theorists argued that memory was most effective when it was mapped onto the brain through visual images, here the monk has access to a visual memory map by looking at his own clothing" (Krawiec 2014: 61). Evagrius's text, dating to the latter part of the fourth century, is the oldest surviving example of that type of description. It represents perhaps the first phase of the Christian tradition of investing monastic garments with symbolic meaning (Krawiec 2014: 57): "The *koukoullion* is a symbol of the grace of God our Saviour, which protects their ruling faculty and keeps fervent their youth in Christ, with a view to those who are always trying to batter and wound them" (Evagrius, *Praktikos*, Prologue 2).

Cassian's *Institutes* may be dated between 419 AD and 425 AD (Goodrich 2007: 3). Although Evagrius's and Cassian's descriptions share an interpretative biblical context, they differ in several ways. The differences reveal that while there was some consensus about what the habit "meant," it did not reach the level of details. There was some fluidity in the interpretation of the various items, as well as in the evaluation of their importance in relation to each other. This indicates that monastic clothes were interpreted according to the circumstances in which the interpretations were made. Several interpretative contexts are at work in the two descriptions (Krawiec 2014). Evagrius makes the monastic habit into a combat dress. He connects each item to a monastic virtue and often to a biblical passage. In Krawiek's interpretation, "Evagrius thus locates monastic practice in the body by mapping the purpose of monastic dress onto it" (2014: 58). In this way, he combines practices of incorporation and inscription. Combined with biblical references, the dress becomes a memory aid for monastic behavior (Krawiec

2014: 60–61). At the same time, Evagrius is eager to legitimize this inscribing by connecting it to the teachings of the Egyptian monastics

> now then we will recount all that we have learned from the holy fathers about it [the habit] (*Prologue* 1).[16] Cassian makes even stronger claims, when he identifies his *Instituta Aegyptiorum* with the original practice and tradition of monasticism, stating that it goes back to the time of the foundation of the church and even to the Old Testament prophets.
>
> (Goodrich 2007: 126)

Comparing Evagrius's and Cassian's descriptions, Krawiec observes that "whereas Evagrius' monk engages in social memory as an extension of preparing for demonic combat, Cassian's monk remembers the authentic and authoritative Egyptian tradition that Cassian, as writer, establishes for him" (2014: 65). In Cassian's thinking, she argues, the habit connects the monastic "to a respected monastic lineage" (Krawiec 2014: 62). The monastic identity is realized both by the monk's habit and by his access to books (Krawiec 2014: 65).

In addition to combat and lineage, the descriptions of the habit anchor it in various other interpretative contexts. Some are made more explicit than others, and the two authors sometimes differ in their interpretations. Evagrius, for instance, sees the hood as a symbol of humility, while Cassian associates it with the innocence of childhood (Goodrich 2007: 90–91). The latter also associates the monastics' white linen with burial clothes and the leather girdle, "the dead skin" (*Institutes* 1.11), with mortality.

The dominant strategy in these interpretations is a shift from literal to metaphorical meanings. For instance, when Cassian describes the staff as a means of defense against dogs—turning them into vile creatures—he explicates that "the carrying of the staff spiritually teaches that they ought never to walk unarmed among so many barking dogs of faults and invisible beasts of spiritual wickedness" (*Institutes* 1.8). Steven D. Driver (2002: 73) appositely remarks that the "several layers of the garment possess layers of meaning ranging from the regulation of character to the constant reminder of the wearer's vocation." While capturing clothes in writing is a way of transforming textiles into text, in this case by inscribing monastic values onto them (Krawiec 2014: 56), this type of inscribing meanings implies that the meaning production of the habit is driven in one direction; it also implies an attempt to make this meaning permanent.

While the inscribing of memories on the habit depends on the cognitive mechanism of associations, in some cases it also depends on the age-old technique of making lists. Lists reflect and produce knowledge, create order and systems, and empower institutions and individuals who make and use them. By establishing boundaries, order, and hierarchy, lists assist those in charge of promoting, organizing, and administrating an institution—in this case, a monastic community.

Like the short list of monastic garments in the story about Paphnutius in the *Historia Monachorum* and the slightly longer list in the Pachomian Rules, Evagrius and Cassian mention all the items that constitute the monastic habit (see Belknap 2004: 15). Both lists are retrospective (see Goody 1978: 80–81), as they refer to the traditional Egyptian monastic habit. Both mention Old Testament and New Testament heroes in their descriptions. Both Evagrius and Cassian intended their lists to function as strategic tools with the purpose of affecting the monastic experience of wearing the habit. Their lists include the following items, in this order:[17]

Table 5.1 Evagrius and Cassian's lists of monastic garments

Evagrius	John Cassian
	Girdle (*cingulum*)
	Clothing (*vestis*)
Hood (*koukoullion*)	Hood (*cucullus*)
	Tunic (*colobium*)
Scapular (*analabos*)	Cord/scapular (*resticula/analabos*)
	Cape (*pallium*)
Belt (*zone*)	
Sheepskin (*melote*)	Goatskin (*melotes* or *pera*)
Staff (*rabdos*)	Staff (*baculum*)
	Shoes (*calceamentum*)
	Girdle (*cingulum*)

Evagrius's description in *Praktikos* progresses from the head to the legs and from the innermost to the outermost. Cassian follows a similar order in his *De institutis* when he describes the habit of the monastics, but he begins and ends with the girdle. His second object is the clothing of the monastics (*de veste monachi*), and then follow the various parts of the habit.[18] Since the order of the items on a list is significant, this means that the girdle is given a special position and meaning. In his first subchapter, Cassian mentions the biblical precedents of the girdle, and in the last subchapter, he presents its more profound Christian and Scriptural meanings, raising it to an epitome of the entire habit. Cassian's list includes more items than Evagrius's. His descriptions of the various items are also much longer.[19] Particular to Cassian is also that he specifically says that some items should not be used in Gaul. Thus, while anchoring the various items of the habit firmly in the religious universe of Christian origins and transferring symbolic values and effects to them, he nonetheless discards some of them, removing them from actual use in Gaul.

Cassian offers a dual reason for removing these items from actual use: they suited neither Gaul's climate nor its prevalent vestimentary code. He suggests that the monastics in Gaul did not have to use those parts of the habit that were not in accordance with the district's customs:

> For the severity of the winter does not allow us to be satisfied with slippers or tunics or a single frock; and the covering of tiny hoods or the wearing of a sheepskin would afford a subject for derision instead of edifying the spectators.
>
> (*Institutes* 1.10)

It is difficult to know why people in Gaul laughed at monastics when they were dressed in the hood and the *melote*. The offending garments should be compared with what other ascetics, as well as laypeople, were actually wearing in that area at the beginning of the fifth century. The most obvious reason for derision seems to be that these items of clothing were otherwise not used, as Cassian indicates. However, it is worth noting that the role of the hood and the *melote* seem to have been ambiguous in other places as well. Headgear, such as hoods, which were usually associated with children, might look awkward on grown-ups. In his *Letter to Eustochium*, Jerome pokes fun at female ascetics who wore hoods (*cucullis*) in an attempt to return to childhood, but—in his eyes—only managed to look like owls (*Letter* 22.27). In Egypt, it seems that the *melote* went from functioning as a coat to something closer to an apron and perhaps over time was considered more of an ideal garment of old than a useful garment for that time.

Cassian's deliberation raises a more general point. If the various versions of the habit were to function as uniforms in a growing monastic movement, they had to be distinct from ordinary dress and clearly show that their wearers belonged to a separate, special group in society. At the same time, if their robes were too distinct, the monastics and ascetics might not be easily accepted by the laypeople, which was probably Cassian's concern in Gaul. According to Richard J. Goodrich, "the ascetic project in Gaul was well under way by the time John Cassian arrived on the scene" (Goodrich 2007: 32). This means that Cassian had to accept—at least partly—what was already established practice to ensure admiration instead of derision. It is easy to see Cassian's point when he concludes that the novelty of the garb might give "some offense to men of the world" and that the idea is to stick to its "honourable simplicity" (*Institutes* 1.10). The Egyptian habit, rooted in Cassian's mythical *Instituta Aegyptiorum*, was still the ideal, but because of the circumstances in Gaul, the monastics who lived there had to be content with less than this foreign and old-fashioned ideal for their daily wear.[20]

In Evagrius's description, as in Cassian's, an implicit question is how special the monastic habit could and should be. His addressee of *Praktikos*, Anatolios, had asked about the symbolism (*symbolikon*) of the habit (*schema*) because "you have considered that it is not by chance or superfluously that it is so different (*parallagen*) from clothing of other people" (*Prologue* 1). The challenge of the habit in Egypt, which it also posed in Gaul, was to strike the right balance. The habit should definitely be a distinct sort of dress, and it should be a dress that people generally saw in a positive light. At the same time, it should not be so strange that its wearers became objects of scorn.

A presupposition shared by Cassian and Evagrius was that an interaction took place between the items of the habit and the "inner" man. By making the habit's function explicit, the two authors sought to take control of this interaction and of the way it affected its wearers. The attempted interaction between the habits and their wearers was, among other things, the fruit of the explicitly stated strategy of Evagrius's and Cassian's lists and inscribing.

How did the two authors conceptualize the interaction between the inner man and the habit? Whereas Evagrius only implies an interaction between the habits and their wearers, Cassian makes the interaction more explicit. Cassian's point was that appearance was significant for inner development. His own experience of wearing the habit and living in a community with men dressed like him was informed by what he had read, especially by what Evagrius and Basil had written about the monastic dress (Goodrich 2007: 120). Cassian begins his description by noting a parallel between the monastic's dress and his inner self, saying that he will first describe "the actual dress of the monks" because he wants to "set the outward man" before the eyes of the readers before "he shall be able to expound in due course their interior life" (*Institutes* 1.1). The final chapter in Book 1, which is about the girdle, is more explicit about the intended interaction. One point is that the girdle both protects the monastic and helps him move more freely because it functions in such a way that the monastic is not hindered by the dress. Another point is that girding the loins with "the dead skin [the girdle] signifies that he bears about the mortification of those members in which are contained the seeds of lust and lasciviousness" (*Institutes* 1.11). In this way, Cassian establishes a direct connection between the inner self and the girdle in relation to both its physical and its symbolic functions. The girdle keeps the tunic in place and divides both the garment and its wearer's body into a purer upper part and an impure lower part, which is a source of sexual desire and procreation. At the same time, the material of the girdle, the "dead skin," is ascribed the essence of death, which is motionlessness and lifelessness. This means that wearing the girdle had a physical effect, which was informed by its symbolic significance. The way it divided the body and closed the garment and the symbolic significance of its material were intended to work together and protect the wearer against sexual impulses, thus ensuring a virtuous life.

Both Cassian and Evagrius tried to take control of the meaning production of the habit by attributing fixed meanings to it and intending that the habit interacted with the wearers in prescribed and normative ways. By reminding the wearers of the meanings and symbolism of its various items and of their references to the clothing of the Old Testament prophets and John the Baptist, the habit should act on the inner self in intended and specific directions. While the "performance" of monastic life could be informed by how the habit was inscribed, just like Cassian and Evagrius intended, it was not limited to such inscriptions. In real life, wearing the habit was a bodily practice that incorporated certain traditions, memories, ideals, and norms and contributed to the way its wearers "performed" monastic life, but their "performance" was also based on their individual emotional investments in their garments, for instance in the special feelings connected to an inherited item of clothing or to an item of clothing, which had been part of a monastic's habit for decades. This implies that the meaning production of the habit was not restricted to specific references and fixed symbolism, such as Cassian and Evagrius tried to inscribe on it, but it had more varied sources.

In this chapter, I have suggested that on an embodied level, crafting interacted with ascetics and monastics in an absorbing way and accompanied the development of special moods. These moods functioned as catalysts for meditative states of mind, imagination based on biblical stories, and mimesis. Clothes were channels to emotions, knowledge, and memories and sometimes functioned as healing mediums. In some cases, clothes were intended to participate in cognition as part of the extended mind of the monastics and to be more like a notebook, inscribed with explicit values and scriptural references. While the Pachomian Rules present a habit that incorporated monastic ideals and functioned as a uniform, and Evagrius and John Cassian were rather intent on establishing a habit with a fixed meaning, this type of uniformity and textual fixity was not necessarily regarded as ideal by all ascetics and monastic groups. Other ideals are also present in the ancient texts, which—in addition to processes of standardization of the habit—also reveal deviations from the norm and sometimes promote more radical ascetic ideals. The tension between economic and spiritual values and gains, which was distinctly present in the stories about John the Little, was played out in the discourse on ascetic and monastic clothes. The topic of the next chapter is how the tension between the spiritual economy—the economy of salvation—and the economy of this world is reflected in clothes. The chapter further discusses the ways in which monastic garments were connected to power and succession, and, more specifically, how the handing down of monastic garments from a deceased monastic father to his successor incorporated different types of authority.

Notes

1 Bentley Layton (2014: 14–32) surmises that the anonymous protagonist is Pshoi, whose so-called Red Monastery later became part of the White Monastery federation.
2 There has been a tendency in the research on Christian monastic and ascetic literature to read the hagiographic accounts as historical reports (see Cameron

1999). This tendency has been criticized, and some, like Samuel Rubenson, have argued for a more nuanced position (see Rubenson 2013b).

3 According to Cassian, the monastics "are in all respects stripped so bare that they have nothing whatever except their shirt, cloak, shoes, sheepskin, and rush mat (*psiathium*)" (*Inst.* 13).

4 Codex ZA 224, translated in Layton (2014: 275) as Shenoute's Rule 429.

5 Codex XS 353–354, translated in Layton (2014: 175) as Shenoute's Rule 211, cf. Layton (2007: 66), note 119.

6 SBo 113, cited in Veilleux (1980: 165–166); G¹ 87, cited in Veilleux (1980: 356).

7 In several perceptive articles, Inbar Graiver has combined cognitive science with the study of monastic texts, especially those written by Origen, Evagrius, and Cassian (Graiver 2016, 2017, 2018). She explains that various strategies were prescribed to the ascetics to keep "their attention focused on the thought of God and slow the usually incessant flow of thoughts, in order to restore the mind's contemplative nature" (Graiver 2018: 89). One of the points that Graiver makes is that a shift in the understanding of the self is brought about among the desert fathers when "thought" is assigned with the semantic role of agent (2017: 261). The use of formulations such as "the thought tells me" indicates that the thought is induced by external agents. The linguistic term for this form is "inverted experiential construction," and Graiver notes that she has not been able to find the term elsewhere in non-Christian Greek writings (Graiver 2017: 267). This is part of the monastic cognitive strategies, which makes the process of thinking passive and dependent (Graiver 2017: 267–271). It is also part of what she labels "a systematic demonological anthropology," originally developed by Origen (Graiver 2018: 82–83; see also Brakke 2006: 246–247). According to Graiver, the "ease with which monastic authors moved between the personal realm of thoughts and the cosmic realm of external influences suggests that their self-understanding embraced both these realms" (2018: 84).

8 This explorative theoretical approach, which Malafouris calls Material Engagement Theory (MET) and has presented in several articles and a book (2013), is relevant to our exploration of the meaning and function of monastic crafting. According to Material Engagement Theory, there are three aspects of the interaction between humans and things: extended cognition, enactive signs, and material agency. Extended cognition means that artifacts and living beings are constitutive for human cognitive processes and that cognition is intertwined with material things (Malafouris 2013, see also Clark and Chalmers 1998; Clark 2011). Enactive signification implies that material signs are not representational mechanisms connected to arbitrary assignments and representations; on the contrary, unlike linguistic signs, a material sign "in most cases, does not stand for a concept, but rather substantiates a concept" (Malafouris and Koukouti 2018: 165; see also Malafouris 2013: 97). Material agency implies that humans are parts of networks of interactions where things are conceived of as actors in line with brains and bodies (Malafouris 2013: 2).

9 The woman, who had been bleeding (*haimorroousa*) for 12 years, touched the fringe of Jesus's cloak (*himation*), and she was immediately cured.

10 In his *Historia Religiosa*, Theodoret of Cyrrhus describes the people who flocked to the pillar-saint, Simeon Stylites, and tried to touch him to get some blessing from his garments of skin (*himation dermatinon*) (25.12).

11 One example of healing by means of oil is the case of John of Lycopolis. According to the *Historia Monachorum*, he did not perform healing publicly, but he used to give oil to the afflicted, thereby curing them (*HM* 1.12; see also 1.16).

12 See also N 172.

13 According to Entwistle (2015: 191–195), the term "fetish" is used in three ways: it can refer to a sacred object with a magical potential, to the way in which commodities in a capitalistic society acquire a special value and appeal, or to objects, sometimes detached from a person, that arouse sexual feelings, as is the case here.

14 Susan Ashbroke Harvey has written an exciting book about ancient Christianity and the olfactory imagination (2006). In relation to the story about the monastic and the infested tunic, she mentions a story about Syncletica, where she advises her fellow nuns to ward off sexual temptation by representing "the body of the beloved as a wound that smells oppressive, and is inclined to putrefy, briefly put, as resembling a corpse" (Pseudo-Athanasius, *Life of Syncletica*, 29, quoted in Harvey 2006: 214). In a story in the *Historia Lausiaca*, a demon has transformed into an Ethiopian girl, sitting on the lap of the monastic. After striking her, the monastic says, "For two years I could not stand the stench of my hand" (*HL* 23.5).

15 Richard J. Goodrich notes that Cassian's *De Institutis* was built on his own experience from his stay in Egypt, which he uses as an argument against other authors, such as Jerome and Basil, who wrote about asceticism but did not have the same kind of hands-on experience as Cassian (2007: 65–115).

16 Evagrius mentions the connection to the teaching of the fathers two more times (*Prologue* 8 and 9).

17 In her doctoral dissertation, Jinha Kim made a diagram with a comparison between the symbols of the monastic habit in three texts: the *Apophthegmata* (Systematic Collection 10, 192; N 55), Evagrius's *Praktikos*, and John Cassian's *Institutes* (Kim 2002: 79–80).

18 Cassian distinguishes between clothes as covering and clothes as vesture, where the point is that monastic clothes should be simple (*Inst.*1, 2, 1). Commenting on the distinction that Cassian makes, Boniface Ramsey remarks that Cassian

> himself has *operimenta* ("covering") rather than *vestimenta* ("vesture"). What seems here to be a fairly insignificant and even arbitrary distinction marks the difference, as he will make clear in the subsequent lines, between purely functional wear, or "covering", which is appropriate for a monk, and more elaborate dress, or "vesture".
>
> (Ramsey 2000: 30)

19 Richard J. Goodrich shows that Cassian's book on the monastic habit borrows many of its ideas from Evagrius and Basil and that his first two chapters build on Basil, while Chapters 3–8 are based on Evagrius (Goodrich 2007: 120).

20 Goodrich (2007: 144–149) points out that in his Preface to the *Institutes*, Cassian places his Gallics near the bottom of the monastic hierarchy in relation to the Egyptians.

6 The economy of salvation and the economy of this world

The two economies

Monastic institutions in late-antique Egypt were religious enterprises. They were also economic enterprises and places where people had to work for a living but were provided for when they got old and sick.[1] This was a sort of life insurance and must have been part of the allure of joining a monastery. While large monasteries had more extensive economies than small ascetic communities, the combination of work and religious activities was similar. The theme of this chapter is how clothes relate, on the one hand, to the economy of salvation, which is a metaphorical way of describing the pursuit of religious goals and rewards, and, on the other hand, to the economy of this world, which is about producing goods for consumption, barter, or sale. The two economies, the spiritual and the physical, were closely intertwined, and to a certain point convertible, which made the tension and the need to establish borders between them a recurring theme in the sources and part of a more general discourse on clothes. The second part of the chapter discusses the way in which various forms of authority, worldly and otherworldly, are expressed by means of clothes.

Literary sources are not direct channels to historical facts. *Vitae*, apophthegms, and travelogues do not relate what really took place. They propose ideals and speak to concerns of ascetics and monastics. Literary sources have agendas. They take part in the shaping of the monastic ideal and are actors intended to engage and influence readers (Sheridan 2015). How were clothes represented in the literary sources as part of the negotiation between the two economies? What was the discourse on dress? In what ways were clothes carriers and transmitters of the various types of religious authority?

Over time and in parallel to the process of structuring and defining the monastic groups, their interaction with their surroundings became more prominent, and the monastic economy became interwoven with the broader Egyptian economy (Giorda 2015). According to Shenoute, his monasteries sold baskets, sacks, books, ropes, and linen and bought grain and wool (Layton 2007: 49, note 20). Some monasteries formed federations. The documentary papyri reveal that monastics were more involved in the worldly economy than the literary sources admit (Wipszycka 2011). According to Roger Bagnall (1993: 299), they "reveal those less successful or less extreme monks."

Although economic realities of the monasteries are not witnessed as often in the literary sources, narratives about the tension between the heavenly and worldly economies are frequently included. The point of departure is the Pachomian *koinonía* ("fellowship"), but narratives about other types of monastic and ascetic living are also drawn into the discussion. The Pachomian monasteries were situated at the borders of cultivated lands and in abandoned villages. The inhabitants cultivated the lands, interacted with local people, and traded with places as remote as Alexandria. *The Life of Pachomius*, for instance, refers to the sale of mats and baskets and to boats on the Nile. Palladius says about Aphthonios, the second-in-command in the Pachomian monastery at Tabennesi, that the brothers "send him to Alexandria to sell their products and to purchase what they need" (*HL* 32.8). The monastics cultivated their own lands or worked as agricultural day laborers and manufactured and marketed basketwork, ropes, and mats (Rousseau 1999: 81–84, 153–158).[2]

Monasteries received donations and gifts and were endowed with properties and livestock from people who joined them or inherited them from deceased monastics (Wipszycka 2011: 163–172; Brown 2016: 95). Sometimes they were bestowed with family estates and agricultural units. For example, Petronios, a rich man, "donated to our father Pachomius' *Koinonia* all he had: sheep, goat, cattle, camels, donkeys, carts, and all he possessed, including boats" (SBo 56, G[1] 80; see also Rousseau 1999: 153). The documentary sources further show that individual monastics also inherited property and continued to own land (Bagnall 1993: 298).

The monastic federations of Pachomius and Shenoute seem to have had different attitudes toward wealth. Ariel G. López notes that whereas "the Pachomian corpus displays a painful realism in describing the monastic economy, and a marked suspicion toward any show of wealth, with Shenoute wealth and its circulation came to bear a far greater symbolic weight" (2013: 67). According to López, "there is very little that is miraculous in the economy of the fourth-century Pachomian communities" (76), whereas the Shenoutean economy of the fifth century is what he calls a "miraculous economy" (67–95). The difference lay in the generous gifts that Shenoute seems to have received in abundance "from the local laity, imperial magistrates, and, above all, from the emperor himself" (86).[3]

Regardless of whether a monastery's material economy was on the poor or on the more affluent side, the purpose of monastic life was also to pursue spiritual goals and salvation. After all, this was their declared *raison d'être*. This required effort and diligence. According to Emile Durkheim (1915: 385), religious beliefs are associated with costs in terms of time, work, and mental exertions. These costs helped to make religion meaningful and to give it value. Ideally the two economies—the worldly economy and the economy of salvation—should be blended so that both were fulfilled at the same time, but sometimes monastics had to divide their time between pursuing religious goals and contributing to the monastery's income.

Balancing these double demands was not without obstacles. After all, it was not easy to ignore the emphasis that Jesus himself had placed on the spiritual economy: "If you wish to be perfect, go, sell what you have and give to the poor, and you will have treasure in heaven. Then come, follow me" (Matt. 19:21). He had also declared that "it is easier for a camel to go through the eye of a needle than for a rich man to enter the kingdom of God" (Matt. 19:24). Ascetics idealized in literary texts followed these principles to the letter:

> They used to say of Abba Serapion that, such was his life that it was like that of one of the birds. Not a thing of this world did he possess, nor did he remain in a cell. He used to go around like an incorporeal being, wearing a sheet and carrying a little gospel book.
>
> (*AP* N 565/S 15.116)

In Athanasius's *Life of Antony*, after the death of his parents, Antony entrusted his sister to a community of virgins, sold his inheritance, and distributed the money to the poor, in line with the teachings of Jesus (2.1–3.1). Max Weber argued that salvation religions, such as Christianity, are characterized by a fundamental mistrust of money and power. The opposition to trading religious goods for money is classically expressed in the New Testament story about Simon Magus, who wanted to buy the Holy Ghost, only to be met with Peter's categorical refusal (Acts 8:9–24; see also *The Letter of Bishop Ammon* 16). Selling God's gifts—in effect converting pecuniary to religious capital—was not allowed. True religion is free of charge (Mikaelsson 1999: 200–203). Although the sources inform us of a stream of people visiting monastics and ascetics to be prayed for and healed, what these healers got in return for their services is usually not part of the story, for exchanging religious benefits with material resources was viewed with suspicion, to say the least.

Striking an acceptable balance between the two economies and integrating economic activities with the religious system were particularly challenging in Egypt. Unlike the elite Manichaeans and the wandering, begging monks of Syria, who dedicated themselves exclusively to their salvation and were supported by laypeople, monastics in Egypt, whether living in monasteries or solitary cells, had to work for a living (Brown 2016; Giorda 2015; Caner 2002; Hedstrom 2017). Peter Brown aptly illustrates the conflict between the two ways of living using the apophthegm about John the Little as an example (2016: 80–81; see also Muehlberger 2013: 170). According to the story, John says to his elder brother, "I should like to be free of all care, like the angels, who do not work, but ceaselessly offer worship to God." After saying that, he takes off his cloak (*himation*) and goes into the desert, thus signaling his departure from the world of humans. However, he returns 1 week later, knocking on the door of his elder brother and saying who he is. The elder brother does not open the door, saying, "John has become an angel, and henceforth he is no longer among men." When the brother finally opens the door, he says to John, "You are a man, and you must once again work to eat" (*AP* A John the Little 2). As Brown fittingly remarks, "there was no room, in Egypt at least, for 'angelic' wannabes" (2016: 81). In Egyptian monasticism, work was an economic necessity, but it was also seen as a contributor to the spiritual progress of the monastics and as part of their socialization (Thelamon 1994: 189).

As discussed in Chapter 5, other stories about John the Little convey the ideal of promoting spirituality by being so deeply immersed in crafting that the result of the activity was completely forgotten. This was a solution—at least the solution adopted in the literature—to the dilemma of weaving for profit versus weaving for salvation. However, the bias of the sources toward the spiritual gains that crafting afforded cannot mask the economic side of the activity. When the *Praecepta* urge the monastics not to "tread upon the rushes which have been dipped in water in preparation for the plaiting of ropes lest even a small loss should come to the monastery through someone's negligence" (*Praecepta* 4), they betray not only the reality but also the urgency of the activity as an economic endeavor. Plaiting, which took place during the synaxis, illustrates the intertwining of the two economies and the respective types of capital involved: income and spirituality. It is worth noting, however, that not all types of crafting were necessarily considered neutral or even beneficial to the economy of salvation. One apophthegm, for instance, associates linen making with traders (*pragmateutes*), unlike plaiting ropes, weaving rush mats, making sieves, and scribing. These latter activities are in line with being a monastic; making and selling linen is not, for "that handiwork is of the world and it is not beneficial for many" (*AP* N 375). The production of linen was a very profitable business for some, which made it suspicious from the viewpoint of the economy of salvation.

Pierre Bourdieu offers a theoretical approach to extending the concept of capital to the symbolic domain of culture. Cultural capital, he posits, includes highly rated knowledge or educational qualifications, while social capital pertains to membership in a group and to social obligations and connections (Bourdieu 1986). Various social actors strive to obtain different forms of material and symbolic "capital" (Bourdieu 1985; Jenkins 1992: 86). According to Bourdieu (1986: 241), the substance of capital is accumulated labor. Seen through this prism, both the religious and the material economies of the monasteries were built through monastic effort. Bourdieu views cultural and social capital as transubstantiated forms of economic capital and self-interest as a driving force behind them.[4] Although his approach is one-sided, ignoring altruistic motivations (Urban 2003: 367), it is useful to think of the monastics as being concerned with different types of capital and with maximizing their religious capital. It is also helpful to view the various types of capital as convertible to a certain extent (Giorda 2015: 281–282). Stories in the *Apophthegmata Patrum* about monastics donating clothes sometimes specify their rewards in the heavenly economy. For instance, when a father gives his *lebiton* to a pauper, Christ appears in his dream wearing the garment (*AP* N 358).

The different types of capital were sometimes confused. When Abba Serapion wanders like an incorporeal being (*asómatos*), wearing only a sheet and crying because he has lost the wealth (*ploutos*) with which his master had entrusted him, people give him bread because they do not understand that he refers to his spiritual wealth (*AP* N 565; S 15.116). This narrative clearly invites the reader to see the point. Much textual effort went into showing why religious capital should *not* be converted into economic; this would devalue it and ultimately make it worthless. According to monastic ideals, the two economies were inversions of each other: growth in one could mean decline in the other.

The middle way

Much as the literary sources could afford to present the spiritual economy as superior to the worldly, real life was more complex. The Pachomian *koinonia* promoted a type of ascetic living that was neither too austere nor too lenient. This middle way that the Pachomians pursued was probably part of their success; it would most likely have been more difficult to maintain monasteries that pursued an extreme asceticism for a long time.[5] The literary sources keep returning to the efforts to prevent the pecuniary economy from getting the upper hand at the expense of the religious, stressing, for instance, the depravity of selling things at a higher price or making more things than prescribed.

In the *Paralipomena*, a collection of anecdotes about Pachomius, the conflict between the heavenly and the worldly economy and the necessity of *not* letting the worldly economy get the upper hand are recurring themes. According to one story, Pachomius punished a brother who charged more money than the shoemaker had asked him to when he sold sandals for the monastery (*Paralipomena* 23; see also Wipszycka 2009: 531–533).[6]

Some overachievers did more crafting than they were supposed to—and for the wrong reasons. In one anecdote, a brother, who has made two mats during the day instead of the prescribed one, places them in such a way that Pachomius will see them, expecting praise: "He did it, uplifted by a thought of vainglory, thinking that in this he would be praised by the Great Man for displaying such zeal, since the rule was for each Brother to make one mat a day" (*Paralipomena* 34).

However, in monastic thinking, mats made for display betrayed vainglory. Instead of praising the brother, Pachomius exclaims, "From morning till now he has given all his toil (*kopos*) to the devil and has left nothing whatever of his work (*ergon*) for the comfort of his own soul" (*Paralipomena* 15.34).

Toiling for the devil is contrasted with working for the soul. Although both require effort, the former, which fetches material gains, is contrary to the latter, which serves the soul and the spiritual economy.

In another anecdote, a brother is in charge of cooking for the other brothers, while Pachomius is away visiting another monastery (*Paralipomena* 15–16). After Pachomius has left, the brother stops cooking vegetables, which are a staple ingredient in the frugal meal of the brothers, because he has noticed that they are not eaten. Instead, he weaves mats every day. When Pachomius returns and sees the brother's doings, he burns the 500 mats that the brother has made during his absence. The vegetables should have been cooked, Pachomius explains, because the brothers would then have had the option to abstain from eating them and thus be rewarded:

> Do you not know that if something is set on the table and the brothers do not taste it because they practice abstinence for God's sake, they shall have a great reward (*misthos*); but if no cooked food is given them, the abstinence from what they do not see shall not be credited to them? For the sake of eighty measures of oil you have cut off so great a harvest of virtues!
>
> (*Paralipomena* 16)[7]

The economic arguments in this story are that the brother thought "it was not right to throw out so great an expenditure (*analoma*)" by spending oil on unnecessarily cooking vegetables and at the same time secured profit for the monastery by making more mats than prescribed—a double economic gain. The counterargument is that economic profit led to spiritual loss. What was lost is described in economic terms: profit (*opheleia*) and reward (*misthos*). Material substance (*hule*) is contrasted to virtues: "May the whole substance (*hule*) of the world be destroyed rather than one small virtue be cut off from the soul" (*Paralipomena* 16). The solution was to pursue the middle way, to weave one mat per day—neither more nor less. Only then was balance brought between the spiritual and the worldly economy. The story makes clear that an economic overachiever is a religious underachiever.[8] The gravity of this argument is rammed home when Pachomius orders the mats burned.

Like everything else in the monasteries and desert cells, clothes and textiles were part of the two economies, the religious and the worldly. When the Pachomian Rules stipulate "no wool tunic (*tunica*), no mantle (*pallium*) and no soft sheepskin (*pellem*) with unshorn wool" (P 81 and P 89), they indicate that clothes that were excessively warm and comfortable were forbidden. Such clothes were too close to one of the poles in the continuum of vestimentary values by being too luxurious. The other pole, clothes that were too poor, should be avoided as well. When Cassian reports to the Gallic brothers what he learned among the monastics in Nitria and Kellis, he strongly argues against wearing particularly poor clothes because they signaled vanity and pride (*Institutes* 1.2).

The ideal of the Pachomian federation was to ensure equality among the monastics. This implied that all had to wear the same clothes, and all had to work. However, this was not the only possible way of monastic life. In his monastery in Thagaste, Augustine allowed those who came from the elite to keep their high-quality clothes and other extras if they wished (*Praeceptum* 3.4; see also Brown 2012: 176–177). Since clothes are so essential to human identity, this indicates that the hierarchy of secular society was partly maintained in the monastery.

The fact that people joined monasteries from different walks of life created dilemmas and tensions. Such dilemmas are illustrated by an apophthegm about Arsenius. According to the story, Arsenius had been a senator and tutor to the sons of Emperor Theodosius I before he became a monastic. The change was dramatic, "just as none in the palace had worn more splendid garments than he when he lived there, so no-one in the Church wore such poor clothing" (*AP* A Arsenius 4). In other words, Arsenius had excelled in both domains, but because he had forsaken such a high position in the worldly economy, his merits in the religious economy were even higher. Once, when Arsenius is ill and is put on a bed with a small pillow under his head, he is criticized by an old monastic, who considers the pillow an unnecessary luxury. The apophthegm immediately counters the criticism. The priest who put Arsenius to bed asks the old monastic about his trade before he joined the monastery. The old man replies that he was a shepherd and that he lives more comfortably in the monastery than he did in his village. The priest then says,

> Do you see this Abba Arsenius? When he was in the world, he was the father of the emperor, surrounded by thousands of slaves with golden girdles, all wearing collars of gold and garments of silk. Beneath him were spread rich coverings. While you were in the world as shepherd you did not enjoy even the comforts you now have but he no longer enjoys the delicate life he led in the world. So you are comforted while he is afflicted.
>
> (Arsenius 36)

The old shepherd immediately repents and is edified.

This story presents the contrast between the two economies by means of a contrast between the most splendid garments of gold and silk and the poorest clothing. The former type belongs to the top level of the worldly hierarchy, while the latter is at the bottom. Because of the inverse relation between the two economies, being low in the earthly economy, expressed by the former senator's current poor clothes, helps him to obtain a high status in the economy of salvation. The small pillow is a reminder of his former worldly status, moderating the inversion of the status hierarchy, which indicates that the symbolic capital of his earlier existence is to a certain degree still valid (Bourdieu 2000: 241).

However, when the apophthegm contrasts between people from diametrically opposite ends of the status hierarchy, the solution is similar to the one Augustine chose for his monastery's inmates. The treatment of the former shepherd is also in line with how Augustine warned the poor brothers in his community that "they should not consider their present good fortune to consist in the possession of food and clothing which were beyond their means elsewhere" (*Praeceptum* 1.5; see also Brown 2012: 176).

Discourse on dress

Texts obviously negotiate the two economies according to various agendas and intentions. In relation to the preferred middle way, the ancient sources describe clothes that skew to both sides. It was generally agreed upon that too opulent clothes were not allowed. This is a commonplace in monastic literature, described more or less eloquently. When Jerome concludes his *Life of Paul the First Hermit* with a contrast between the materially wealthy and his hero, the ascetic Paul, he contrasts in a similar way as in the story about Arsenius above the worldly elite's tunics of wrought gold with Paul's lack of even "the raiment of the meanest of your slaves" and their silks with his glory (17).[9]

Extreme poverty could also be a problem. To what extent should it be restricted? The ideal among those living in Nitria, Kellia, and Scetis was that a monastic should have a dress in such a shape that he could leave it outside his cell for 3 days without anyone trying to steal it (*AP* A Pambo 6; see also Freiberger 2009: 214). However, there was a difference between clothes that showed humility—and, accordingly, monastic excellence—and poor and deviant clothes worn for show-off, thus betraying hypocrisy. The difference depended on the circumstances and was subject to negotiation.

Monastic rules are explicit about what the monastics should wear. The Pachomian Rules in particular score by definition high on normativity. What ascetics wore according to the apophthegms and travelogues was not regulated to the same degree, but it definitely played a role. There are several references to clothes in the Apophthegms, including several examples of deviant and unacceptable clothes. For instance, Isaac from Kellia labeled a brother wearing "a little cloak" (*mikron koussoulion*) a secular person (*kosmikos*) and turned him away from the Church of Kellia (*AP* A Isaac from Kellia 8). What seems to be a minor anomaly is here regarded as a sign of secularity, probably because the offending garment was considered too luxurious.[10] It was usually more acceptable to wear clothes that were on the poor side. The same Isaac is attributed with saying, "Our Fathers and Abba Pambo wore old, patched up clothes made of palm-fibre; now you are wearing expensive clothing. Go away from here" (*AP* A Isaac from Kellia 7a). "Old," "patched-up," and "palm fibers" signify three qualities that score low in terms of clothing in the earthly economy but—exactly for that reason—high in the heavenly economy.

Nostalgia for the desert and the biblical heroes is also reflected in a story about Jonas, an old gardener in a Pachomian monastery, who "was dressed in this fashion: he joined three goatskins together and these were sufficient to cover his whole body" (*Paralipomena* 11.29).[11] Jonas had only one tunic, which he had owned for 85 years, always kept clean and only used during divine service (*Paralipomena* 11.29).[12] The story presents the challenge of striking the right balance between marginality and ascetic excellence on the one hand and playing by the monastic rules on the other. While Jonas wore the daily attire of the desert, he kept the one tunic for rituals, thus conforming to the monastic group; however, he still showed that he was unique by owning only one, not two tunics, which was normally the rule (see Veilleux 1981: 69).

However, it was not always *comme il faut* to wear inexpensive and poor clothing.[13] When a brother comes to church dressed in a little cloak (*maphorion*) darned all over, Abba Joseph of Pelusia contrasts him with the other brothers who are "looking like angels for the Synaxis in the church" (*AP* A Cronius 5). When the brother explains that he has no other dress, Joseph takes him to his cell and gives him a tunic (*lebiton*) and other things that he needs. The brother, previously so poorly dressed, becomes like the others: an angel to look at.

Why did Abba Joseph of Pelusia not find it laudable or even acceptable for the poor brother to come to the church in his little darned cloak? Was it not a sign of humility and poverty—exactly the attitude applauded in the other examples? The changed attitude to dress could have been the result of a change in the degree of monastic organization; the apophthegm indicates that wearing a special dress to church was now common (see Freiberger 2009: 215). Although the apophthegm specifically refers to Abba Joseph and a monastery and church in Sinai, its message has something to do more generally with monastic centers such as Kellia developing into magnets for pilgrims (Hedstrom 2017: 255–263). When monastics were seen in the synaxis in the church, dressed in uniform garments, they must have been a magnificent and edifying sight, easy to liken to an assembly of angels and attractive to look at for visitors.

Variations in dress are common in the monastic texts and part of a discourse on asceticism. In his comparative analysis of asceticism in the Upanishads and the Apophthegms, Oliver Freiberger stresses that a discourse contains not only shared beliefs and values but also particularly contested ones (2009, 2019: 170). He suggests a model for the asceticism discourse, defining asceticism discursively:

> Asceticism is a combination of practices of self-restraint, at least some of which are viewed as extraordinary in the respective cultural context. How this combination is ideally designed—what practices are included,

what form and intensity each should have, and how they are ranked—is
the subject of the asceticism discourse.

(Freiberger 2010: 189–191; see also 2019: 193)

The model of this discourse and its sub-discourses has, according to
Freiberger, three characteristics: (1) There are two opposing approaches
to the various aspects of ascetic life: the regulatory/selective approach,
which seeks to define and regulate behavior, and the antiregulatory/indif-
ferent approach, which leaves it to the ascetic's discretion. (2) The various
ascetic practices relate to each other in a value hierarchy. (3) The spectrum
of ascetic practices implies that each practice varies according to its form
and intensity (Freiberger 2010: 185–190, 2019: 190). On one end of the
spectrum of ascetic practices is dressing without restrictions, which implies
that an ascetic is dressed in clothes similar to those of a lay person; on the
other end of the spectrum is nakedness (Freiberger 2019: 192).[14]

Generally speaking, ascetic and monastic clothes relate to the totality of
clothes in society and social norms pertaining to status, gender, and age; to
personal and institutional relationships; and to the lived religion of monastics and ascetics. Thus, they contribute to reflecting, creating, and participating in ascetic and monastic life and are accordingly used in the discourse
on this life.

The rag and the diadem

Clothes embody religious attitudes and spiritual states of mind. For those
who know the vestimentary codes, their meaning is immediately striking.
For this reason, they are also easy to use in texts to describe persons and
make the reader understand their characters. The underlying presupposition for this to work is that persons are normally what they wear or, as in
the case of the old man clad in the mat, what they want to be. Authors and
readers tend to share the presupposition that we are the clothes we wear, a
presupposition that we also share with the crocodile in the Introduction.[15]

The use of deviant materials and strange garments illustrates unique status of the monastic fathers. Strange things could be used as clothes, at least
for rhetorical effect. One apophthegm tells the story of a monk who heals
a rich man possessed by a demon. By way of thanks, the rich man offers
the monk a basket filled with gold. The monastic does not accept the gold,
but, as he does not wish to upset the giver, he takes the basket and makes
a tunic out of it, "hairy and hard" (*trichinon kai skleron*), and he wears it
for a long time so that it will wear down his flesh (*sarks*) (*AP* N 662/694).
The tunic made out of the basket fulfilled functions similar to a hair shirt.
It is specifically said to be "hairy" and to affect the body in a troublesome
manner in order to subdue it. In another apophthegm, a "hard-working old
man" is dressed in a mat (*AP* A Ammonas 4). In this case, however, the mat
is associated with three possible ways of living, all of which are extreme.

Abba Ammonas advises the old man not to pursue any of them but to lead a modest life in his cell. Nothing further is said of the mat, but if the old man heeded the advice to lead a "normal" ascetic life, the mat probably had to go. Because of their texture, "clothes" made out of baskets and mats would have affected the body in an uncomfortable and even painful way, similar to hair shirts. But at least in the example of the man who wore a tunic made out of a basket, the anomalous garment did not carry the same ambiguity as a hair shirt (see Chapter 7), while in the example of the man dressed in a mat, it probably did.

In addition to deviant types of texture and material, clothes could also be worn in non-prescribed ways. When an important person visited Theodore of Pherme, the latter received him in a torn habit, with his chest bare and his hood dangling down in front of it. The narrator says that he tried to cover him, but he was rejected because Theodore claimed that one should not respond to other people's expectations but remain as one was (*AP* A Theodore of Pherme 28). Here, a superior state of mind finds its outlet in disarranged clothes, which illustrate Theodore's attitude toward the world, indicating that he is no longer bound by it. There are also examples of monastics taking off their clothes, pretending to be mad or possessed by demons to avoid people worshipping them or for other reasons (*AP* N 61; S 4.35).

Sometimes, women were also given an elevated status, and, in a similar way, this new status was reflected in their garments. This can be seen in one of Palladius's stories from a Pachomian female monastery. Palladius claims to have visited the male Pachomian monastery in the south, in Tabennesi. It has been questioned whether Palladius was really there and whether what he presents is an eye-witness account, as he claims (Katos 2011: 15, 107).[16] Some of the things that he mentions are not consistent with what others say about the Pachomian monasteries; for instance, Palladius says that they bred pigs, which has been debated (Leyerle 2005: 154; Grumett and Muers 2010: 13). On the other hand, one can argue that such details make his stories more credible because reality is seldom a blueprint of a normative ideal. At the very least, this kind of information could reflect that he had talked with people from the monastery. He mentions, for instance, Aphthonios as "my true friend" (*HL* 32.8).[17]

A characteristic of Palladius's descriptions of the male and the female monasteries is that they are strikingly different. After Palladius describes the Pachomian male monasteries at Tabennesi and their various activities, he turns to the women's monastery (*HL* 33 and 34).[18] However, while Palladius promotes one of the women in the female Pachomian monastery to the status of *amma*, "mother," he does not pay much tribute to the other women in the monastery. In the story, the woman remains nameless and is described both as a fool (*sale*) and as holy (cf. *AP* S 18.24).[19] She pretends to be insane, and she is loathed by everyone: "She had bound a rag (*hrakos*) round her head (all the others were shorn and wore hoods)" (*HL*

34.1).[20] However, an angel appears to the holy man Pieroum and reveals the holiness of this woman to him. One purpose of the angel's revelation is to show an almost unattainable spiritual ideal: "Do you want to see a woman more pious than yourself? Go to the women's monastery at Tabennesi and there you will find one with a diadem (*diadema*) around her head. She is better than you are" (*HL* 34.3). Pieroum travels to the monastery, where he is allowed in because of his age and holiness, sees the woman with the rag on, falls at her feet, and says, "This one is our *amma*"—and Palladius comments, "That is what they call spiritual women (*pneumatikas*)" (*HL* 34.6). Palladius/Pieroum likens her rag to a diadem (*diadema*). The women fall at Pieroum's feet, repent, and begin to treat the sister with great respect. She, however, cannot tolerate the new esteem. She flees the monastery and vanishes into the desert.

When *Historia Lausiaca* places the nameless nun in the heavenly economy as a hero and likens her fillets to a diadem (*HL* 34.1; 34.3; 34.6), the metaphorical description connotes a martyr's crown. A rag and a diadem are normally situated at opposite ends of the continuum of headdresses. In this story, the rag functions as a charismatic item of clothing through which the spiritual status of its wearer is revealed. The nameless woman is further characterized as "suffering" (*paschousas*), a characteristic especially attributed to Christ and to martyrs. In the end, however, a charismatic female of lowly origin is obviously too difficult to accommodate after she and her unorthodox head garment have made their point;[21] hence, she vanishes from the monastery and from the text. It is also worth noting that even if she receives the honorary title of *amma*, she is not given the status of having a name.

Dress and authority

The nameless monastic with her diadem represents charismatic authority, as Kari Vogt notes (1987: 104–106). Different garments were used to express different types of authority in the monastic and in the Christian movement in general. These garments refer to the two economies and their dilemmas.[22] A brief look at the religious landscape of Egypt suggests a general rise of religious authority in the years when monasticism was institutionalized. Authority, which had theretofore been local and relatively independent and had allowed for diversity, was increasingly subjected to attempts at doctrinal and ecclesiastical control. In parallel with this process, an institutionalization of monasticism was also underway.[23] This is reflected in the formulation of monastic rules, including a standardization of the monastic habit. Since the habit is an instrument for establishing authority in monastic life, my hypothesis is that different types of monastic garments corresponded to different types of authority and that garments particularly associated with charismatic authority came under scrutiny and criticism. What types of authority were embodied, experienced, enacted, and expressed by means of the monastic garments described in the monastic literature of late-antiquity Egypt? What types of clothes were carriers of charismatic authority?

Authority has been a hot topic in the research on ancient Christianity, especially in connection with the so-called "holy man." The notion was first put forth by Peter Brown (1971). The "holy man's" charismatic power was seen as an alternative to the power of the Church and the bishops (see also Cameron 1999).

Claudia Rapp (2005) is among the scholars who have discussed the changing dynamics of authority in late antiquity, particularly in relation to bishops (cf. Demacopoulos 2007; Leyser 2000; Sterk 2009). Rapp offers an explanatory model built on Max Weber's model of charismatic, traditional, and legal–rational authority,[24] which she adapts to early Christianity. Instead of Weber's categories of authority, she discerns between spiritual, ascetic, and pragmatic authority. Spiritual authority stems from a source outside the individual: "It is given by God as a gift" (Rapp 2005: 16). It is a personal form of authority that is self-sufficient and "can exist in the individual independent of its recognition by others" (Rapp 2005: 16, 56–99). Spiritual authority is especially connected to teaching and miracles. The source of ascetic authority, on the other hand, is based on the individual's personal efforts to subdue the body and live a virtuous life. Ascetic authority is earned through work. It is visible in appearance and lifestyle and depends on the recognition of others (Rapp 2005: 17, 100–152). Unlike ascetic authority, pragmatic authority is not directed toward disciplining the self but toward others and toward the administration of religious institutions. Pragmatic authority is public and dependent on social position and wealth (Rapp 2005: 17, 23–55).

In Rapp's tripartite model, ascetic authority plays a prominent role: "The usefulness of this tripartite scheme lies in the fact that it accords a special place of relevance to ascetic authority as the vital link to the other two" (Rapp 2005: 17; see also 16–18, 101–105). On the one hand, ascetic authority prepares the individual for receiving spiritual authority; on the other hand, it motivates and legitimates pragmatic authority. Unlike Weber, Rapp does not contrast charismatic with institutional authority, and she downplays the opposition between ascetics and bishops (Rapp 2005: 17, 137): "Weber's notion of charismatic authority functions in specific contradistinction to institutionalized authority, a dichotomization that this study hopes to transcend by introducing a model that embraces three types of authority: spiritual, ascetic, and pragmatic" (Rapp 2005: 17). Rapp convincingly shows that the pragmatic authority of a bishop might include the ascetic and spiritual authority (cf. Sterk 2009: 7).

Rapp's model is dynamic and fruitful for a study of the relationship between different forms of institutional power in Christianity in late antiquity. Two of her categories of authority, ascetic and pragmatic, are immediately attractive, as they both build on two types of practice: a life of abstinence and training and a life as a church leader. However, for the purposes of this analysis, we will retain Weber's characterization "charismatic." Although his use of "charismatic" is ultimately derived from Christianity, via church historian Rudolf Sohm (see Riesebrodt 1999: 5–8), the term has been universalized and is well established.[25] In our analysis, the third category is understood in line with Weber's original definition:

> The term "charisma" will be applied to a certain quality of an individual personality by virtue of which he is considered extraordinary and treated as endowed with supernatural, superhuman, or at least specifically exceptional powers or qualities. These are such as are not accessible to the ordinary person but are regarded as of divine origin or as exemplary, and on the basis of them the individual concerned is treated as a "leader."
>
> (Weber 1968: 241)

Although charismatic authority characterizes extraordinary personal qualities in individuals, Weber stresses that "what is alone important is how the individual is actually regarded by those subject to charismatic authority, by his 'followers' or 'disciples'" (1968: 242). In other words, charisma is not based primarily on self-understanding but on the understanding of the followers (Riesebrodt 1999: 10). Charismatic authority may continue to be inspirational after its holder's death. When the monastic literature describes eminent ascetics, it shows a preference for the charismatic ones, thus promoting their authority.

The independence of office of charismatic authority and its potential preservation in tradition posthumously make it a type of authority that flourishes in anecdotic texts. If a holder of charismatic authority has caused friction in life and challenged other types of authority, when his or her story is adapted and incorporated in a text, it is aimed as a general inspiration to lead a Christian and ascetic life and functions as a supplement to ascetic and pragmatic authority. One way of expressing charismatic authority is through descriptions of specific garments that the ascetics and monastics used. Before we focus on clothes and charisma, let us address the more general question of how monastic garments incorporate and express different types of authority.

Incorporating and transferring authority

The monastic habit symbolized a special type of life, and the monastic was expected to live up to the ideal that it represented. This is reflected in the literature, for instance in the *Apophthegmata Patrum* (*AP* S 4.68, 4; *AP* S 5.4, 12; *AP* S 10.192, 3; *AP* N 55; *AP* N 373b). Even if the items of clothes that constituted the monastic habit changed through the centuries and differed from place to place, and although monastics might have worn work clothes in their everyday life and reserved the habit for more solemn occasions

(Mossakowska-Gaubert 2015), some items of clothing were assigned a special significance.

According to Rollason (2016: 151), some clothes "have greater symbolic capital, and this appears to stem from their associations with spiritual authority." This is an apt observation; it should be added, however, that their greater symbolic capital was due to their dependency on the other types of authority as well—for instance, the pragmatic authority incorporated in the monastic rules. Ability of the clothes to mold the body and thus form the experience of the monastics must also be taken into account. Both social expectations and physical molding are part of the habit. A look at descriptions of monastic garments reveals both their capacity to physically mold the body and their symbolic capacity to reflect, express, and transfer authority. Authority is built into the monastic habit. By means of physical constraints and symbolic power, the habit forces the monastics to conform to the rules and subjects them to the pragmatic authority of the institution in which they belong. The habit is a witness of ascetic life and transmits the wearer's ascetic authority to the surrounding world.

What does it take for a garment to incorporate and transfer charismatic authority? How do different types of garments relate to different types of authority? Two stories about the deaths of illustrious ascetics describe intimate connections between garments and types of authority. One of these stories is part of Bishop Athanasius's *Life of Antony*, composed *c.* 360. The other is found in Jerome's biography of the hermit Paul, dated *c.* 375. Antony was a real person, whom Athanasius molded in a way that he saw fit. Paul was probably made up by Jerome to compete with Athanasius's hero, who was the first ascetic to live in the desert. Despite Jerome's effort to promote Paul, however, the *Life of Antony* became "the definitive hagiographical model" (Brennan 1985).

The role that clothes play in these two stories has been discussed by several scholars (Dihle 1979; Brennan 1985; Krawiec 2009: 135–136), and a main observation is that these stories describe a transfer of authority by means of clothes (Brakke 1998: 246–247; Rollason 2016: 130; Bremmer 2020). The focus has been on Antony's *melote* and Antony's and Paul's mantles, whereas two other garments appearing in these stories, Antony's hair shirt and Paul's tunic of palm leaves, have attracted less attention.

According to his *Vita*, Antony always wore "a garment of hair (*trichinon*) on the inside, while the outside was skin, which he kept until his end" (47.2). Athanasius says that no one ever saw Antony naked before he was dead (47.2). He says that he wore the same dress in old age, and the text conveys the impression that the dress was pretty much part of him. When Antony is about to die, Athanasius makes him say,

> Divide my clothes (*endumata*). Give to Bishop Athanasius one of my sheepskins (*melote*) and the cloak (*himation*) I rest on. He gave it to

me new, and it has aged with me. Give the other sheepskin (*melote*) to Bishop Serapion, and keep the hair shirt (*to trichinon enduma*) yourselves.

(91.8–9)

The hair shirt that is present at the scene of Antony's death is probably the same hair shirt mentioned earlier in the text. It attracts less attention than the other items of clothing. According to Athanasius,

both those who received the sheepskin and the cloak (*himation*) worn by him kept them as a treasure. To look at them is like seeing Antony, and he who is clothed in them seems to bear his admonitions with joy.

(92.3)

The first quotation includes three garments—the cloak (*himation/pallium*), the sheepskin (*melote*), and the hair shirt (*trichinon enduma*). However, unlike the cloak and sheepskin, the hair shirt, which is the only garment connected to Antony in the earlier part of the text, is not commented upon.[26]

Like the sheepskin, the cloak came to be invested with great symbolic capital. The latter points to the authority of a bishop, whereas the sheepskin (*melote*), as part of the monastic habit, points to the authority of an ascetic (Rollason 2016: 130).[27] The cloak originally belonged to Athanasius, who had given it to Antony. The return of the cloak to Athanasius and the gift of the sheepskin to him represent a transfer of ascetic and charismatic authority from the desert ascetic Antony to a bishop (91.8–9). By means of this gift, Athanasius brings his ascetic hero safely under the mantle of orthodoxy (Rollason 2016: 150–156). That Bishop Serapion gets only a sheepskin implies that Athanasius alone receives the special mixture of ascetic and clerical authority that the *himation/pallium* and the *melote* together represent (Rollason 2016: 154). The hair shirt is not part of the transfer of authority from the ascetic to the bishop, but it is handed over to Antony's two anonymous disciples and disappears from the story.

In Jerome's *Life of Paul, the First Hermit* (*Vita Sancti Pauli primae eremitae*) the story of Antony's mantle differs from Athanasius's narrative in crucial ways. When Paul is about to die, he asks Antony, who has come to visit him, to

'go and fetch the mantle (*pallium*) Bishop Athanasius gave you, to wrap my poor body in.' The blessed Paul asked this favour not because he cared much whether his corpse when it decayed were clothed or naked (why should he indeed, when he had so long worn a garment (*tunica*) of palm-leaves stitched together?); but that he might soften his friend's regret for his death

(12)

Antony fetches the mantle from his cell (13) and returns to Paul's cave. But before he reaches it, "he saw Paul in robes of snowy white ascending on high among the bands of angels, and the choirs of prophets and apostles" (14). It comes as no surprise to the reader that Antony finds Paul dead when he returns to his cave. There, Antony "took for himself the tunic (*tunica*) which after the manner of wicker-work the saint had woven out of palm leaves" (16), and "on the feast-days of Easter and Pentecost he always wore Paul's tunic (*tunica*)" (16). The fact that the tunic is worn only at the feasts of Resurrection and the descent of the Holy Spirit shows not only that it is believed to have a unique quality and status of holiness, but also that it is not considered fit for daily wear. This might be due to its state of preservation, but more likely it reflects Antony's position in relation to Paul in Jerome's eyes. Paul is a full-time and exceptionally charismatic ascetic; Antony is second to him.

In Paul's case, we observe a dramatic change of dress from the tunic of palm leaves, which he wore when he was alive and which was his only garment, to the heavenly snowy white robes in which he is seen in Antony's vision and to Bishop Athanasius's cloak, in which he was buried.[28] A *melote* is not mentioned. In the last part of Paul's *Vita*, Jerome makes a sharp contrast between Paul's garment of Christ and the dead who are clothed in silk and grave clothes of gold (17). As a final touch, "the sinner Jerome" states that he "would much rather choose the tunic of Paul with his merits than the purple of kings with their kingdoms" (18).

In Jerome's narrative, Athanasius gives his mantle to Antony, but Antony passes it on to Paul, with whom it is buried. This implies that the mantle cannot be returned to Athanasius. The narrative also ordains Antony as Paul's successor by having him take over the latter's palm tunic (Rollason 2016: 156). In Rollason's well-argued interpretation, Antony "is functioning to legitimate Jerome's claim that Paul was the founder of eremitical monasticism," and "the pallium becomes a visual symbol of this attempt to appropriate Antony's fame for a western saint" (155). She notes that "important qualities of the holy man were imbibed by his clothing" (136; see also 154), arguing that the garment contributed to transform a monk who had been given it by making him partake of the original owner's qualities. Rollason stresses the competing authorities of charismatic saints and bishops and remarks that the clothing gift of the *pallium* is refashioned "to suit the literary agendas of authors" (149).

Four garments stand out in the two stories, embodying and expressing different types of authority. The cloak (*himation/pallium*) expresses the authority of the clergy and especially the bishop—in other words, the pragmatic/ecclesiastic authority. The sheepskin (*melote*) expresses the authority of the ascetics. The hair shirt and the tunic of palm leaves express charismatic authority. The last type of authority is not so easily accommodated and institutionalized. In addition, there exists not only the heavenly snowy white garment, but also the luxurious golden and purple vestments of damnation. It is worth noting that shortly before Antony dies, he mentions Egyptian burial customs whereby the saintly dead are dressed in white and kept in houses for veneration (90–91). He disapproves of the latter part but says nothing about the former; this suggests that Athanasius/Antony approved of dressing the dead in white.[29]

In both stories, clothes move in two dimensions. They move vertically between salvation (white linen clothes) and damnation (luxurious gold and purple fabrics), and move horizontally from strict asceticism and charisma in the far reaches of the desert (hair shirt and tunic of palm leaves), to the asceticism of structured monastic life (*melote*), to the ecclesiastical authority of bishops and the clergy (*himation/pallium*).

The *Life of Antony* stresses the transition from the ascetic authority to the pragmatic authority of the bishop. This transfer of authority speaks of the parallel institutionalization of church and monasticism that took place in late antiquity.[30] The *Life of Paul* represents an infusion of the stronger charismatic authority of Paul into the ascetic/charismatic authority of Antony and, accordingly, an exchange between charismatic and ascetic authority. It is also partly a routinization of Paul's charisma through Antony's regular use of his tunic of palm leaves on the most important religious and churchly feast days, even though Jerome does not go so far as to let Antony use this garment full-time.

Clothes and charisma

In the words of Brian Brennan (1985: 211), "*Vita Antonii* reflects, on a literary level, the process by which Athanasius routinized Antony's potentially dangerous charisma." This argument, shared by other interpreters of the text as well, is in line with Rapp's model and her description of the authority of Christian bishops. Nevertheless, Antony's and Paul's charisma was not completely routinized. Did the hair shirt and the tunic of palm leaves escape, at least partly, institutionalization and the routinization of charisma?

As noted, in the *Life of Antony*, the garment of hair is given to Antony's two anonymous disciples, and nothing more is said about it. Such garments were not part of the standard ascetic or monastic equipment, even if some monastic heroes wore them, like Antony did, according to Athanasius. In one of the stories in the *Apophthegmata Patrum*, Abba Daniel inherits the hairshirt of Abba Arsenius along with his leather tunic and palm-leaf sandals (*AP* A Arsenius 42). Pachomius, the father of cenobitic monasticism himself, used a hair shirt day and night before he became leader of the monastery, but only during the night afterwards (*The First Sahidic Life of Pachomius*, in Lefort 1965: 102). The hair shirt is not part of the list of items of the monastic habit in the Pachomian Rules, which stipulate that superfluous garments would be removed (*Praecepta* 81). Pachomius's biography, however, makes a sort of compromise between monastic norms and charismatic exceptions by having himself wear the hair shirt only during the night. In this way, Pachomius conforms to the Rules but still shows his extraordinary status and holiness by means of his hair shirt. Wearers of hair shirts must be worthy of them. In Abba Arsenius's case, it is said that his appearance is angelic and that he has wept so much that his eyelashes have fallen out (*AP* A Arsenius 42). Nobody can doubt Arsenius's holiness. He looks like an angel and is constantly grieving over this sinful life; he is therefore worthy of wearing a hair shirt.

In a biblical context, the hair shirt might refer to the clothing of John the Baptist, which is also a reference to Elijah's *melote* (see Chapter 2). Has the prophetic and charismatic model of Elijah/Elisha and John the Baptist split into the sheepskin of the monastic habit and the coarse clothing of hair of charismatic heroes? Although both these garments have charismatic references, the *melote* was colonized to a higher degree, becoming part of the standard monastic outfit.

The tunic of palm leaves is less controversial than the hair shirt. Paul's tunic is first mentioned in Jerome's description, when we learn that in his youth, Paul made his abode in a cave in a rocky mountain. It had no roof, but it was shaded by "the spreading branches of an ancient palm" (5). "The palm tree supplied his few needs of food and clothing" (6). Paul seems to have almost returned to a prelapsarian state, where he does not need to toil for his food and clothes—but not quite; his tunic of palm leaves required some sort of wicker work, which means that it was not completely without toil.

Palm leaves are on the simple and inexpensive side compared to other types of materials, such as linen and wool. Palladius says that until "his death, [presbyter of Scete] Isidore never wore linen other than a headdress, never took a bath, and did not partake of meat" (*HL* 1.2). Abba Helle was characterized by his humility and poverty, was dressed in a rag with many patches, and is praised by a priest: "You have a most beautiful mantle (*himátion*) for your soul (*psyché*), brother" (*HM* 12.7). This manner of praise reveals the inverse relationship between the heavenly and the earthly economy.

Common among several items of clothing that reflect charismatic authority is their inexpensiveness. As we have seen, the economy is an important issue in the monastic literature. When its great hero, Antony, goes into the desert, he gives up all his money in imitation of biblical models (Brennan 1985: 215–217). The connection between charisma and economy was also central to Max Weber's thinking. In his view,

> charisma quite deliberately shuns the possession of money and of pecuniary income per se, as did Saint Francis and many of his like; but this is of course not the rule. . . . But charisma, and this is decisive, always rejects as undignified any pecuniary gain that is methodical and rational. In general, charisma rejects all rational economic conduct.
>
> (Weber 2007: 247)

This means that when clothes are described as especially poor, this is a way of describing charismatic authority in contrast to other types of authority.

Monastic authors sometimes allowed women to wear clothes that underlined their charismatic authority, as was the case of the nameless female monastic with the rag around her head. Melania the younger, a high-status Christian woman and a favorite of monastic literature, had, according to Krawiec (2009: 138), "the ability to use her clothing as a male monk might, but only because she took on male clothing and, by extension, its divine authority." Her authority is manifested, for instance, when Palladius mentions that it was she who re-dressed Evagrius in monastic clothes (*HL* 38.9). And while Melania did not wear the sheepskin mantle (Krawiec 2009: 138), even that garment is bestowed on her in Palladius's history (although he does not explicitly state that she wears it). When Macarius of Alexandria miraculously cured a hyena cub of blindness, its mother "brought the fleece of a large sheep to the holy one" (*HL* 18.28). According to Palladius, Melania had told him that Macarius gave her that fleece as a token of his friendship (*HL* 18.28). Melania's case, however, is unusual. Even though, as a woman, she scores low in the ancient hierarchy of gender, she scores high in hierarchies relating to status, wealth, kin, and—not least—in incarnating all Christian ascetic virtues. We note in passing that the story about the fleece also illustrates how a charismatic holy man might get an item of clothing in a miraculous way—in this case, given to him by a grateful hyena. Melania, a woman of high status, is on one end of the spectrum of charismatic monastic females; the nameless monastic in *Historia Lausiaca* is on the other.[31]

With the increasing institutionalization of monasticism, charismatic authority became more problematic. It also ran the risk of being labeled heretical. According to Guy Stroumsa (2016: 173), in

> Weberian sociology, then, there are two main kinds of religious authority: that stemming from charismatic prophecy, and that embedded in the routine of ecclesiastical hierarchy. The tension between prophets and bishops soon becomes an opposition between orthodox rulers and heretical leaders.

At the same time, legitimate charismatic authority flourished in hagiographic texts, which, in the words of Claudia Rapp, served "the apologetic purpose of presenting a whitewashed version of the life of a controversial figure" (Rapp 2005: 295), or, in the words of James Goehring, "filtering the received tradition through the newly defined categories of orthodoxy and heterodoxy" (Goehring 1999: 218). Whereas rules are normative texts that tell monastics what to do (and in this case, what to wear), the anecdotic literature creates identity (Assmann 2006: 38).

Monasticism was a form of literary culture whereby a Christian *paideia* was developed through reading and writing (Rubenson 2013a: 89–90; Lundhaug and Jenott 2015). Ascetic "practice and the making of texts were parallel enterprises. Both involved the manipulation of raw material to produce holy identities" (Krueger 2001: 195). It is tempting to include the making of ascetic garments as a third parallel practice that "involved the manipulation of raw material to produce holy identities." This manipulation took place not only in the production of textiles and clothes in the monasteries and among the ascetics, but also in the incorporation of ascetic and monastic garments into texts and their adaptation to the purposes of each author.

In late fourth- and early fifth-century Egypt, the legal–rational authority of monastic rules was propagated by identity-making stories, such as *apophthegmata* and *vitae*, which idealized the authority of charismatic heroes (Horsfield 2015: 288).[32] Charisma is routinized in the construction of monasticism and at the same time "domesticated" by means of textualization. Recent research has revealed the diversity of emergent monasticism, especially in Egypt, with "parallel models of ascetic authority" (Choat 2013: 63). The intersection, overlap, and competition between the different types of authority (see Rapp 2005: 73) were played out in various ways in Christianity in late antiquity, including by means of monastic clothing. Claudia Rapp convincingly shows how ascetic authority became a key category that mediated between the pragmatic authority of the bishop and the spiritual authority of desert dwellers.

In this chapter, the discussion has focused on the two economies of ascetic and monastic life, the spiritual and the material economy, and on how literary texts present charismatic authority by means of clothes. While a *melote* (sheepskin) tends to express a colonization of ascetic and charismatic authority, other items of clothing reflect charismatic authority in a more direct and untamed manner, such as the hair shirt and the tunic of palm leaves.

The hair shirt, the tunic of palm leaves, and such garments as patched cloaks and headgear made of rags are exclusive pieces of clothing that do not easily fit into the processes whereby ascetic authority and episcopal power were institutionalized and sometimes converged and fused during late antiquity. These items of clothing retained their charismatic power; they evaded colonization by institutional power in the same way as the *melote* and were reserved for the select few—the charismatic super-achievers. In the next chapter, we will see how nakedness became the preferred costume of ascetic superheroes—at least in texts—and how some items of clothes came to be considered heretical.

Notes

1 According to Max Weber (2007: 334), "temples and monasteries have everywhere become the very loci of rational economies."
2 Regarding monasteries in the fifth and sixth centuries, church historian A.H.M. Jones (1960: 86) says that "they were always financially autonomous, being supported either by the offerings of the faithful or by the labor of their inmates, or, to an increasing degree as time went on, by their own endowments."

3 The archaeological evidence suggests that the White Monastery "was a self-sufficient community capable of not only meeting its own daily needs, but also accumulating monetary wealth and land as well as undertaking major building projects and maintaining an intricate built environment" (Blanke 2019: 149).

4   So it has to be posited simultaneously that economic capital is at the root of all the other types of capital and that these transformed, disguised forms of economic capital, never reducible to that definition, produce their most specific effects only to the extent that they conceal (not least from their possessors) the fact that economic capital is at their root, in other words—but only in the last analysis—at the roots of their effects.

(Bourdieu 1986: 54)

Bourdieu is not particularly concerned with religion, and when he specifically addresses the subject, the outcome is usually reductionistic (Urban 2003: 355).

5 A classic example of a monastic middle way is found in the Pali Canon of Theravada Buddhism, where the middle way is presented as the preferred type of ascetic life. In the first speech that according to tradition the Buddha gave after his awakening, he said:

Monks, these two extremes ought not to be practiced by one who has gone forth from the household life: There is addiction to indulgence of sense-pleasures, which is low, coarse, the way of ordinary people, unworthy, and unprofitable; and there is addiction to self-mortification, which is painful, unworthy, and unprofitable.

"*Dhammacakkappavattana Sutta*: Setting in Motion the Wheel of Truth (SN 56:11)," translated from the Pali by Piyadassi Thera. Access to Insight (BCBS Edition), www.accesstoinsight.org/tipitaka/sn/sn56/sn56.011.piya. html (accessed September 1, 2020)

However, what qualifies as "middle way" is culturally dependent.

6 Ewa Wipszycka considers the story fictional, positing that it was probably written in the late fourth or the beginning of the fifth century (2009: 532). The story might be fictional, it is difficult to know, but it presents a relevant problem.

7 In addition, on behalf of a young boy who had complained that no vegetables had been cooked, Pachomius says to the errant brother, "Or do you not know that boys especially are not able to continue in virtue unless they are granted some relaxation or small comforts?" (*Paralipomena* 8.15–16).

8 Making one mat per day did not necessarily equal spiritual progress, as seen in the apophthegm about the drunken elder who used the money he got for the mat on drink (*AP* N 340; S 16.27).

9 Similar eloquence is displayed by the Cappadocian Basil when he contrasts the clothes of those of the highest status in the world with the biblical models wearing fleece:

Let each consider for himself whom the Christian more fittingly resembles—those who live in royal palaces and are clothed in soft garments, or him, the messenger and herald of the Lord's advent, than whom no greater born of woman has arisen, John, I mean, son of Zachary, whose garment was of camel's hair. The saints of old, moreover, also went about clad in sheepskins and goatskins.

(*The Long Rules* 22)

10 According to Thomas Andrew (2009: 65, note 208),

Guy claims that the Greek κουσσουλιον has been incorrectly translated as "cucullum" in the Latin (in a note to the Greek Systematic version), because

of Cassian's description of the desert uniform, which includes a hood—
Cassianus, *de institutis*: I.4: *de cucullis Aegyptiorum*. There is nothing to say,
however, that Isaac was not simply reacting to the traditions of a uniform that
diverged with his own standard: either as a development in his community, or
simply originating from a different geographical area (which is most likely, as
the hooded monk seems to be arriving).

Freiberger (2009: 214, note 83)

Freiberger concludes that this was probably not a simple, inexpensive garment.

11 The story about Jonas also includes a thematization of the two economies connected to a fig tree that bore a lot of fruit, but where an evil spirit dwelt (*Paralipomena* 11.28 and 31).

12 Armand Veilleux (1981: 69) compares the story about the old gardener with
the story of Theodore of Pherme, who allowed thieves to steal all his belongings
except his *lebiton*, which he wore at the assembly.

13 Freiberger (2009: 213–217) points to the contrast between the two examples
about Isaac and the one referring to Abba Joseph (*AP* A Isaac from Kellis 7 and
8, Cronius 5).

14 Freiberger has applied this model on several sub-discourses of asceticism, such as
the ascetic habitat (2010) and dressing (2009, 2019). He notes that clothing "is
not very often addressed in the Apophthegmata, but the passages that discuss it
reflect a range of approaches" (2019: 187).

15 This also means that clothes can deceive (see also *AP* N 287). One apophthegm
makes the point that clothes do not really change who people are (*AP* A Joseph
of Panephysis 1).

16 Armand Veilleux presents an overview of the research history of Palladius'
chronicle of the Tabennesiots and argues that the historical value of the chronicle
does not justify its popularity (Veilleux 1981: 5–6).

17 It has also been suggested that Palladius wrote down what he had heard a long
time after he heard it, which can mean that his memory is not always to be
trusted (Draguet 1945: 41).

18 Here, his description is no longer firsthand, which is reasonable since men
were normally not admitted into female monasteries. The impression is rather
that Palladius passes on rumors and slanders about female monastics that
he has heard from male monastic milieus. His work is addressed to Lausus,
an administrator of the royal bedchamber, who was close to the emperor's
powerful sister. Unlike the *Historia Monachorum*, Palladius includes several
holy women in his travelogue. This could be because of his target readership.
A purpose of his work was to entertain and edify the ladies of the court.
According to Demetrios S. Katos (2011: 105), "the HL paid homage to aristocratic women."

19 The woman is sometimes presented as the first example of the holy fool (Rydén
1981: 106–107). Kari Vogt (1987: 99–100) notes out that Palladius uses both
the terms *moros* and *salos* with the meaning of "insane." Cf. Ivanov (2006:
52–53).

20 Another occasion when a rag plays a special role, though not equally prominent,
is when Abba Arsenius had a rag on his lap while he was working to mop up the
tears falling from his eyes (*AP* S 3.3; cf. Arsenius 41). Most likely, he was crying
because of the sinfulness of life in this world.

21 Another story is about a young nun who ran into a seamster (*hráptes*) who was
looking for work (*HL* 33). *Hráptes* not only means "one who stitches," "seamster," "clothes-mender," but also has the secondary meanings of "deviser" and
"plotter" (Lampe 1997: 1215). The term indicates that there may be a certain

ambiguity about who this person was and what he wanted. The nun explained that the monastery had its own tailors. Afterwards, she was, according to the story, falsely accused of misconduct by another nun who had seen the incident, and a few others repeated the accusation, which led to her drowning herself and eventually her accuser hanging herself.

22 The rest of this chapter is based on an article written in honor of my esteemed colleague Professor Håkan Rydving (Gilhus 2018b).

23 Andrea Sterk remarks that it is puzzling that "such a class of seemingly iso-lated, world-renouncing, and often recalcitrant monastics should have become an increasingly normative model for leadership and eventually an institution within the hierarchy of the post-Constantinian church in the East" (2009: 5), noting that there is simultaneously "a process of asceticization of an institution, the episcopate, and the near institutionalization of asceticism in the ascendance of the monk-Bishop" (2009: 7).

24 *Authority* is a translation from Weber's *Herrschaft*.

25 Martin Riesebrodt (1999) notes that Weber developed "charisma" in two dif-ferent contexts: as a sociological concept for a specific type of authority and as a central concept of his sociology of religion. In the former case, it is built on Sohm's concept; in the latter case, it is a much looser concept—more in line with the then-popular concepts of *mana* and *orenda*. Earlier generations of historians of religion used the Polynesian word *mana* ("energy," "power") as a general category and a universal concept and compared it with other concepts, such as the Iroquois word *orenda*.

26 According to Brennan (1985: 223),

> The monks inherit Antony's "hairy garment," a piece of clothing possibly associated with the garment worn by Elijah in 2 Kings 1.8, but this "hairy garment" does not have the qualities attributed in Chapter 92 to Antony's sheepskins and *himation*.

Scholars tend to comment very little on the hair shirt.

27 According to Rollason, this perhaps implied

> the superiority of the clergy in religious authority over monks, for while the latter may have colonised the *melote* and its associations with the charismatic power of the Old and New Testament prophets, the clergy were distinguished by the garment favoured by Christ and Peter.
>
> (2016: 145; see also 222)

28 Jan N. Bremmer has pointed out that Jerome "lets Paul have only one garment, woven from palm leaves instead of Antony's elaborate wardrobe with its four mantles" (Bremmer 2020). See also Bremmer's discussion of the single gar-ment as a symbol of marginality from early Pythagoreans to late antique monks (Bremmer 1992: 206–207).

29 According to Jonathan L. Zecher (2014: 172), "Athanasius' Antony polemizes as much against burial practices as against Arians and Melitians, effectively numbering mortuary religion among the famous heresies that preoccupied the bishop for so much of his career." Lynda L. Coon (1997: 56) notes that "the pre-dominant fabric of the gospels is linen, which symbolizes Christ's resurrection," arguing that "it represents bodily purity, righteousness, and resurrection."

30 Rapp (2005) focuses especially on the transition from ascetic to pragmatic authority and the relation between monks and bishops.

31 Averil Cameron (1999: 41) raises the interesting question of "how far the asceti-cism we see in the texts of late antiquity really did operate in society at large. Might it not be primarily a textual matter, internal to writings?"

32 Guy Stroumsa (2016: 173) makes the apt point that "scriptural authority too can be either charismatic and routinized." According to him, "charismatic interpreters are either heralds or contenders of routinized scriptural authority. The 'Scriptural Movement' "represents the systematic construction of new interpretative layers over existing scriptures" (172).

7   Prelapsarian nakedness and wolves in sheep's clothing

Holiness and heresy

The lives of ascetics varied in the degree of organization and communal activities, including the uniformity of dress: some were dressed uniformly and others more individually. There were also discrepancies between what ascetics were expected to wear, what they actually wore, and how their outfits were described or depicted. According to the monastic literature, eminent ascetic heroes sometimes wore strange garments or wore their regular garments in peculiar ways. This set them apart from others, revealing their holiness. At the same time, the way they were dressed was used to make educational points. Some of these oddly dressed males and females were praised in the literary sources for their ascetic excellence and were held up as moral examples for later generations of monastics and other readers. One example is Abba Silvanus, who went out to water the garden with his face hidden in his cowl to avoid seeing the trees and being distracted (*AP* A Silvanus 4).

The fourth century witnessed an institutionalization of monasticism, which in various ways contributed to consolidating norms of ascetic behavior— not least to designing monastic uniforms and promoting views on preferred types of dress. But even when clothes were part of monastic orthodoxy, there was room for deviance. How deviance was interpreted was not obvious. The meanings of garments were negotiated by their wearers, the observers, and those who wrote about them; clothes could be regarded as heretic, secular, or holy. Depending on context and circumstances, the same garment could be a sign of holiness or heresy.

Clothes could moreover be deceptive, hiding the true nature of people who, according to critics, were "wolves in sheep's clothing" (Matt. 7:15). Church historian Socrates describes how Emperor Julian in his youth wore "plain clothes" and was educated by Christian teachers but then started to study Pagan philosophy secretly. To allay people's—especially the emperor's— suspicions, Julian became very anxious to lull the suspicions which had been awakened, and therefore began to assume the external semblance of what he once was in reality. He was shaved to the very skin, and pretended to live a monastic life: and while in private he pursued his philosophical studies, in public he read the sacred writings of the Christians, and moreover was constituted a reader (anagnostes) in the church of Nicomedia.[1]

Just as Julian hid his pagan inclinations behind a monastic appearance, there are examples of monastics who were accused of using the monastic dress to usurp spiritual status and holiness while in reality nourishing heretical beliefs.

This chapter discusses extremes of ascetic dressing, from angel-like dressing and prelapsarian nakedness to disguises, cross-dressing, and clothes of heretics. What were the meanings and functions of angel-like clothing on the one hand and ascetic nakedness on the other? What do clothes tell about faking asceticism, and how do they tell it? When clothes were part of the negotiations between heresy and orthodoxy, how did they make their wearers look suspicious?

Angel-like dressing and prelapsarian nakedness

There was a certain fluidity between angels and ascetics. One aspect of the angel-like life, *angelikos bios*, was that it was a life, which was cleansed of sexuality and reproduction that could be anticipated while still in this world. To shun marriage and be like angels was an ideal already present in the gospels. According to Luke, Jesus said to his disciples,

> Those who belong to this age marry and are given in marriage; but those who are considered worthy of a place in that age and in the resurrection from the dead neither marry nor are given in marriage. Indeed, they cannot die anymore, since they are like angels (*isangeloi*) and they are children of God, being the children of the resurrection.
>
> (Luke 20:34–36)

Luke contrasts marriage and procreation in this life with the angel-like state of being in the world above.

Being clothed like angels contributed to a feeling of belonging and to boosting moral. It was a foreshadowing of the future glory of the monastics, when they would really become angels or like angels. To be like angels was sometimes a collective vestimentary enterprise but other times characterized individual spiritual eminence.

In Chapter 6, we saw that Abba Joseph wanted all the brothers to look like angels for the synaxis in the church and dressed them accordingly (*AP* A Cronius 5). No details are given of how they looked, except that they were *not* dressed like the brother who came in a little cloak, darned all over, and to whom Joseph gave "a tunic and whatever else he needed." Then the brother is explicitly said to be "like an angel to look at." The uniform wearing of the habit seems to be what created the angel-like impression. Uniform dressing according to a certain standard was staged for the benefit of the participants, as well as for onlookers and readers, as a visualization of the ideal life of the present as well as the future life among angels (Rubenson 2009). Such attires reflected the ideals of organized monasticism.

Whiteness was a quality that had the power to make monastics look like angels.[2] When the *Historia Monachorum*, describing the deeds of the holy man Apollo, says that a community of 500 brothers formed around him, the community is depicted as an army of angels: "One could see them looking like a real army of angels, drawn up in perfect order, robed in white" (*HM* 8.18). Here, not only the collective but also the militant aspect of the angelic appearance is brought to the fore. These "armies of monks" (*HM* 8.20) are presented as a realization of the words of Scripture, "for more are the children of the desert than the children of the married wife" (Isa. 31:1, 54:1), and further as a fulfillment of the words in Romans 5:20, "Where sin abounded, grace did much more abound." Sin is described in the subsequent passages of the *Historia Monachorum* as the Egyptian worship of "dogs and apes and other animals," which is characterized as "polytheism" (*HM* 8.20–21). The abounding grace is materialized in the army of angellike monastics dressed in white. In this way, and by means of clothing, the text evokes a cosmic setting of angelic armies of monastics versus the pagan worshippers of animals and demons.

Besides such collective angel-like appearances based on uniform dressing and sometimes whiteness, there are examples of spiritual eminence of individual monastics who are similarly likened to angels. When individual monastics appear like angels, their faces usually shine, as is the case of Abba Or: "He looked just like an angel. He was about ninety years old and had a snowy white beard down to his chest. And his face was so radiant that the sight of him alone filled one with awe" (*HM* 2.1). Radiant light is regarded as an expression of an inner, spiritual state (Muehlberger 2008: 458). Sometimes, the monastic's entire body is radiant. When a brother came to Abba Arsenius's cell, he saw "the old man completely like a flame (*pyr*)" (*AP* A Arsenius 27).[3] The apophthegm comments that "the brother was worthy of the sight (*idea*)" and notes that when Arsenius saw the look on the brother's face, he wondered if he had seen something, but the brother denied it. Only those worthy of it were able to see this type of bodily appearance, and they were expected not to talk about it. This mode of visual perception is described by means of metaphors of light, which Patricia Cox Miller characterizes as perceiving "the body of plenitude" or "the body from nowhere" (1994: 137–153; see also Upson-Saia 2014: 165–169). These expressions refer to the spiritual body and seem to have little or nothing to do with actual clothes.

Among the varieties of ascetic dress and of anticipating the future angel-like state, the most extreme approach was to appear in the nude. Generally, ascetic and monastic nakedness was not acceptable. The crocodile in the Introduction functioned as a pedagogical tool when it ate the naked bathing monastic. Unlike the unfortunate bather, Amoun of Nitria hesitated to take off his clothes when he was about to cross a ford, lest his disciple Theodore saw him naked. Amoun was then transported to the other side by an angel (*HL* 8. 6). In another version of this story in the *Life of Antony*, Amoun felt ashamed even to see himself naked and was suddenly borne over to the other side of a river (*Vita Antonii* 60.5–9; see also Muehlberger 2008: 461).

Although the pedagogics of crocodiles and angels may function on different levels and with different procedures, the message is clear: under normal circumstances, monastic clothes should stay on. This is made explicit in Shenoute's *Third Canon*, where he—in his usual style—rambles on about all kinds of situations in which nakedness may occur but definitely should not, and routinely anathematizes potential violators of his rules. Shenoute obviously has a vivid imagination, conceiving of astonishingly many situations in which nakedness occurs or may occur:

> Accursed are men and women who will peer to look with lust upon the nakedness of their neighbours in their bedrooms, or stare at them in any other place, either when they are on a wall or up a tree, or when they urinate or walk in mud or bathe, or when they are sitting down and uncover (themselves) inadvertently, or when they are dragging a log up to a high spot, or when they are working with one another or washing their clothing in the flow at the canal or by the cistern, or when the brethren who make the bread reach into the ovens or (are busy) at any other task which some would be doing in our domain or in your domain too and unwittingly bare (themselves). And those who will gaze at them in lust with a shameless eye shall be accursed. And also those who will look passionately upon their own nakedness shall be accursed. Men or women among us who will defile themselves in any [way. . .]
> (Shenoute's *Third Canon*, translated in Young 2000: 271–273)

In Shenoute's canon, excessive exposure of the body and various forms of involuntary and voluntary nakedness pertain to everyday behavior that involves partial or complete removal of clothes, special situations in which they have to be pulled up, or cases where clothes for some reason accidentally ride up or slip down. The description applies to the movements of partly draped clothes kept in place by a girdle and emphasizes the attention that these clothes demand so that their monastic wearers do not become indecently exposed.

While nudity was usually regarded as highly improper, it could under certain circumstances be a sign of holiness. In apophthegms and biographies (*vitae*) there are several examples of situations in which monastics are admired for appearing naked. When nakedness was admired, it happened for pedagogical reasons or for transcendent purposes—or both. An example of pedagogical nakedness is a brother who asks an elder how to be saved and is answered by means of an educational performance. The elder takes off his *lebiton*, girds his loins, and holds his hands up to heaven, saying,

"This is how the monk ought to be: stripped of the material things of life (*apo tes hules tou biou*) and crucified" (*AP* N 143a, S 6.20). By stripping off, the elder visualizes his message to the younger brother. The version of this apophthegm in the Systematic Collection extends the story and continues with a comparison between monastics and wrestlers. Since ancient wrestlers competed in the nude, the comparison makes clear that the story is about nakedness. At the same time, however, the elder is explicitly said to gird his loins so that the offensive image of a completely naked ascetic is avoided.[4] In another story, nakedness is used to expand on a theme from the gospels (see Matt. 25:35–45). Here, Abba Serapion takes off his frock/tunic (*chitona/himation*) and gives it to a pauper (who turns out to be Christ), and his disciples then find him walking about naked (*AP* N 566; cf. *AP* S 15.117). The story is about the merits of giving to the poor and of humility.

These are pedagogical examples of monastics who undress to embody Christian attitudes and morals. Permanent nudity is another matter, as it implies a more radical violation of the dress code. Most extreme were naked ascetics far out in the desert, of whom the texts provide some rare glimpses. They are unnamed in the Apophthegms, and they are not the protagonists in any of them. The purpose of these stories seems to be to point to an ideal unattainable for ordinary monastics.

One example is an anchorite who goes into the desert wearing only a *lebiton* (*AP* N 132.5, S 20.13). Since the story begins with an ascetic who reduces his dress to just one garment, it suggests to the reader that clothes— or a lack thereof—are a point of the story. After 3 days, far into the desert, the anchorite sees a naked (*gumnos*) old man grazing like a wild animal: "He got down (keeping out of sight) and laid hands on him. The elder was naked and he felt faint because he could not tolerate the smell of men." When the anchorite runs after him, the elder ascetic runs away and does not stop until the anchorite has taken off his *lebiton*—his only garment. The naked elder characterizes this garment as "the material of this world" (*ten hulen tou kosmou*) (*AP* N 132.5; *AP* S 20.13) and explains why he finally stopped: "When you threw away from you the material of the world, I waited for you." [The brother] besought him saying: "Father, utter a saying for me [showing] how I may be saved." He said to him: "Flee from men and be silent—and you shall be saved."

In another story, an anchorite goes far into the desert, where he finds a dead monastic in a cave. When he touches the dead body, it is reduced to dust, as is the dead man's tunic, which is hanging there (*AP* N 132.2; *AP* S 20.15). Obviously, the deceased had not been wearing the tunic when he died, but it is left to the reader's imagination if and how he was clad. The anchorite then found another man amid buffaloes, naked, only concealing his private parts with his hair. The man tells his personal story. He had been working as a linen weaver, set up a monastery, made a lot of money, and started to live in sin with a virgin. After that, he fled into the desert. His hair grew, and his clothes wore out over time. He also tells a story about the miraculous healing of his liver (it was cut out, manipulated, and put in again by an angelic being). He then dismisses the visitor with a prayer. According to the apophthegm, this story was told by the anchorite to the brothers of Raithou, and it ends with the words, "This I have told you for your benefit" (*AP* S 20.15).[5] This and similar stories describe these naked men in the wilderness as a type of higher-level ascetics practicing advanced asceticism.[6]

How do we interpret these naked ascetics, and what sort of benefits can be gained from stories about them? Because clothes are so intimately connected to the human body, but still possible to part with, they act here as signs of the material world. Accordingly, they are characterized as "the matter of the world" or "the material things of this life." Renouncing their clothes means that the ascetics renounce this world. Generally, the lack of clothes tends to refer to the innocence of babies and small children on the one hand and to sexual behavior on the other. Both connotations are potentially present in Genesis in the contrast between Adam and Eve's prelapsarian and postlapsarian nudity. In line with the Genesis account, it obviously made sense that being naked was accompanied by a feeling of intense shamefulness. People do not walk around naked, even when much is at stake. According to Eusebius, after young Origen's father had been imprisoned, his mother hid all the boy's clothing to keep him from joining his father and becoming a martyr like him (*Ecclesiastical History* 6.5). In the Apophthegms and in vitae, sexual nudity is usually associated with women who show themselves to monastics to tempt them. These women are usually revealed to be demons in disguise.

Contrary to sexual nudity, nudity of ascetics in the wilderness refers to the paradisal state before the Fall—and before humans wore clothes (see Chapter 2). It is primarily male nudity. Palladius's story about Serapion Sindonios illustrates this preference for male nudity (see Introduction). Serapion challenges a virgin to walk naked through the city center to prove her claim that she has died to the world. When she refuses, it shows, according to Serapion/Palladius, that she has not reached the state of holiness that dying to the world implies. One subtext in this story is that women will never reach a state of transcendence such that they can appear naked in public without being emotionally affected. Serapion himself has obviously reached this state. Still, judging by his nickname Sindonios ("sheet-clad"), his nakedness is not permanent. Permanent male nakedness in the apophthegms and in *vitae* is mainly a wilderness phenomenon, and it is not always complete. The former linen weaver who roamed with the buffaloes concealed his private parts with his hair.[7] The elder who took off his clothes to show his detachment from the material world girded himself. There seems to be a certain reluctance to describe completely naked ascetics.

Naked ascetics have renounced everything. They roam in the wilderness with animals or live in caves like them. Cold and heat do not affect them. Meeting with these super-achievers—even superhumans—in remote deserts and mountains are examples of encounters with human transcendence—or something very close to it. These ascetics are ideal and are closer to eternal life than to this life. Stories about them illustrate not only the need to renounce the things of this world, but also make clear that this type of life is an unattainable ideal for ordinary monastics and ascetics.[8] Those who meet naked ascetics in the wilderness return to their orderly, communal way of life in desert cells and monasteries. Accordingly, the stories put ordinary monastic life into perspective. In this realization lies the pedagogical value of these stories. It is doubtful whether these naked ascetics ever existed. It is more plausible to think of them as fictional pious characters who served as illustrations of one extreme in the spectrum of ascetic practices. However, it can be argued that in these cases, nakedness was regarded not as a pole in the spectrum of ascetic dressing but as a transcendence of the spectrum.[9]

Disguise and cross-dressing

Naked ascetics and monastics dressed like angels were dressed, or not dressed, in a way that foreshadowed their future elevation to a higher level of being. Their garments, or lack thereof, pointed to a permanent transformation. These manners of dressing are different from disguises. A disguise implies changing one's appearance to hide one's true identity. In the Apophthegms and in vitae, disguises indicate a discrepancy between the dress and the wearer's characteristics or inner state or between a being who appears to belong to one category in the hierarchy of beings but in reality belongs to another, for instance, when a demon masquerades as a monastic.

There is a wide range of disguises. Some are seen as positive and others as negative, but they are seldom regarded as neutral. Angels who appear as monastics are seen in a positive light; a monastic whose dress hides his pagan or heretical sentiments is regarded as deceitful. Cross-dressing is sometimes regarded as positive (at least when it appears in texts and for an acceptable purpose) but usually as ambiguous or downright negative.[10] The negative perception of cross-dressing has a biblical forerunner in Deuteronomy, where it is stated that "a woman shall not wear a man's apparel, nor shall a man put on a woman's garment; for whoever does such things is abhorrent to the Lord your God" (Deut. 22:5). In his treatise *On the Spectacles*, Tertullian condemns a man who dresses like a woman, citing Deuteronomy (*De spectaculis* 23). In the ascetic literature, however, some women are staged to do exactly what is here forbidden: dress in male clothes.

Cross-dressing was a destabilization of gender roles. It was a challenge to the gendered dress system in general and the monastic dressing code in particular. It usually implied that female ascetics appeared in a male garb, either as a matter of routine or as a disguise to escape danger (Davis 2002). However, there are also examples of men dressed as women; in some martyr stories, for instance, a man and a woman sometimes swap clothes. Palladius tells the story of a Christian virgin who was forcefully taken to a brothel because she refused to become a magistrate's lover. She prayed to God, and God sent "an intelligent and handsome imperial officer, with a burning desire to die" (*HL* 65.3). He came to her private quarters, "undressed her and changed her clothing for his own, the shirts, the mantle, and all the men's clothes" (65.4). The virgin escaped, "pure and unadulterated," and the officer was thrown to the wild beasts.[11]

Less dramatic is the story of a female monastic who was "dressed in tattered rags" (*perischisméne kai rakophorusa*) and pretended to be a drunkard but was in reality a virtuous, holy woman (*AP* N 596.7). When her deception was revealed and the contempt with which she had earlier been treated turned to admiration, she took the staff (*rabdos*) and cowl (*epirriptarion*) of Abba Daniel, who was visiting her monastery, left a message, and escaped stealthily into the night. Dressing like a man may have been wise for an unaccompanied woman in the middle of the night—and perhaps the reason that in this story it is acceptable for a woman to wear male clothes. In both stories, cross-dressing is incidental and a solution to an acute crisis. However, there are also examples of more permanent cross-dressing. Stories about female anchorites who permanently dressed like men appear both in vitae and in the Apophthegms in several variations. However, in these cases too, cross-dressing was usually a response to a serious crisis, which is what made it acceptable.

According to the Anonymous Collection, a eunuch was living alone in the inner desert of Scete (*AP* N 596.2). When he was about to die, he sent for Abba Daniel and asked that they *not* strip him of his clothes when he died. When he did, Abba Daniel took off his own clothes and asked a disciple to dress the dead in them "on top of what he is wearing." Upon dressing him, the disciple discovered that "he had the breasts of a woman, like two dried-out leaves." According to the apophthegm, the dead woman was wearing an undergarment of palm fibers (*phaskidion sebentinon*),[12] which might be pictured as straps pressing her breasts to her body, and a patched cloak (*kentonion*).[13] The apophthegm explains that she was a patrician who had fled from the emperor.[14] She resorted to cross-dressing to avoid persecution; it is thus a crisis that forces her to dress in male clothes. This means that females sometimes have an excuse for wearing such clothes and that their cross-dressing is acceptable to ecclesiastical and monastic leaders (Upson-Saia 2011: 102).

In this story, Abba Daniel knew all along that the dead eunuch was actually a woman. The twist in the plot may have come as a surprise to readers who had not heard or read similar stories before.[15] In a similar story in the Alphabetical Collection, neither Bessarion nor his disciple knew that a monk whom they had seen in a cave, plaiting a rope, and later found dead in the same cave was in reality a woman (*AP* A Bessarion 4; see also *AP* S 20.1). They only realized when they took the body to bury it. The revelation is a surprise to the reader as well: "Filled with astonishment, the old man (Bessarion) said, 'See how the women triumph over Satan, while we still behave badly in the towns.'" In this story, the female cross-dresser is used to shame male monastics.

Monastics encounter not only angels disguised as monastics but also demons. This means that the discrepancy between what people looked like and what they really were extended to supernatural categories. Demons had a wide spectrum of disguises, sometimes masquerading as animals, other times as secular women or male monastics, and even as angels (Shaw 1997: 127).

One may wonder why there are so many stories in the monastic literature about discrepancies between the appearance of characters and true identity. What is the function of these stories? Early Christian mythology and cosmology are characterized by a pronounced polarity between God and Satan, between angels and demons, between those who are saved and those who are damned, between Christians and pagans, and between those considered orthodox and those regarded as heretics. In narratives and pictures, the categorical belonging of the actors and their moral *habitus* are revealed and easily identified, which means that disguises are always seen through. A main point in the stories is to unmask pretenders, reveal their true nature, and expose evil powers—and in doing so, teach a moral lesson. In addition to being highly entertaining, these stories are pedagogical instruments helping their readers and listeners cope with life in the world, where things were not so clear and distinctions could be much more subtle.

Wolves in sheep's clothing

In the literary sources, some of the habit's items, especially the hood (*koukoullion*) and the sheepskin/goatskin (*melote*), symbolize monastic life more than others. As previously discussed, the *melote* was a chief characteristic of male monastics and pointed to monastic succession, maleness, and biblical models, that is, the mythical world of biblical and ascetic heroes. It also appears in accusations of heresy and of faking asceticism, as in Epiphanius's well-stocked medicine chest against heresy, the *Panarion*, which contains descriptions and refutations of eighty heresies.

In his description of the so-called Archontics, Epiphanius describes Peter, an old man who lived in Palestine. Peter had been a presbyter and a member of many sects in his youth, and he was convicted of being a Gnostic. Epiphanius begins his narrative with a description of Peter's garments:

> To begin with, this old man had an extraordinary (*ekplekton*, "astonishing") garment (*endyma*), stuffed with hypocrisy. For he actually wore a sheep's fleece (*kodion probation*) on the outside, and it was not realized that on the inside he was a ravening wolf. He appeared to be a hermit because he lived in a certain cave, gathered many, supposedly for the ascetic life, and he was called "father," if you please, because of his age

and his dress (*schema*). He had distributed his possessions to the poor, and he gave alms daily.

(*Panarion* 40.1. 4)

The adjuration in Matthew 7:15, "Beware of false prophets, who come to you in sheep's clothing but inwardly are ravenous wolves," is used here to characterize a heretic. The reference is applied several times in the *Panarion* and was widely used in heresiological literature.[16] In the description of the hapless Peter, the metaphor of the sheep's clothing is used about the actual garments of a live heretic the better to make him into a metaphorical wolf. This particular reference to Matthew 7:15 and materialization of the metaphor seem to be rare but not unique (Shaw 1997). When Jerome in his famous letter to Eustochium characterizes the virgins "among the heretics and among the followers of the infamous Mani" not as virgins but as prostitutes, he says that

> it is because they know that the name virgin brings glory with it, that they go about as wolves in sheep's clothing (*sub ovium pellibus lupos tegunt*). As antichrist pretends to be Christ, such virgins assume an honorable name, that they may better cloak a discreditable life.

(*Letter* 22.38)

Jerome uses the reference to the "wolves in sheep's clothing" metaphorically, having earlier pointed out that their actual clothes were among the things that made these women fake virgins (*Letter* 22.13; Undheim 2018: 167–170).[17]

Epiphanius does not use *melote*, the accepted term for the sheepskin cloak worn by an ascetic/monk, to refer to what Peter is wearing. It seems like he avoids this term with its honorable references because, in his opinion, the wearer is unworthy, and the garment has become a hiding place for a heretic. By not using the term *melote*, characterizing instead the garment as "a sheep's fleece" (*kodion probation*), Epiphanius reduces Peter's traditional monastic garment to a deceptive, as well as secular, garment. According to his narrative, in this case it is not possible to discern heretics from what they are wearing because they are clad in a traditional ascetic or monastic dress. The dress does not reflect but instead conceals the true spiritual status of its wearer. This means, in line with the general intention of the *Panarion*, that it takes a person with real insight—that is, Epiphanius—to tell the difference between an orthodox and a heretic. Though there was nothing wrong with Peter's practice and how he wore his sheepskin, there was something terribly wrong with what he taught, according to Epiphanius.[18]

While the goatskin was mandatory in the Pachomian Rules and the sheepskin frequently appears in stories about the desert fathers, the hair shirt is rarer. Hair shirts and sackcloth are garments that act upon their wearers by irritating the skin and making them constantly aware of their bodies' vulnerability and mortality. This means that in Christian interpretations, the hair shirt works through physical mechanisms to promote spiritual goals. All garments interact with the body, but some do it more aggressively; the hair shirt involves the largest sensory system, the skin's network of receptors. Unlike the hood and the sheep- or goatskin, hair shirts and sackcloth were not standard items of the monastic wardrobe.

The *First Sahidic Life of Pachomius* belongs to the oldest part of the biographical tradition (Goehring 2000: 19). It speaks about Pachomius and the

> hair-[tunic] (*kooune*) that he wore bound around his loins so that the ashes (*krmec*) ate away at him, and he was in pain. He hardly ever wore his linen tunic (*kiton*). But from the time he gathered together the (monastic) community, he no longer wore the hair-tunic (*kooune*) except at night.
>
> (S¹ Fragment II, 4).[19]

Why did Pachomius always wear this garment before he founded his monastery but only wore it at night afterwards? One explanation is that it was not part of what later became the monk's standard uniform; but, more importantly, it was an ambiguous piece of clothing, only viewed positively under certain circumstances.

The hair shirt and similar garments were intended to inspire humility. Only Melania's aunt knew that she wore a "coarse tunic" (*himation khondron*) under her traditional Roman dress (Gerontius, *The Life of Melania* 4). When a couple of pious ascetic women living as virgins are held up as a model in the *Apophthegmata*, a point in the story is that their wearing hair shirts was kept secret: "At night we wear hair-shirts and our ordinary clothes by day. No-one has known of this till now" (*AP* A, Eucharistus the Secular 1). Hoods and hair shirts work on their wearers in expected ways— hoods openly for all to see, and hair shirts secretly. If the wearer does not possess the necessary spiritual qualifications, the hair shirt might reflect the opposite of true charisma: pride and heresy. Charisma is a difficult entity, usually surrounded by ambiguity, which also implies that a charismatic person runs the risk of being branded as a heretic.

The heretical aspect of the hair shirt is illustrated in a story in the *Paralipomena*. In this story, two men are boasting of being extraordinarily gifted and able to walk on water (*Paralipomena* 33). The story begins by stating that they were wearing hair shirts: "Some heretical (*hairetikoi*) monks who wore hair garments (*trichinas*) heard about holy Pachomius" (*Paralipomena* 33; see also Halkin 1932: 158). They talk with some brothers in Pachomius's monastery and through them challenge Pachomius to cross the river walking on the water with them. Pachomius explains to the brothers that the heretics walk on water with the devil's help. He admonishes the brothers to work on their salvation and not exalt themselves with such achievements (*Paralipomena* 33). The ability of "heretical" monks to walk on water is not doubted; what is questioned and condemned is their motive for doing so and the source of their supernatural ability—unsurprisingly, the devil.

The hair shirts in this story are not explicitly commented upon, and their meaning is never spelled out. The plot, however, makes them into a sign of hypocrisy because, like the other elements of the story, they imply that the heretics exalt themselves, work miracles to show off, and turn asceticism into a competition. Instead of charisma, their garments reflect their *hybris* and heresy.[20] The hair shirts belong to the economy of this world rather than to the economy of the kingdom (see Chapter 6).

A similar example, this time with sackcloth as the offensive garment, is found in Palladius's *Lausiac History*. According to the story, "a spinster in Jerusalem wore sackcloth (*sakkophoreo*) for six years." As this was an expression of "excessive pride" and "human display," she "met with a fall" (*HL* 28). Like hair shirts, sackcloth was usually made of goat hair, and the terms are sometimes combined in *trichinos sakkos* (see Tertullian, *On Modesty* 13). It was a sign of penitence, but it could also characterize a person who made a show out of his or her asceticism.

The hair shirt and the sackcloth were ambiguous garments. They were tolerated as part of the most holy saints' outfit but were otherwise seen as dubious. They were often shown to belong to someone who wanted to pass off as holy and saintly but in reality was not. Epiphanius is very clear about the sackcloth in his *Panarion*. He mentions a Mesopotamian sect, the Massalians, who wear their hair like women and openly wear the controversial garment (*Panarion* 80; see also *De fide* 13.2). Epiphanius is adamant that "visible sackcloth is out of place in the Catholic church" (*Panarion* 80.6.5). Openly worn sackcloth or hair shirts were a type of show-off, which was incompatible with orthodoxy. Those who wore it under their clothing, on the other hand, were, according to Epiphanius, "the ones who wear it properly, for virtue and repentance" (*De fide* 23.6).

In the same group of ambiguous and sometimes offensive things to wear were chains. Jerome, who early in his career had tried out an anchorite life in the Syrian desert, tells us that "sackcloth disfigured my unkempt limbs (*horrebam sacco membra deformis*)" (*Letter* 22.7). He complains about how he was "rolling in sackcloth and ashes (*in sacco et cinere volutati*)" and further about "chains (*catenae*), squalor (*sordes*), and long hair (*comae*)" (*Letter* 17.2). The monastic Apollo in the *Historia Monachorum*

> severely censured those who wore iron chains and let their hair grow long. 'For these,' he said, 'make an exhibition of themselves and chase after human approbation, when instead they should make the body waste away with fasting and do good in secret'.
>
> (*HM* 8.59)

Sometimes, the texts reveal a discrepancy between what monastics wear and how they behave. According to the *Bohairic Life of Pachomius*, a brother

> wore a sackcloth tunic throughout his life and would eat nothing at all except bread and salt. On the other hand, if a brother somehow offended him, he would hate him and nurse his anger against him so as to repay him for evil.
>
> (*SBo* 116)

The *Life* continues with a description of a vision that Pachomius had, in which he saw the brother in "a scorching hot place, fastened like a dog to a tree laden with fruit" (*SBo* 117). The brother lived off the fruit, but he was stuck to the tree. The ambiguous hair shirt is obviously also effective in showing how great spiritual ambitions can be combined with a defect in monastic character.

Besides the symbolic connotations of the hair shirt and sackcloth, the way they functioned made them controversial. Their peculiar way of acting on their wearer was the raison d'être of these garments in the first place. Their aggressive material aspect was stressed in John Cassian's condemnation of the use of hair shirts (*cilicium*) by monks.[21] He claims that the fathers of the monastic movement disapproved of it because it encouraged vanity and pride, as well as obstructing work (Cassian *Institutes* 2; see also Krawiec 2014: 61–65). As previously noted, the garment continuously involves the body's sensory system. Conrad Leyser (2000: 55) notes about Cassian's construction of monastic life that the "very purpose of casting asceticism as a technique and a tradition was to safeguard against the possibility of aberrant charismatic leadership, which had dogged the ascetic movement in Gaul." Philip Rousseau (2010: 189) posits that with Cassian there is a "decline of the charismatic master." In line with his critical view of charismatic authority, Cassian does not approve of either hair shirts or traditional Egyptian monastic items of clothing, such as the hood and the *melote* (*Institutes* 1.10). Even if he writes eloquently about their spiritual meaning, their Egyptian background, and their prophetic models, they are simply not suitable for use in Gaul (see Chapter 5). If the wearer's main occupation was to chastise his or her body, the hair shirt might have been an apt garment; but if earning a living was part of ascetic life, as was the case for Cassian and Egyptian monastics, a hair shirt was distracting.

The use of hair shirts and sackcloth reflected *hubris*, and, according to Cassian, they obstructed and hampered the monastic in his work. Moreover, they were sometimes worn by alleged heretics. It is clear that characterizing groups in terms of their clothes could be an effective literary tool. We previously saw that Jerome described the wandering ascetics, whom he disliked, by what they were wearing: "long sleeves, big booths, clumsy dress" (*Letter* 22.43; see Chapter 3). In Apuleius's novel *Metamorphoses* (*The Golden Ass*), the priests of the Syrian goddess Atargatis have painted faces and are dressed in several colors, saffron-colored vestments of linen and silk, tunics with purple stripes, and yellow shoes (8.27). These priests are seen as strange and effeminate because of their clothes and behavior. This literary example leads to a more general question: how important were clothes as markers of heresy?

At roughly the same time, when monastic habits were developed in Egypt, urban Christian virgins were singled out by means of their dress (Undheim and Ivanovici 2019), but other than those people, the various groups of Christians as well as the Manichaeans do not seem to have worn garments strikingly different from what other people were wearing.[22] While Christians in Egypt were divided by theological doctrines, this does not seem to have been reflected in dress to a great extent—or it was reflected in subtle ways and is not documented in the surviving sources.[23] This means that heresiologists were mostly unable to use clothes to brand their victims as heretics.[24] Although, as we have seen, clothes could be markers of heresy or fake asceticism, and identification of heresies based on their clothes did occur, such use of clothes is not prominent in the surviving sources, and the heresiologies have, in fact, not much to say about heretical garments and dressing.[25]

Notes

1 Socrates, *Church History* 3.1. See also Sozomen, *Church History* 5.2. According to Shaw (1997: 127), Julian "feigned Christian piety and external behaviours, going so far as to associate with clergy and dress like a monk, while secretly holding and nurturing pagan sentiments."

2 It has been debated whether monastics were dressed in white. Karl Suso Frank claims that the characterization of monastic clothes as *schema angelikon* refers to their simplicity: "Dort lag das tertium comparationis des Verhältnisses Mönchskleid-Engelkleid in der Bedürfnislosigkeit und Unansehnlichkeit des Mönchskleides" (1964: 98–99, note 10). In the literary examples cited here, angel-like qualities are reflected in the whiteness of the dresses and in the sheer number of monastics who are so dressed.

3 Other examples in the Alphabetical Collection are Abba Pambo's face, which shines like lightning (Pambo 12); Abba Sisoes's face, which shines like the sun (Sisoes 14); and Abba Silvanus, who shines like an angel (Silvanus 12; see also Miller 1994: 141–142).

4 In another variant of the story (*AP* N 406; *AP* S 7.58), the monastic's nudity is only implied in the comparison with the wrestler.

5 The story is also found in a more elaborate version. In this story, the naked ascetic is named Timothy, and the one who meets him is Paphnutius (Onnophrius 3–9 in *Paphnutius*). Paphnutius also meets Onnophrius, another naked ascetic: "Now suddenly I looked, and I saw a man in the distance; he was very terrifying because his hair was spread out over his body like a leopard's. Indeed, he was naked, and leaves covered his male member" (Onnophrius 10 in *Paphnutius*).

6 Abba Macarius the Egyptian encounters two naked ascetics living in the desert on an island in the middle of a sea (*AP* A Macarius the Egyptian 2; *AP* S 20.4).

7 Kristi Upson-Saia (2014) argues that descriptions of ascetics' hair did not allude to sexuality but—quite on the contrary—were a means of marking their spiritual status.

8 According to Freiberger (2009: 217), these naked ascetics stand outside the monastic circles of the *Apophthegmata*. Their way of life is hailed but not imitated.

9 Kallistos Ware distinguishes between "natural" and "unnatural" ascetics and provides an example pertaining to clothes: "Thus, it is a form of natural asceticism to wear cheap and plain clothing, whereas it is unnatural to wear fetters with iron spikes piercing the flesh" (Ware 1998: 8). Nakedness is an interesting example in relation to the natural and unnatural because, though it is the natural state of the body, from a social point of view, it is in most cases considered an unnatural state. Freiberger (2009: 251) suggests using the terms "active" and "passive" instead of "natural" and "unnatural."

10 Sozomen criticizes Christian women who dress like men in Armenia (*Church History* 3.14), and Tertullian criticizes men who dress like women in theatrical shows (*De Spectaculis* 23).

11 Ambrose of Milan tells a similar story about a virgin from Antioch (*Concerning Virgins* 2.22–33).

12 Lampe 1997: *phaskidion*, "strap," thong"; *sebeninos* (and variants) "made of palm fibers."

13 Lampe 1997: *kentone*, "patched cloak"; *kentonion*, "rag covering," "much patched garment."

14 Kristi Upson-Saia (2011: 88–102) has analyzed stories about female saints' cross-dressing, composed between the fourth and seventh centuries and compiled in *vitae*. Generally, in these stories, false accusations of rape or paternity cause sexual anxiety. The saints' naked bodies tend to be exposed in the end, and their true gender is revealed by their breasts or nipples. The exposure usually happens when they are dead. Upson-Saia further shows that "the narratives generally used feminine terms when writing from the omniscient voice and used masculine terms in direct speech between the cross-dressing monk and those who considered her to be male" (97).

15 Upson-Saia (2011: 100–101) notes that the authors usually state the female cross-dressers' gender from the beginning so that the readers are aware of the discrepancy between their sex and their dress. This means that the deception only worked in the story itself but not on the reader. It further means that radical cross-dressing was domesticated in the literary sources. Upson-Saia (2011: 89, 148 note 21) mentions another story in which the disguise remains a secret until the end: the *Life of Bishop Paul and Priest John*.

16 Alain Le Boulluec (1985: 488) points out that Matt 7:15 is used to stress the subtle difference between orthodoxy and heresy. Irenaeus, for instance, uses the reference in *Against the Heresies* to describe heretics:`

> Lest, therefore, through my neglect, some should be carried off, even as sheep are by wolves, while they perceive not the true character of these men,— because they outwardly are covered with sheep's clothing (against whom the Lord has enjoined us to be on our guard), and because their language resembles ours, while their sentiments are very different.
> (*Against the Heresies* 1. Preface 1.2)

Athanasius refers to Matthew 7: 15 in his letter to Egyptian and Libyan bishops (*Circular to Bishops of Egypt and Libya*, 1991: 3; see also Kim 2015: 93).

17 Jerome describes the dress of fake virgins as follows:

> Their robes have but a narrow purple stripe, it is true; and their head-dress is somewhat loose, so as to leave the hair free. From their shoulders flutters the lilac mantle which they call 'maforte'; they have their feet in cheap slippers

and their arms tucked up tight-fitting sleeves. Add to these marks of their profession an easy gait, and you have all the virginity that they possess.

(*Letter* 22.13)

Jerome's idea of an ideal dress for a virgin is reflected in this admonition to Eustochium: "Let your dress be neither too neat nor too slovenly; neither let it be so remarkable as to draw the attention of passers-by, and to make men point their fingers at you" (*Letter* 22.27).

18 The genre of heresiology flourished from the late fourth century concurrently with the processes of building churches, founding monasteries, and defining orthodoxy (McClure 1979: 190). Epiphanius's grand oeuvre *Panarion*, his "Medical Chest against All Heresies," is a prime example of the genre. Epiphanius is mainly interested in what heretics believed and thought, their theology, but also in their rituals and behavior. However, he does not say much about dressing and rarely uses clothes to identify or mock heretics. The Sacccoforians and the previously mentioned sheep fleece of Peter are rather exceptions; even then, the fleece is mentioned only briefly, and the sackcloth is only implied in the name of a specific sect, and nothing more is said about its use. However, in addition to the references to sheepskins and sackcloth, Epiphanius also offers an example from the extreme end of the spectrum of ascetic dressing: nakedness. One of the eighty groups that he describes and condemns, the so-called Adamites, aspired to resume the prelapsarian state of Adam and performed, according to Epiphanius, their rituals in the nude. The Adamites are also mentioned by Augustine. The example again indicates that nudity was highly ambiguous and only tolerated for characters who most likely were pious fictions.

19 Translated in Goehring (2000: 24); see also Lefort (1965: 102).

20 A modern commentator on a picture of the saint Theodore Trichinas ("the hair shirt wearer") says that "under his rough tunic we can imagine, tightly bound around his waist, the hair" (Tradigo 2006: 324). In other words, we are invited to imagine a hair shirt that we cannot see in the picture. A hair shirt seems to have its intended and optimal effect only when it is invisible.

21 The *cilicium* originated in the Roman province of Cilicium (south-eastern coast of modern-day Turkey) and was made of goat's hair.

22 The fact that we do not know in any detail what Egyptian Manichaeans wore indicates that they did not stand out from the crowd, though some clues about their clothes are found in the documentary literature from a Manichaean community in the Dakhleh oasis. Many of the fourth-century letters from what was then the town of Kellis are about the production of textiles and garments, and some mention gifts of clothing (see *Coptic Documentary Texts from Kellis*, vols. 1 and 2; P. Kellis Copt. 18, 21–23 and P. Kellis Copt. 58, B21–30, see also Teigen 2018: 323–325 and 357; Franzmann 2013: 41).

23 A similar point is made by Steven Fine in an article about Jewish costume in the Roman Empire, where he raises the question, "How do you know a Jew when you see one?" He contends that, while it is difficult to distinguish Jews from other inhabitants of the Roman Empire, their garments may have had details discernible only by insiders (Fine 2013: 25).

24 The dominant position of Christianity in the fourth century was accompanied by a drive to define and formulate orthodoxy and to classify and refute heresies. The processes of consolidation and exclusion are also reflected in the compilation of laws in the Theodosian Code. A great part of the last of the code's sixteen books is concerned with heretics. The Theodosian Code mentions clothes as markers of status or occupation and makes such distinctions as between civilian clothes, military garbs, togas, "shaggy coats or hood" of slaves (14.10.1–4),

and clothes of actresses (15.7.11–12). However, when it comes to laws specifically targeted against heresies, garments are not a focal point (16.5). Among the thirty-seven heretic groups listed in the code, only one is characterized by what its members wore: the Saccoforians, or "sackcloth wearers." In the Theodosian code, they are associated with the Manichaeans (16.5. 9 and 11).

25 According to Sulpitius Severus (ca. 363–425), who wrote about the persecution of Priscillian "heretics" in Spain, garments could be used as reasons for accusations of heresy: "For in such circumstances, a judgement was formed simply by appearances, so that one was deemed a heretic rather on his turning pale from fear, or wearing a particular garment, than by the faith he professed" (*Dialogue* 2.11).

8   Dressing death, clothing eternity

The dressed stages of monastic life

The dressed stages of monastic life included the would-be monastics standing outside the gates of a monastery, clad in secular clothes, asking to be let in. Once inside, and after a due period, they took off their secular clothes, put on the monastic habit, and began a life in asceticism and toil, alternating between their work clothes, the clothes in which they slept at night, and the full monastic habit, worn for ritual purposes. Most of those who joined monasteries seem to have already been baptized, but there were also some catechumens in the Pachomian monasteries (Lundhaug 2011: 1350).[1] Finally, when they were about to die, the monastics were clad in the habit for the last time and were after death shrouded and buried. In other words, monastic life began with an initiation ritual that involved changing clothes and ended with a final transition ritual whereby the monastic was dressed, shrouded, and placed in a tomb. However, a further stage can be added: the longed-for heavenly state, where the dead were clothed in the imagined garments of salvation.

Generally speaking, ritual dressing, undressing, and redressing are parts of rites of passage that mark movements in social and geographical space and can be seen in line with the *rites de passage* model of Arnold van Gennep (1960) with its rituals of separation, transition (*limen*), and incorporation. However, when the stage of the afterlife is added to the stages of this life, the orientation of these rites is altered. In line with Victor Turner's (1969) interpretation and elaboration of the original *rites de passage* model, monastic life can be seen as a phase of prolonged liminality between life in the secular world and the afterlife. This is what Turner called "institutionalization of liminality" (1969: 107). According to this version of the model, separation rites effectuate leaving secular society and entering the monastery,[2] while incorporation in the form of burial rites transports the monastic to the afterlife. Dressing is part of both rituals. The initial gate scene, where the monastic is about to be allowed into the monastery, is similar to the way in which monastics are sometimes depicted outside the gates of paradise.[3]

They are shown praying, with their arms in an orans position, richly dressed in what are presumably heavenly garments.[4]

The latter version of the *rites de passage* model implies that in death, there are two scenarios, which are sometimes intertwined. In the first scenario, the body is dressed in the monastic habit, shrouded, and interred. The second scenario is about salvation and is represented in texts and images depicting the monastics wearing heavenly garments.

This chapter starts with a discussion of the clothes of dead and buried monastics and then proceeds to explore the characteristics, meanings, and functions of the imagined clothes of spiritual transition, transformation, and salvation. Egyptian burial customs and ideology, Graeco–Roman philosophical views of the body and soul, conflicting Christian theologies of resurrection, and the rich monastic narrative tradition are brought into the discussion. Among the sources examined in this chapter are the Nag Hammadi codices (NHC), which were found near the Pachomian monasteries and most likely belonged to and were read by the monastics, informing their views of this life, reinforcing their sense of belonging in an elite, and nourishing their hope for future transcendence. How do the various sources present the two versions of postmortem clothing—the material dress of the buried body and the imagined garments of salvation? What is the connection between burial clothes and garments of salvation, and how do the various garments interact with the deceased?

Dressed for death

The Pachomian *vitae* contain six examples of monastic funerals (Veilleux 1968: 371–379). These are the funerals of Pachomius (SBo 123, G[1] 116), Petronius (SBo 130, G[1] 117), Theodore (SBo 207, G[1] 149), Pachomius's teacher Palamon (SBo 18, G[1] 13), a monastic named Erôn (SBo 205, G[1] 147), and an anonymous female monastic (SBo 27). Armand Veilleux (1968: 371–372) noted that these funerals were similar and assumed that they were modeled on Pachomius's burial. The description of the latter's funeral underlines its general function as a model: "They prepared his holy body for burial just as they did all the other brothers" (SBo 123). Perhaps it is safer to say that the text reflects that a standardization of funerals had taken place in the Pachomian tradition and that the description of Pachomius's burial followed an already established tradition.

According to these narratives, a funeral consisted of holding a vigil, dressing the dead at the hour of the synaxis, and performing the Eucharist, followed by walking in a solemn procession to the burial place. Reciting, singing psalms, and praying are mentioned as part of the vigil and the funeral procession. While in most cases the texts mention preparing the body without providing any details, the dressing of the deceased is explicitly mentioned in Theodore's case: "When morning came, at the time of the synaxis, they prepared his body carefully for burial with fine linens and offered

for him the holy liturgy, the body and the blood of our Lord Jesus Christ"
(SBo 207). Regarding the nameless sister, it is said that "their mother covered her with a shroud" (SBo 27). The brothers are sent for, and after they
have chanted psalms, she is placed on a bier and carried in a procession with
the virgin sisters following, their monastic mother walking before them and
their monastic father walking behind them to the mountain where she is to
be buried (SBo 27; see also *HL* 33.1; *Paralipomena* 5).[5]

How were the bodies of the monastics dressed in death? Several textual
sources document that they wore their habits on their deathbed and were
interred in them. In one apophthegm, the brothers surrounding the bed of a
dying elder "put him in the habit" (*AP* N 279; see also *AP* S 11.115; *AP* N
63; *AP* S 5.11). In another apophthegm, where the tradition is described in
more detail, Apa James

> hid himself in a withdrawn cell, outside the *lavra*, and put on his
> garments of burial, as though preparing himself for death. For the
> Egyptian fathers have the custom of keeping the cloak and cowl in
> which they took the holy habit until their death, only wearing them
> on Sundays for the Holy Communion and taking them off immedi-
> ately afterwards.
>
> (*AP* A Phocas 1)

This means that the clothes in which the monastics were buried were the
actual garments—the ritual dress—that they had worn when they were alive
and, in a way, had also saved for that final moment in their lives (Patrich
1995: 217). In addition to the habit, which conveyed who they were in life
and death, their bodies were shrouded, which means that the habit and
shroud together constituted the garments of death.

Do these descriptions fit with the archaeological evidence? Most textiles
from burials are lost, partly because excavations were not conducted carefully, as archaeologists did not necessarily find monastic burial clothes and
shrouds valuable, and partly because of illegal diggings.[6] Some of the excavated textiles survive only as fragments devoid of context. In some monastic
tombs, however, the outfits of the dead have been preserved with their material, texture, and shape intact, confirming that monastics were buried in
their habits. Examples of well-documented monastic burials are the Monastery of Epiphanius and the monastery in Deir-el-Bachit (Apa Paul) in Western Thebes, the Monastery of Apa Apollo at Bawit, opposite Antinoopolis,
and the Monastery of Abu Fanah in the Western Desert.

Clothes found in tombs are no longer part of the lived life of the monastics: We cannot hear the rustling when these garments moved with their
wearers, nor do we feel their texture when they pass us nor smell them; so
even if the clothes from these burials are the ones that the monastics wore
when they were alive, they no longer reflect life and motion. They are situated in death, reflecting how monastic death was ritualized and perceived.

What did these burials look like? Françoise Dunand (2007: 163) notes that "until a very late period, Egyptian people were buried with the same rituals which had been elaborated in much older times." She stresses that according to the evidence from burials between the fourth and seventh centuries, "most people, clerics as well as laymen, continued to consider it very important to preserve the dead body from decay" (174). The attempts at preservation, however, were usually based on simplified techniques. In Egyptian monastic burials, the ingredients tended to be not only salt and juniper, as is the case with the bodies in Epiphanius's monastery, but also sometimes resin, as in the monastery in Deir el-Bachit.

These procedures have their antecedents in Egyptian mummification techniques. Dunand notes that compared to earlier Egyptian burials, with Christian funerary practices, "the problem becomes more difficult and complex" (2007: 163), but she also points out that "it is probable that in Coptic Egypt, as in other Christian societies, most people thought that it was essential to put dead bodies in good, secure tombs to grant them resurrection" (177). The Christian idea of resurrection and concern for the body in the afterlife most likely had a special resonance in traditional Egyptian conceptions and practices, which aimed at physically preserving the dead body for eternity.[7]

In a dissertation about mummification in Coptic Egypt, Gudrun Fischhaber (1997) examined the materials and their details, making seven salient points: the body is to be protected against decay; mummification techniques were still applied; east–west burials indicate that the interred were Christians; body preservation techniques were limited, for instance, using crystalline salt; the body was not opened; there was a new emphasis on shrouding; and grave goods were not as common as they had previously been. The main conclusion is a continuity from ancient Egyptian practices of body preservation, though these practices had become more restricted. Instead, shrouding now had a prominent role. Fischhaber comments on the shrouding in the following way (my translation):[8]

> Greater emphasis was placed on shrouding, which took over the protective and preserving functions of the preparation of the body. Particular attention was paid to the head, which was often either additionally wrapped or protected with hood-like cloths or other structures. What is important is not only the protective aspect, but primarily the desire to preserve the body in an aesthetic manner.
>
> (Fischhaber 1997: 44)

Sheets or shrouds are worth commenting upon. In Theodore's funeral, "fine linen" was especially mentioned. Charles Wilfred Griggs notes that in burials in Fayoum, which can be identified as Christian because the dead were buried with their heads facing west, the textiles of the shrouds "appear to have been made and used for the first time in that context" (2005: 190). In Epiphanius's monastery, which was founded in the last part of the sixth century and excavated at the beginning of the twentieth century, archaeologists found artifacts and texts, including remnants of looms. Looms were also found in Deir el-Bachit, which suggests that textile craft was a main occupation of the monastics and that the grave clothes of the monastics with their shrouds and ribbons for binding were most likely made in the monastery (MacCoull 1998: 313). According to Ewa Wipszycka (2011: 178), linen shrouds for burials were made on narrow weaving looms, which were simpler to operate than ordinary looms. Even so, considering that they were made with the sole purpose of accompanying the dead in the hereafter, the effort expended to make them is suggestive of their value and importance.

Similar care for the dead body through the use of textiles and clothing, but in this case in an ad hoc way, is reflected in several apophthegms. In one story, Abba Ammonas commands that six fine linen sheets be given to a young pregnant girl for fear that "when she comes to give birth, she might die, she or her child, and have nothing for the burial" (*AP* A Ammonas 8). In another story, a monk divides his *lebitón* in two to bury a naked ascetic (*AP* N 132.3, S 20.16). An interesting point is that while the only clothing of the ascetic had been the white hair on his head—in other words, he was naked—in death, it was important to get him dressed. In an embellished story about a dead female monastic disguised as a male, in addition to her own clothes, she is shrouded in the clothes of Abba Daniel, who found her body (see Chapter 7). In this literary example of an ad hoc burial, the body of the dead woman was wrapped in several layers of textiles, much like dead bodies were wrapped in shrouds in ordinary burials. What does this practice tell us about the function and meanings of such layers of textiles for monastic burials?

In an insightful study, Christina Riggs (2014) scrutinizes wrapping practices in Ancient Egypt spanning four millennia. She argues that "wrapping the dead in textiles was the common denominator of a set of practices characterized as mummification" (223). She suggests that there was "a close association between cloth and concealment as well as wrapping and regeneration" (223) and that the relationship between "that which was wrapped, and that which wrapped" was "symbiotic, not oppositional" (225). Wrapping is a material action that conceals, protects, and transforms the body. As Riggs shows, in societies where clothes are frequently wrapped and not tailored, the dividing line between clothes and shrouds is blurry. Although wrapping the body in shrouds and covering the head including the face was a practice mainly associated with death, Riggs notes that it also signified holiness, as seen in many wrapped statues in ancient Egypt (23–27, 215–217).

Monastic burials in late ancient Egypt continued the tradition of burying the dead in layers of linen shrouds. In the Monastery of Abu Fanah in the Western Desert (fourth–fifth centuries), Apa Kafka and Apa Herakleides were wrapped in several layers of fine linen bound with ribbons, while the body of Apa Bane (Fanah) was buried in even more expensive linen, and parts of his clothes were colored purple (Fischhaber 1997: 38–39).[9] The burial practices in the monastery of Deir el-Bachit, close to ancient Thebes, dating from the sixth to tenth centuries, consisted of mummies wrapped in thin linen sheets and tied with strips. The sheets and strips were glued with a resin-like mass and coarse salt, and juniper berries, probably used as fragrance, were found on the bodies and between the inner layers of the sheets (Lösch et al. 2013: 31). As many as six or eight linen shrouds, as well as aprons and belts, were used. The bodies were then covered with sleeping mats (Dunand 2007: 171–172; see also Fischhaber 1997: 41–42). According to the excavators, the preservation state of the mummies "seems to correlate with the applied number of linen layers" (Lösch et al. 2013: 31). Wrapping the dead was a means to control death by establishing a new setting for the body, in which the transformation to the afterlife was to take place. The wrapping prepared the monastic body for eternity. Combined with preservative fluids, this generous shrouding seems to have been effective in the preservation of the dead body. Strengthened with salt and juniper, and sometimes resin, these linen textiles were thought to both preserve the bodies from deterioration and participate in the transformation whereby the body assumed immortality. In other words, the wrappings played a role in the processes of sealing the body from this world, preserving it, and transforming it for eternity.

While monastic burials were a continuation of the ancient Egyptian mummification tradition, they took place in a new religious and ideological climate, where the Osirian afterlife was replaced with a belief in resurrection in Christ. General similarities between the ancient Egyptian and the Christian tradition are evident, especially in their common idea of a continuity after death, which in the Christian tradition, too, tended to involve the body rather heavily. However, concepts of this bodily continuation varied from the belief in the resurrection of the fleshly body to the belief in the resurrection of a spiritual body (*soma pneumatikon*), as suggested by Paul (1 Cor. 15:44), and these beliefs were a topic of intense debate (see Clark 1992; Schroeder 2007; Lundhaug 2017).

David Frankfurter (2018: 178) suggests that

> the treatment of and craft surrounding the corpse should successfully transform the deceased into an ancestor or (for monks) intercessory figure, or at least should afford the deceased a measure of protection against mortuary demons, a concern attested by the elaborate inscription of some monks' tombs with apotropaic blessings.

Frankfurter warns against viewing mummification and its details as representative of belief, arguing that it was rather the result of a local "mortuary craft." He posits that funerary practices lay outside institutional religion and stresses that "modern efforts to connect these practices with Christian doctrine tend to be speculative at best" (2018: 179). However, even if burials were not a central part of institutional religion but were based on traditional Egyptian practice, they now took place in a new Christian setting—in the case of monastics, an elite Christian context. For this reason, it is obvious to connect the Christian metaphorical imagery of resurrection to the shrouded bodies of the deceased monastics.

What do we see when we relate the Christian metaphorical language pertaining to resurrection to the shrouded bodies of the deceased monastics? The most frequently used Christian metaphors for resurrection are compatible with burials of bodies wrapped in shrouds. Examples are the processual metaphors of seed and plant, sleep and awakening, and pregnancy and birth (Bynum 1995: 6–7; Lundhaug 2017: 228–229). The seed represents the dormant stage of a plant, between life and death, while it awaits germination. The metaphor indicates that the transformation of the dead is a metamorphosis that takes place in secret and implies a dramatic transition from one state to another. The metaphor of sleep and awakening similarly suggests transformation and a new beginning. Like the seed and plant, sleep and awakening symbolize a passage from darkness to light. The wrapping of the dead can further be seen as a parallel to the customary wrapping of newborn babies. When the baby is swaddled, "the wrapping material may be perceived as containing elements that carry over from the womb and help to move the infant from a liminal, transitional state to viable personhood" (Russell 2014: 43).[10] In an analogous way, the shrouding of the dead facilitates their transition to a new life in heaven.

It seems likely that the traditional Egyptian mortuary craft of wrapping in linen shrouds and binding was reinterpreted in its new Christian setting. The wrapping of the body was seen as a means of influencing the postmortem state of the deceased so that a transformation could take place. It is obvious that Christian metaphors and imaginations gradually replaced the traditional Egyptian conceptions. Wrapping facilitated the transfer of the dead monastic to the future state of salvation and rebirth in eternity, in line with the prevalent Christian metaphors of resurrection.

Influencing the postmortem state

The burial of the body in the earth or in a cave signified that its owner was no longer part of the world of the living. Besides closure, the clothes and shrouding of the body and the covering of the face of the deceased also indicated care and a wish to actively influence their postmortem fate.

Monastic burials reflect the universal human urge to take care of dead bodies belonging to a certain social group. They also reflect the idea that this matters to the dead themselves. The dressing of the dead expresses who and what sort of person he or she was and, in a way, continues to be. In other words, the clothes reflect the *persona* of the dead. When it comes to saintly death scenes and burial clothes, the description of the death of Melania the Younger in her *vita* is frequently quoted:

> Her burial garments were worthy of her holiness. I think it is necessary for me to describe them for the benefit of those who may read this account. She had the tunic (*sticharion*) of a certain saint, the veil (*mophorion*) of another servant of God, another garment without sleeves (*lebetonos*), the belt (*zone*) of another, which she had worn while she was alive, and the hood (*koukoullion*) of another. Instead of a pillow, she had a hood made from the hair (*koukoullion trichinon*) of another saint, which we made into a cushion and placed under her honoured head. For it was fitting that she be buried in the garments (*ta himatia*) of those whose virtues she had acquired while she was living. She had no burial cloth ('*othone*),[11] except the linen (*sindonion*) with which we wrapped her from without.
>
> (*Vita Melaniae* 69)

Melania's burial garments are specifically said to be in harmony with the qualities of their wearer. Their main function is arguably to convey who Melania was by emphasizing her high status in the economy of salvation. The language of saintly dress is translated into a language of virtues in a spectacular textual display of holiness (see Krawiec 2009: 139). While the function of these funerary garments together and the hair from dead saints were not thought to better Melania's chances in the hereafter, they were a statement of her virtues. They are, after all, the actual clothing in which Melania transitioned to the afterlife (at least according to her *vita*). Thus, they did not contribute to but indicated her salvation.

Besides expressing the dead person's posthumous continuity and transformation, the use of burial clothes and textiles can also be seen as an attempt to influence their postmortem fate in more specific ways. Deviations from the norms for burials reveal that a dead body could be treated in ways that radically influenced its postmortem fate. The doctrinal content of such beliefs was an object of debate. In *On the Care to Be Had for the Dead* (2), Augustine is adamant that the fate of the deceased in the hereafter is determined exclusively by what they did when they were alive. What others piously do for them afterwards does not influence their fate (see also *The City of God* 21.24). Contrary to Augustine's assertion, however, many people believed that it was possible to help the dead. As Rebillard (2013: 240) puts it,

> while Augustine would deny that funerary rites were useful at all, popular belief would hold that the body retains 'traces of the soul' and that its burial is useful for salvation. These popular beliefs would also lead to the practice of inhumation *ad sanctos*, close to the bodies of martyrs and their relics.
>
> (See also Rebillard 2003: 53–54)

The monastic tradition offers several examples of the belief that it was possible to influence the postmortem state of others. Clothes play a role in many of these examples, which shows how closely they were associated with the deceased person. One story recounts how Paul the Simple saved his disciple from hell with his good deeds. Paul had a vision of his dead disciple being carried by two persons and "had become completely hard like a shell (*ostrakon*) from head to feet. There was no sign of activity, mental or corporal, no speech whatever; he was as though petrified" (*AP* N 599). The vision is a reference to Matthew 22:13: "Bind the one without a wedding garment (*endyma gamou*) hand and foot and cast him into outer darkness; there shall be weeping and gnashing of teeth." After this vision, Paul intensifies his asceticism and his good deeds, thanks to which "the all-holy Mother of God" (*Panagia Theotokos*) revives his disciple. Paul sees the disciple "coming all joyful, walking of his own accord and laughing." The wedding garment symbolizes a contrast to being fettered and lifeless because of sin. In this case, the heavenly wedding garment is not produced by the disciple's own effort but solely by that of his master.

Another way to help the deceased in the afterlife was to treat their dead bodies rather brutally to redeem them from sins that they had committed when they were alive. One example is a story about a monastic who asks another brother to throw his body naked into the desert after his death:

> When I fall asleep in the Lord, take up my corpse and cast it into the wilderness so the wild beasts and the birds can devour it, for it has greatly sinned against God and is not worthy of burial.
>
> (*AP* N 520).

Three days after his corpse has been cast into the desert, the dead monastic appears to the other brother in his dream and tells him that because of his great humility, God had destined the deceased monastic to be with Antony (who clearly represents the summit of saintly ascetics). While the postmortem fate of the dead body is staged by the deceased himself, it is clear that the desired result depends on the other brother's cooperation, for which he is rewarded.

What happened to the dead body in this story is telling of the values inherent in an ordinary monastic funeral. The apophthegm implies that being stripped of all clothes after death and appearing naked was regarded as shameful.[12] The story describes the ultimate humiliation and bodily destruction, like stories about Christian martyrs where their naked bodies were consumed by animals in the arenas. In the end, the apophthegm reflects the idea that the deceased should be worthy of a proper burial. The moral is that being willing to endure the humiliation of being stripped of one's clothes and eaten by animals after death meant redeeming for sins committed in this life, which would otherwise have warranted damnation. The story invites the general question of how far one could go to influence the postmortem fate of another.

Another narrative, which Armand Veilleux (1968: 375) calls "a curious story" (*un curieux récit*), goes to great lengths to humiliate a dead monastic. The story has several versions, in all of which the clothes of the deceased play an important role. In the *Paralipomena* version, Pachomius encounters a funeral procession of a dead brother:

> From a distance the brothers saw the Holy Man coming toward them, and they set the bier down on the ground so that the Holy Man might come and pray over him. So the brothers stood there singing psalms with the secular folk. When the Blessed Man had come and had prayed, he ordered the brothers not to sing psalms any more in front of [the dead brother]. He had the dead brother's clothes brought [to him] and ordered them burned in front of everyone. Then, when tney had been burned, he commanded [the brothers] to take up the body and to bury it without psalmody. And when the brothers and the parents of the dead brother threw themselves at his feet and entreated him to let them sing psalms over him, he would not endure it.
>
> (*Paralipomena* 5–6)[13]

The narrative describes a conflict between the family and the monastics, who were in charge of the burial. Generally, ordinary funerals were the responsibility of the family and did not necessarily involve clergy. According to Eric Rebillard (2003: 55), "the memory of the dead and their salvation are two different questions, and only the second is the concern for the Church."[14] In monastic settlements, things were different because the monastics had left their biological families when they joined the monastery and, in doing so, had become brothers and sisters in their new ascetic family. Burial places were connected to the monasteries. In this story, however, the biological family is present and objects strongly to the unexpected turn that their son's funeral is about to take and the brutal treatment of his dead body. Their opposition contributes to sharpening the plot. The point of the narrative is made when Pachomius explains in a rather long answer that he did this because of the disobedience of the brother, concluding,

> For this reason, I entreat you: that his punishment may be lightened. Take him away without psalms. For God, who is good, knows how to give him release because of this dishonour inflicted upon him, and to call him again to life. Had he listened to me on the several occasions on which I admonished him, he would not have come to this.
>
> (*Paralipomena* 6)[15]

This and similar stories highlight the difference between a dead human body, which is dressed, and a human corpse—a carcass, which is stripped and reduced to an object. They also reflect the idea that it is possible to influence what happens to the dead in the afterlife in a positive way. Clothes imply that the dead body retains part of its social and personal identity and its dignity because it is still treated—at least partly—as a subject. One may wonder whether clothes that were burned were seen as a stand-in for a dead brother, as their burning anticipated and substituted his looming postmortem punishment.

Resurrection and Christian theology

What did Christians think about the connection between the body and the psychological and spiritual elements of the person? What happened to these elements when a person died? These are ontological questions. They were a rich source of imagination and had several answers and normative solutions. The Christian religion encompassed complex traditions with a continuum of views ranging from spiritual to bodily resurrection and with nuanced understandings of the relationship between body and soul. The ingredients of the Christian afterlife came from several traditions, including Judaism and the Greco-Roman tradition, as well as from the New Testament (Bremmer 1983, 2002: 69–70).

In the fourth and fifth centuries, there were several types of monastics and ascetics in Egypt and as many opinions about resurrection and the constitution of human beings. This is clear from the influential writings and legacy of Origen and Evagrius; from several so-called apocryphal texts—most prominently the thirteen codices found in 1945 at Nag Hammadi/Chenoboskion, close to the Pachomian monasteries in Upper Egypt; and from the critical testimonies of the advocates of orthodoxy, like Athanasius and Epiphanius (Lundhaug and Jenott 2015: 234–262).

The idea of the physical body rising from its grave is rooted in the gospels and the resurrection of Jesus, the prototypical resurrection story in Christianity.[16] According to Luke, Peter found Jesus's tomb empty and "the linen clothes by themselves" (Luke 24:12; cf. John 20:5). An imitation of this type of resurrection is found in an apophthegm where the body of a dead pious monastic has been locked in a sanctuary, awaiting a public burial. When the abba unlocked the door, he "found nothing there except for his clothing and sandals" (*AP* N 642). The description alludes to a bodily resurrection, which does not include the dead man's clothes.

At the opposite end of the spectrum of beliefs in resurrection was the idea that the spirit left the body an empty shell. The view that the soul was foreign to the body and was trapped in it because of a "fall" was common. According to Origen, the original creation of pure intellects that contemplated God was followed by a stage where these intellects moved away from God; this was the Fall (*De principiis* 1.4.1). The intellects became souls and were given bodies. The goal was thus to return to the original unity with God, but not as embodied beings. One of the accusations against Origen and his followers was that they denied the resurrection of the flesh.

Between the idea of a physical body rising from the grave and that of a purely spiritual salvation lay several intermediate positions and theological deliberations. These deliberations were part of a rich discourse that offered many opportunities to condemn others as heretics because of their purported views on resurrection (for instance Thomassen 2009: 169–70). In polemics more extreme positions were adopted. For instance, Shenoute, who defended a complete bodily resurrection in line with the orthodox position, accused opponents of characterizing the human flesh as swinish (Schroeder 2007: 148).[17]

The surviving Pachomian tradition is anti-Origenist. In the *Letter of Ammon* (26), Theodore condemns the Origenist stance of a monastic called Patchelphius, and in his Greek *vita*, Pachomius affirms the postmortem resurrection of the body and the present spiritual resurrection (G[1] 56–57). However, as James E. Goehring (1986: 273) notes, "these sections do not appear in the Coptic *vitae*." The early Pachomian tradition was apparently adapted to more orthodox positions in later times (Farag 2018; Goehring 2020). In the surviving monastic literature as a whole, the Origenist position is mostly condemned. In the *Historia Lausiaca*, Macarius the Egyptian goes to great lengths to prove the resurrection of the body: "The rumor did the rounds that, in order to persuade a heretic who did not agree that there is a resurrection of bodies, Macarius raised up a dead person, and that rumor persisted in the desert" (*HL* 17.11).

Several resurrection and salvation concepts and metaphors were ambiguous—not least Paul's highly poetic descriptions about being clothed in Christ (Galatians 3:27) and about the perishable body that puts on imperishability, or the mortal body that puts on immortality (1 Cor. 15:50–54).[18] Similarly, various text corpora, including Hermetic texts and the codices from Nag Hammadi, reflect some of the interpretative possibilities regarding salvation circulating in Egypt in the fourth and fifth centuries.

The body as a garment and clothes of transition

The apophthegms include sayings that liken the body to a garment, such as the following: "Our body is like a garment: if you take care of it, it holds up; but if you neglect it, it wastes away" (*AP* N 174; *AP* S 5.45). It is open to interpretation whether it is an advantage that the body wastes away, or the apophthegm encourages readers to take care of it. Drawing a parallel between the body and a garment, another apophthegm is more critical of the body: "Once the soul tastes the sweetness of God, it almost hates the very garment it is wearing and even its own body" (*AP* N 592.63). Here, the body has more in common with a garment than with the soul.

Several Nag Hammadi texts contain criticisms of literal interpretations of resurrection (Lundhaug and Jenott 2015: 252–262), sometimes expressed through negative views of the body. In the *Gospel of Thomas*, Jesus says,

> It is amazing if it was for the spirit [*pneuma*] that flesh [*sarx*] came into existence. And it is amazing indeed if the spirit [*pneuma*] (came into existence) for the sake of the body [*soma*]. But as for me, I am amazed at how this great wealth has come to dwell in this poverty.
>
> (NHC II, 2, 38:31–39:2 = Logion 29)

This and other sayings construct a duality between spirit and flesh and connect wealth and poverty to spiritual rather than material qualities, and they can easily be interpreted as implying that the fleshly body (or at least its drives and desires) is external to the soul. The latter point is also apparent in two other logia, where clothes are used metaphorically to describe identity and the body. When Mary asks Jesus what his disciples are like, he answers,

> They are like little children who are travelling in a field which does not belong to them. When the owners of the field come, they will say, 'Let us have our field.' They strip naked in their presence, in order to let them have it, to give their field to them.
>
> (NHC II, 2, 36:35–37:6 = Logion 21)

The children can be interpreted as the disciples, the field as the world, and the owners as the evil powers of this world, stripping thus symbolizing freeing oneself from the body and/or the bodily desires.[19] The logion also implies that when the children strip off their clothes, these clothes are left to the owners of the field along with it. This could mean that bodily existence is connected to evil powers.

In Logion 37 in the *Gospel of Thomas*, the disciples ask when Jesus will be revealed to them, upon which he answers,

> When you undress and are not ashamed, and take your clothes (*shten*) and leave them under your feet like little children and tread upon them, then [you will see] the Son of the living one and you will not be afraid.
>
> (NHC II, 2, 39:29–40:2)

This may be an allusion to Adam's prelapsarian nakedness.[20] That bodies are appendages to souls and should be thought of more like clothes does not mean that the body is without its allures. The *Gospel of Thomas* clearly states that the body may have power over the soul. For those, however, who are no longer in the grip of their bodies, bodies are like clothes—they can be taken off and exchanged for something else. Clothes and bodily identity are thus closely connected.

Regarding the body as something foreign to the soul that has been glued to it and dragged it down meant that living in the world could be imagined as a descent from the soul's heavenly home. The idea of a descent was matched by the idea of the possibility of an ascent from this world to return to its original home. Such ideas are occasionally expressed by means of garments, which are sometimes connected to the various planetary spheres. The soul was dressed in these garments when it left its heavenly home, went through the spheres, and was born in the fallen world below. If saved, it escaped the evil material world, doffed its earthly and planetary robes, and was finally clad in the garments of salvation in the spiritual world above.

The idea of the body as the soul's garment has its roots in Greek thinking. It is present in Hermetic texts, with their rethought Egyptian priestly wisdom.[21] Such texts circulated in antique Egypt, including in monastic circles. In one instance in the *Corpus Hermeticum* (*CH*), those who seek salvation are admonished to free their souls of the cage that is the body:

> But first you must rip off the tunic (*chiton*) that you wear, the garment of ignorance, the foundation of vice, the bonds of corruption, the dark cage, the living death, the sentient corpse, the portable tomb, the resident thief, the one who hates through what he loves and envies through what he hates. Such is the odious tunic you have put on. It strangles you and drags you down with it so that you will not hate its viciousness.
>
> (*CH* VII, 2–3)

In this eloquent listing of the evils of the body, the dominant metaphor is the tunic (*chiton*). The metaphorical tunic plays a particularly active role in hindering the spiritual progress of the Hermetic adept (Copenhaver 1992: 146–148). Its prime characteristics are ignorance and death. It is a burden to the soul and strangles it.

In another Hermetic text, the mind of those who leave the body, "since it is divine by nature, becomes purified of its garments and takes on a fiery body" (*CH* X, 16). Here, the soul is described as the garment of the mind and the spirit as the garment of the soul. According to the text, "the earthy body cannot support so great an immortality" as that of the mind, so the mind must be enshrouded by the soul and the spirit (*CH* X, 16). When the mind is free from the earthly body, it puts on a tunic of fire (*CH* X, 17; see also *Poimandres* 25–26).

Similar thoughts about the need for clothes adapted to the various realms of the spiritual and material worlds are found in the Nag Hammadi codices, connected to redeemers, who descend through the spheres to bring the message of salvation to spirits trapped in bodies. These heavenly redeemers change their garments according to their surroundings. In the *Trimorphic Protennoia*, the redeemer says,

> The third time, I revealed myself to them in their tents (*skené*) as Word (*logos*), and I revealed myself in the likeness of their shape (*éikon*). And

I wore everyone's garment (*hbso*), and I hid myself within them, and [they] did not know who empowers me.

(NHC XIII, 1, 47: 13–19)

He also says, "I clothed myself as the son of the chief creator (*Archigenetor*)" (NHC XIII, 1, 49: 12–13). The redeemers' garments seem to function both as a necessary protection in the descent through the spheres and as a disguise so that the spiritual messengers are not detected by the powers in the world below.

The most elaborate wardrobe of a spiritual traveler to the lower world is found in the *Paraphrase of Shem* (NHC VII, 1), in which Derdekeas, a redeemer, reveals his message to Shem.[22] Derdekeas changes clothes according to the circumstances.[23] He speaks of wearing the body and once about wearing "erring flesh" (36: 28). He even says that in Hades, "I put on the beast (*therion*)," using "beast" as a characteristic of the body and something that can be worn, thus mixing metaphorical references (19: 26–27; see also Wisse 1970: 135).[24] In this text, garments are used as metaphors for bodily existence, for transitional states in the planetary spheres, and for salvation in the world above. They reflect the close integration between a wearer and the clothes that he or she wears, as well as the necessity to change clothes according to not only social but also ontological circumstances.

Most fascinating is how certain garments are given names and appear as spiritual powers. Derdekeas names three different garments Chelkeach, Chelkea, and Chelke (33: 4, 33: 9, 33: 12). They are protective, are connected to clouds, and act as a crux between garments and divine beings.[25] The various garments protect Derdekeas, confuse his antagonists, and have a saving power (43: 9–11; see also Wisse 1970: 134).

There is a parallel in the Manichaean *Kephalaia* from Egypt, where garments function as an armor and as the forces of a prominent mythological being called "the First Man." His garments are also described as the five sons (*Kephalaia* I, 148.24–25), identified as the Living Fire and the Garments of the Wind, Water, Light, and Air (I 127.5–7). The First Man "approached his garments, the gods who shine forth" (69.28–29), and he spoke to them and draped them over himself (69, 29–70,1; 177, 20–23). One of the gifts offered to the righteous soul after death is the garment of Light (36.12–21). Garments in Manichaean mythology are sometimes turned into "rags," which indicates that the garments of the First Man were caught in the material world of darkness and were scattered. The garments are spiritual elements imprisoned in darkness and matter, and the Manichaean process of salvation aims at liberating them. In a similar way as in the *Paraphrase of Shem*, the protective role of clothes is here expanded so that they are personified or semi-personified, appearing as mythological entities. Despite their personal names, however, the garments function more collectively than individually. This indicates that there were limits to the extent to which mythological life could be breathed into spiritual helpers in the form of garments.

Garments of salvation

Clothes that are used to describe the spiritual world have special qualities. In the Revelation of John, "the narrative path of the apocalypse is liberally strewn with clothes" (Neufeld 2005: 71), and there is a strong tendency for the divine and apocalyptic heroes to be dressed in white garments, which indicate their moral standing and rank in the spiritual hierarchy. Candida R. Moss points out that "white robes are seen as generic markers of elect status, an ambiguous marker of otherworldly identity, and an almost banal cipher for moral purity" (Moss 2019: 99).[26]

Garments of salvation continued to fascinate. Resurrection is often presented in terms of wedding feasts and bridal chambers, with wedding garments associated with the heavenly robe of glory (see Matt. 22:1–11; see also Hunt 2012: 146–148).[27] In one of the apophthegms, Abba Dioscuros says:

> If we wear our heavenly robe (*to ouranion endyma*), we shall not be found naked, but if we are found not wearing that garment (*to endyma ekeino*), what shall we do, brother? We, even we also, shall hear the voice that says, "Cast them into outer darkness; there men will weep and gnash their teeth" [Matt. 22:13]. And brothers, there will be great shame in store for us, if, after having worn this habit (*schema*) for so long, we are found in the hour of need not having put on the wedding garment (*to endyma tou gamou*). Oh, what compunction will seize us! What darkness will fall upon us, in the presence of our fathers and our brothers, who will see us being tortured by the angels of punishment!
>
> (*AP* A Dioscuros 3)

Three garments are mentioned in this apophthegm: the heavenly robe, the monastic habit, and the wedding garment. The heavenly robe and the wedding garment are metaphorical expressions for clothes of salvation, while at the same time the saying indicates that these garments are produced during the life of the monastics. The evil alternative to the heavenly robe and the wedding garment is the dreaded postmortem nakedness.

There is sometimes an interplay between actual garments and the imaginary garments of salvation. In some images, monastics about to be let into heaven wear clothes that combine the ordinary habit and extraordinary items and signs. One example is a tomb in the inner tomb chapel at the White Monastery that has been associated with Shenoute (Bolman, Davis, and Pyke 2010; see also Chapter 3). A man is depicted in a belted tunic and mantle, a leather apron with a shoulder strap, and a long scarf with four crosses. A square halo frames his head as he reaches out to grasp what seems to be a crown of victory (Bolman et al. 2010: 457–459). Together with what is probably a robed angel (only the lower body remains), the halo and the crown of victory make Shenoute's monastic habit into a heavenly garment.

Combinations of earthly and heavenly garments are also shown in the monastic portraits in the Monastery of Apa Apollo in Bawit (Thomas 2012).[28] In these pictures, the monastic fathers are depicted as apostles and shown together with them and in the same type of dress.[29] Monastics in their ideal typological garments are not just dressed for salvation but depicted in a superior state of salvation; they are closely associated with apostles and prophets and, like them, are understood as intercessors in the Christian mythological universe (Thomas 2012: 59). In a similar way, angelic clothing could be seen as an ideal type of monastic clothing (Thomas 2012: 62). In the state of salvation, the distinction between angels and humans—and between their clothes—tends to be blurred.

The contrast between garments worn in this life and those worn in the world to come was commonplace in various branches of Christian literature. Donning a new garment was probably Tertullian's favorite metaphor for resurrection (Bynum 1995: 40):

> For although they shall be found naked when their flesh has been laid aside, or to some extent sundered or worn away (and this condition may well be called nakedness), they shall afterwards recover it again, in order that, being reinvested with the flesh, they may be able also to have put over that the supervestment of immortality; for it will be impossible for the outside garment to fit except over one who is already dressed.
>
> *(On the Resurrection of the Flesh* 42: 13)

Ideas about special postmortem clothing, the necessity to trade earthly clothes for heavenly ones, and the contrast between these types of garments are found in various Nag Hammadi texts: "O my son, strip off the old garment of fornication (*porneia*) and put on the garment which is clean and shining, that you may be beautiful in it. But when you have this garment, protect it well" (*The Teachings of Silvanus* NHC VII, 4, 105:13–19). Einar Thomassen (2005: 348) points out that the idea of putting on a new garment is central in the *Gospel of Philip*. According to this gospel, "in this world those who put on garments (*hbso*) are better than the garments. In the kingdom of heaven, the garments (*hbso*) are better than those who have put them on" (57: 19–22). Lundhaug identifies "the garments in this world metaphorically with the material body and the garments in the kingdom of heaven with the body, in the post-initiatory and postmortem wearing of the 'perfect' man" (2010: 253–254). This interpretation makes sense of another enigmatic saying in the gospel: "Some are afraid that they rise naked. Because of this, they wish to rise in the flesh, and they do not know that it is those who wear the flesh who are naked" (56: 26–31). The saying uses the conceptual metaphor of the body as a garment but discerns between two types of metaphorical garments: the material body and the body that has been attained through the Eucharist (*Gos. Phil.* 57:1–8). The latter body is the resurrection body, which is also identified with the body of Christ (Lundhaug 2013, 2017: 225–228).

Heavenly baptisms and transformations are described in the *Trimorphic Protennoia* and *Zostrianos*. According to the former, "you (plural) will receive a garment (*stole*) from those that give garments (*stole*), and the baptizers will baptize you" (NHC XIII, 1, 45:16–17).[30] Here, the corporeal body is stripped off, and a celestial garment is bestowed on the baptizand. The postmortem garment is associated with a baptismal dress, and the ascending adept is transformed by means of a garment of light (see Burns 2014: 127).

In the end, in salvation, garments sometimes become alive, similar to the way in which celestial garments are described as living entities in the *Kephalaia* and in the *Paraphrase of Shem*. For instance, the idea of a living garment is found in the "Hymn of the Pearl," which exists in one Syriac and one Greek manuscript (*The Acts of Thomas*, Chapters 108–113). The hymn narrates the story of a king's son, who has to leave his kingdom in the East, take off his splendid garment, go to Egypt, and bring back a pearl. When he arrives in Egypt, he "dressed in their dress, that they might not hold me in abhorrence" (109:29). He eats from their food, forgets who he is and why he has come to Egypt, and falls into a deep sleep. When his parents realize what has happened, they send him a letter, which flies to him. The letter reminds him that he is the son of kings and urges him to remember the pearl and to think of his splendid robe. When the prince wakes up, he comments on his dirty clothing and undresses, "their filthy and unclean dress I stripped off and left it in their country" (111:62), fulfills his mission, and returns to his kingdom. There, he is reunited with his splendid robe, which has the image of the King of kings on it. The robe plays an active role in the reunion:

> And in its kingly movements it poured itself entirely over me, and on the hands of its givers it hastened that I might take it. And love urged me to run to meet it and receive it; and I stretched forth and took it. With the beauty of its colours I adorned myself, and I wrapped myself wholly in my toga of brilliant hues.
>
> (113:93–97)

The hymn's potential to invite a seemingly infinite range of interpretations is one of its strengths.[31] It also possibly explains why it is found in both Christian and Manichaean contexts. It is worth noting, in line with A.F.J. Klijn's observation in his commentary to the hymn, that even if it is called the "Hymn of the Pearl," its main theme is the heavenly robe (2003: 191). One way to interpret this hymn is as an allegory of the soul, which has fallen from its heavenly home but is reunited with its heavenly robe in salvation. It is striking how active this robe is and how it becomes a living entity in its own right. This is a mythologization of dress, which probably had several inputs, for instance, not only in the idea of robes of initiation, such as the baptismal robe in Christianity, but also in the more basic idea that a new status requires a new type of garment.

Heavenly garments continued to take on a life of their own. In one passage in the popular Egyptian text *The Investiture of the Archangel Michael*, the apostles see the gates of heaven open and the Archangel Michael wrapping robes of light around the fruits from the Tree of Life, "and when the robes to which Michael gathers the fruits are filled, the one that is full takes wings and flies away and comes to place itself by the feet of the Saviour, worshipping him" (M593, 35: 8–9). Then, "those of the heavens and the air are filled with holy scarves and every precious robe, flying out of the seventh heaven until they come to the place where the Lord sits with his twelve apostles" (M593 35: 10). One way to interpret these enigmatic fruits is to see them as a metaphorical description of the souls of the deceased who have obtained salvation and are therefore wrapped in the glorious garments of salvation. These glorious garments are the heavenly counterparts of those who are saved.

Ideas about heavenly garments enrobing those who are saved and even appearing as living entities in their own right are found in Christian groups, as well as among Manichaeans. Although they had roots in Jewish interpretations of Genesis and in the story about Adam's former Glory before he was clothed in the garments of skin, they transcended their origins and became embedded in rich traditions of mythological imagination and theological speculation.

Besides their metaphorical meanings, these ideas of heavenly garments have an experiential foundation in the actual wearing of clothes. Clothes have an ambiguous existence because they are integrated with their wearers and are part of their embodiment, while at the same time being extensions of the body, which can be put on and taken off at will. Generally speaking, clothes provide protection against the cold, starting with the swaddling of a baby immediately after it is born, accompanying the person through life, and ending with the shrouding of the dead body. They envelope their wearers warmly, represent safety, express their identity, and support life even in death. These qualities make clothes particularly suited for an active role not only in this life but also in the imagined afterlife, where their function as agents in human life finds a mythical expression in the living garments of salvation.

Notes

1 In the fourth century, baptism included anointment, a triple immersion in water, and coming out of the water and being dressed in a white garment, which functioned as a vestimentary symbol of a new life. After having been baptized, the new Christians were allowed to participate in the Eucharist. According to Hugo Lundhaug (2011: 1347), there are relatively few references to baptism in early Egyptian monastic sources, though there are some passing references. The Pachomian sources focus on baptism as an initiation to Christianity (1349), for

instance in relation to Pachomius' baptism (SBo 8 and G¹ 5) and to the baptism of catechumens (SBo 81). The dominating baptismal metaphors are rebirth and seal (Lundhaug 2011: 1357). In the Shenoutean sources, the dominant baptismal metaphors are "those of seal, cleansing, the putting on of Christ, and dying and rising with Christ" (1373). Examples are found in Shenoute's writings, *There Is Another Foolishness* and *The Lord Thundered*. Both the Pachomian and the Shenoutean sources stress the soteriological significance of baptism (Lundhaug 2011: 1373).

2 Arpad Szakolczai (2000: 220) discerns three types of "permanent liminality," each related to one of the three phases of the rites of passage. Monasticism is a state of permanent liminality seen as a process of a never-ending performance of rites of separation.

3 A parallel between the two gates is suggested in the *Bohairic Life of Pachomius*, where a chapter about Pachomius, who at the end of his life stands before "the gate of life" but has to return to his body for some more suffering, is followed by a chapter where a man arrives at the monastery's gate (SBo 114; see also Maguire 2003: 19, notes 14 and 16).

4 Eunice Dauterman Maguire (2003: 39–42) shows that this last scene is a motif frequently found on textiles and paintings, but she also considers the possibility that these figures are not holy monastics but their namesakes. She further notes that "we may misunderstand what it was that such images sought to communicate if we turn to them for reliable pictures of the real-time physical appearance of monastic persons" (51).

5 The *Praecepta* make no explicit mention of the dressing of dead monastics. They only say that no one accompanying a deceased monastic to the burial ground shall "take his mantle with him while going to the mountain" (*Praecepta* 127).

6 According to Maguire (2003: 41), "unfortunately, since garments have seldom been studied in burials that were still intact, an untold quantity of archaeological information has been lost."

7 According to Éric Rebillard (2013: 3, 62), in North Africa, burial places were not necessarily seen as relevant to Christian identity, and ordinary people were buried in spaces that were not marked as Christian. Rebillard argues convincingly that Christianity was part of a plural lateral identity rather than a hierarchical identity and poses the interesting question of when it was developed (2013: 92). Although it is reasonable to assume that monastics had a predominantly Christian identity, even in their case, other identities were sometimes involved.

8 Original version of Fischhaber:

> Grösser Wert wurde auf die Umhüllungen gelegt, die anstelle der Körperprä-paration schützende und erhaltende Funktionen übernahmen. Dabei wurde vor allem dem Kopf besondere Beachtung geschenkt, der häufig entweder extra eingehüllt oder mit haubenartig angeordneten Tüchern oder andere Konstruktionen geschützt was. Wichtig war dabei nicht nur der Schutzas-pekt, sondern primär der Wünsch, den Körper in ästhetischer Art und Weise zu bewahren.

9 Purple is a royal color, and it may have been used to show the special spiritual status of Apa Bane. Also see Georges Castel's detailed description of the clothes of a monastic mummy from the Church of Saint Mark at Qurnat Mari (1979).

10 P. B. Adamson contends that in Egypt, the swaddling of a baby represented the swaddling of a mummy, thus protecting it from evil spirits (Adamson 1985: 179). However, the opposite may have as well been the case: the wrapping of the dead may have been modeled on the swaddling of babies and similarly contributed to

a transition from one state to another. It must also be noted that the day when a person died was sometimes described as *dies natalis*, "day of birth," because the dead was to be reborn in a state of salvation.

11 *Othone* was a special fine linen usually used in burials.

12 In a study on dying in contemporary Finland, Terhi Utriainen (2004: 135) notes that "dying and dead people, who are (left) undressed, are often regarded as an ultimate token of abandonment and denial of human value."

13 See also SBo 93, G¹ 103.

14 A churchly burial liturgy was developed in the seventh and eighth centuries (Rebillard 2013: 69; Plesa 2017: 34).

15 In the Bohairic version, when Pachomius "burned his clothes and his habit," it was to instill fear in the other brothers so that they would do no evil (SBo 93, G¹ 103). A third version is found in an Arabic translation of the *Life of Pachomius* (Göttingen Ms. 114), where a young boy is in a state of severe impurity. Pachomius orders his clothes burned and the ashes thrown far from the monastery. This is one of the stories recounting that Pachomius had received grace from God to distinguish sinners from non-sinners and serves as an example of this ability. According to Veilleux (1968: 375–376), this is the original version of the story. However, it could also be a late effort to give an unsettling story a rational explanation.

16 The Christian belief in resurrection was probably inherited from the Jews, but Christians developed several ideas, among which was the resurrection of the flesh (Bremmer 2002: 50–55). As we have seen, the traditional Egyptian strife for bodily permanence, reflected in the practice of mummification that lasted millennia, also played a role in Christian burials. Fischhaber (1997: 258) notes that like in the Egyptian Osiris mythology, scenes of destruction in the stories about Christian martyrs are followed by scenes of restoration of mutilated bodies. It must also be noted that the ancient Egyptian idea of several versions or several aspects of the soul was exceptionally sophisticated and may have played a role, at least in Egyptian Christianity.

17 Caroline T. Schroeder (2007: 128) raises the question of "how Shenoute's theological writings on embodiment rhetorically conflate pagans and heretics and what ideological purposes that conflation serves." She makes the salient point that "perhaps religious identity in late antique Egypt was much more fluid than these monikers imply" (133; see also Frankfurter 2018).

18 In the Epistle to the Colossians, Paul says, "Do not lie to one another, seeing that you have stripped off the old self with its practices and have clothed yourself with the new self, which is being renewed in knowledge according to the image of its creator" (Col. 3: 9–10). In Ephesians, he urges the believers "to clothe yourself with the new self, created according to the likeness of God in true righteousness and holiness" (Eph. 4: 24).

19 In addition to death, baptismal allusions also seem to play a part in Logion 21. The same is true of renunciation of bodily desires, as discussed by Simon Gathercole (2014: 302).

20 Jonathan Z. Smith (1966) points to the parallel between what happens in this logion and what happens at baptism. The references to the prelapsarian body and to baptism imply not only that clothes stand for the body, but also that they indicate social identity (cf. Valantasis 1997: 114).

21 Christian Bull has recently made a strong case for the Egyptian background of the Hermetic tradition (Bull 2018: 428–431, 456–460). I am grateful to him for pointing me to relevant Hermetic passages.

22 It has been debated whether the *Paraphrase of Shem* is a Christian text (see Wisse 1970). It is based on Old Testament texts and on the first text of one of

the Nag Hammadi codices (VII). It shares the codex with Christian texts and was most likely read by Christians. Reaves (2019) argues for considering it a Christian text. See also Burns 2015.

23 Derdekeas initially wears a "garment (*hbso*) of light" (8: 33–35, 12: 7–8, 12: 30–31), later appears "without my holy garment" (17: 1), and then says that he has laid down "his other garment" (17: 19). He describes the garment in the lower world as follows: "I took off my garment and put on another garment of fire, which has no form" (18: 4–5, 19: 22).

24 Derdekeas speaks about his "garment of fire" (18: 27) and says that it "rubbed Nature in her covering" (18: 33–34), "I rested with my garment" (19: 11–12), and "I arose with my garment in the power" (22: 17–18). He further declares that his garment "will shine upon the creation" (28: 24–25), speaks of his "invincible garment" (30: 35, 33: 18–19, 41: 28), and declares that "the likeness is my honoured garment" (32: 34–35).

25 Derdekeas enigmatically says that "my unequalled garment will shine forth upon me, and all my other garments which I put on in the clouds which were from the astonishment of the Spirit" (39: 1–6).

26 Rev. 3: 34, 3: 17, 4: 4, 6: 11, 7: 9, 7: 13, 15: 15, 19: 13. White garments were worn by priests, worshippers, the Essenes, heavenly messengers, God, and Roman deities (Neufeld 2005: 73). White continued to be the color of the saved, as well as of angels. In a captivating story of Christian martyrs, *The Passion of Perpetua and Felicity*, Perpetua has a vision of heaven. In a garden, she sees "many thousands of people clad in white garments" (4.9). When her dead brother appears to her, he is in a dark place wearing a sullied dress (7.7), but after Perpetua prays for him, she sees him "all clean, well dressed and refreshed" (8.1). According to a vision of her companion in prison, Saturus, he came, after his death to a place with a gate, where four angels dressed those who entered in white garments (12.1; see Bremmer 2002: 57–64 and Salisbury 1997: 92–115). However, Moss makes the striking observation that when "the aesthetics of the resurrection correspond to the bodies and attire of the rich, salvation becomes a process of enrichment that never deconstructs the social hierarchy that it wants to challenge" (Moss 2019: 113).

27 The idea of a postmortem angel-like life for the righteous and saved is found in the Dead Sea Scrolls and the Synoptic Gospels, as well as in the monastic tradition (Burns 2014: 121).

28 Thelma K. Thomas (2012) divides the depictions of the monastic dress in these portraits into what she has termed schematic and ideal modes of monastic dress. The schematic mode is "the paradigmatic appearance of the monk," which is the recognizable outward form. It does not necessarily include items of clothing used by actual monastics (38). The ideal mode "carries associations of mimetic emulation, that is, deliberately copying of exemplary forms, especially portraits as form of divinities and heroes" (40). That the depicted monastics are in a state of transcendence is seen in the prayers inscribed on the walls (42).

29 Thomas makes the salient point that although the portraits may not show the monastics' actual garments, "art historical inquiry into these different pictorial strategies for figuration through dress should contribute to our understanding of the role of the monastic habit in the monk's salvation" (2012: 46). She notes that the two modes of monastic dress, schematic and ideal, are based on the traditional vestimentary system with the tunic and mantle and were understood in dialogue with the actual habit worn by monastics (48). Depictions of monastics among apostles are also found at the Monastery of Apa Jeremiah in Saqqara and

are in line with the way in which monks are likened to apostles in the monastic literature (43–44).

30 Later in *Trimorphic Protennoia*, the names of those who give robes of light are listed: Ammon, Elasso, and Amenai.

31 According to Robin Darling Young, this enigmatic story "seems to attract metaphorical interpretations that are retrojected as its genuine meaning" (2007: 199).

Epilogue

Paul and the crocodile

In the controversies about the nature of resurrection at the turn of the fifth century, the interpretation of key scriptural passages in Paul's letters were hotly debated (Lundhaug 2017). Paul uses complex anthropological distinctions to describe humans and their potential for salvation building on the concepts of body (*soma*), flesh (*sarx*), soul (*psyche*), and spirit (*pneuma*) (Engberg-Pedersen 2010: 102–105). He often uses vestimentary metaphors when he tries to express the reidentification and transition of the self from the state of mortality to that of immortality (Campbell 2014: 85). In the earliest promise of the rising of the dead found in a Christian text, Paul uses the verb *enduo*, which means "to put on," "to clothe oneself in" to describe immortality:

> For this perishable body must put on (*endusasthai*) imperishability, and this mortal body must put on immortality. When this perishable body puts on imperishability, and this mortal body puts on immortality, then the saying that is written will be fulfilled: 'Death has been swallowed up in victory'.
>
> (1 Cor. 15:53–54)

Paul refers to Christ as a garment that believers must put on (Rom. 13:12–14; Gal. 3:26–27), speaks of taking off the old self and putting on a new self (Col. 3:9–10; Ephes. 4:20–24), and describes the bodily resurrection as a wish "to be clothed over" (*ependusasthai*) (2 Cor. 5:2, 4) and not to be "unclothed" (*ekduasthai*) (2 Cor. 5:4).[1]

Paul uses the metaphor of clothes to speak about bodies. In the words of Frederick Tappenden, "Paul is concerned . . . not with the putting on of different clothes but rather with the putting on of a different body" (2016: 126).[2] However, Paul's repeated use of clothing metaphors suggests that, like his contemporaries—and most people, for that matter—he saw dress as an obvious part of human beings. Although this does not seem surprising, the implication that dress is an integral part of humans, deeply embedded in emotional and cognitive life, is usually overlooked.

Unlike Paul, the crocodile in the Introduction has a rather simplistic view of the human constitution. It thought that the monastic was identified with the habit that he had left on the shore—in other words, it reduced the monastic to his clothes. Paul and the crocodile clearly have different points of departure and different interests: Paul is obsessed with salvation, whereas the crocodile is interested in food. At first sight, the crocodile's view of the human constitution may appear rather absurd: clothes are not us. Or are they? And if so, in what ways and to what extent? Based on what has been discussed in this book, I now wish to tease out some of the complexity of the cultural presence, meanings, actions, and functions of clothes. Let us first recapitulate the findings of the preceding chapters.

Recapitulation

Christian ascetic garments have connotations that point back to ancient Middle Eastern conceptions of wilderness dressing and forward to the standardized monastic dress of the European Middle Ages and later. The wilderness garment of Gilgamesh was compared to the sheepskin cloaks of Old Testament prophets Elisha and Elijah, who are frequently cited as role models for Egyptian monastics. The Old Testament stories about Adam and Eve's prelapsarian nakedness, their tunics of skin, and their being denied eternal life were compared to precursors in Mesopotamian mythology, especially the *Epic of Gilgamesh*. The Middle Eastern myths were seen in relation to later discussions of the human condition, the new Christian hope of immortality, and the institutionalization of ascetic life.

A wide variety of ascetic and monastic life were experienced through clothes, ranging from ascetics and hermits with their rags and nakedness to coenobitic monastics who developed their habit into a uniform. The various items of ascetic clothing were parts of an evolving monastic dressing system and the general dressing system of the Roman Empire. The monastic dress was part of the *rites de passage* of monastic life, as well as of daily and weekly practices and procedures. When monastics were dressed in their standardized habit, its various items acted on them and were worn in ways that contributed to shaping them; for instance, hoods served to limit communication when Pachomian monastics were sitting at the table, eating. Clothes moved with their wearers, enabled them, and restricted them. Deviations from the norms of correct dressing, such as flirty fringes, sloppy dressing, or rags, could lead to alternative ways of behavior. Monastic clothes were also utilized as tools, for instance to carry things in, to punish with, or to hide behind, as well as an interface between the spiritual and material worlds.

The arduous work required in the various stages of the production of clothes, from harvesting material for thread to the finished garments and other textiles, took up a considerable part of monastic life. The making of thread, textiles, and clothes accompanied the efforts of the monastics to recapitulate biblical stories, nourish religious imagination, and create a meditative mood. Thus, crafting acted on their minds and contributed to shaping them in desired ways. Moreover, clothes could evoke memories and arouse and express emotions. Monastic clothes, like potentially all garments, incorporated memories that were not only personal and emotional but sometimes also inscribed on the habit in ways that were intended to fixate their references and meanings on a collective basis.

As most things in ascetic and monastic life, clothes participated in two economies: the economy of salvation, which was based on symbolic and religious capital, and the economy of this world, which was based on material resources and economic gains. A middle way—neither too lenient nor too strict—was established between these economies. Clothes were evaluated on that basis, and deviances in either direction fueled ascetic discourse and constituted points of departure for moral stories. Dress incorporated three forms of authority—ascetic, pragmatic, and charismatic—and made them distinct and palpable.

Clothes could hide the true nature of their wearers and create a discrepancy between them and their wearers. Disguises and cross-dressing were contentious. An ascetic or monastic dress could conceal the character of a person who failed to live up to the intentions that it expressed. Some items of clothing were controversial. A prime example is the hair shirt, which not only tended to imply hubris but also hindered a monastic's activities because it irritated the skin. The meaning of clothes (or lack thereof) was pushed to the extreme when the holiest ascetics were imagined in a state of prelapsarian nakedness.

When monastic habits were developed in Egypt in the fourth century, these uniform garments marked their wearers as special. The habit was part of the development of a new type of Christian organization, monasticism, incorporated a type of life that was mandatory in its institutions, and shaped the monastics. However, whereas monastics and ascetics were recognized through their dressing, the various Christian subgroups do not seem to have been similarly identified, and heresiologists seldom referred to clothes as indicators of heresy. This also suggests that those who were branded heretics did not necessarily intend to wear special clothes that identified them as separate groups or indeed to appear as separate groups at all.

Dead monastics were carefully wrapped in linen before they were interred. Even in the afterlife, it was obviously painful to think of the deceased as naked; on the contrary, nakedness in the hereafter usually meant damnation. Using the dress code was a means of describing salvation as a superior state of being, for instance, by means of color—being dressed in white; by means of radiance—shining clothes; or by means of movement and celebration—wedding garments. There are also examples of garments of salvation, which were imagined to be alive and appear as persons. This can be seen as a mythologization of a general tendency of clothes to sometimes appear as actors in their wearers' lives.

Dimensions of dress

While the motivation behind this book was to shed light on the use of ascetic and monastic clothes in late-antiquity Egypt, it was also driven by an ambition to understand the general importance of clothes in human life. However, it can be argued that the source material has been rather restricted and one-sided, which may have made it difficult to fulfill this last ambition. The source material is mainly textual, and the wearing of those ancient monastic clothes is no longer observable. On the other hand, this stripped and restricted material, connected to a simple and specialized way of life, has been extremely helpful in illuminating some of the fundamentals related to wearing clothes. Not least, the sources have shown how multifunctional and, importantly, how multidimensional clothes are in human life.

Wearing clothes can be described according to four dimensions: the bodily and material dimension, the sensual and emotional dimension, the social dimension, and the cognitive dimension. The division is, of course, artificial; in real life, these dimensions are closely interconnected, and it is their interplay that makes clothes so significant in human life and explains why we are so deeply entangled in them. However, such a division may still be helpful for analytical purposes.

The bodily and material dimension

Ascetic and monastic clothes were physical artifacts made by humans. Because clothes are material, they partake in continuous processes of change and decay. Clothes are intimately connected to the body, affect their wearers, and mediate the contact between the wearer and the world. They become actors through their constraints and affordances, although their influence can range from weak to strong and significant. Wearing monastic garments molded the bodies and minds of the monastics.

The interaction between clothes and their wearers implies that the monastics ideally controlled them, but at the same time, the habit also controlled the monastics by guiding how they should walk, sit, and act. Clothes were part of the interaction between the inmates of the monasteries and the ritualization and systematization of their lives.

The sensual and emotional dimension

Wearing the habit had an impact on ascetics and monastics' self-perception, their interaction with their surroundings, and their feelings, thoughts, and actions. The perception of clothes is based not only on their social but also on their sensual aspects. They afford not only social integration but also safety and protection from the sun, heat, cold, and insects. Naked babies stop crying when they are enfolded in blankets; the terror of death is more manageable when dead bodies are dressed and shrouded.

Clothes tend to be conceived as part of the body. Therefore, experiencing the world is intertwined with being dressed. The habit was obviously an external representation of monastic life, but it was more than that. Generally speaking, clothes contribute to creating and sustaining emotional dispositions, they trigger emotional episodes, and they nourish or change affective states (Colombetti and Krueger 2015: 1163; Colombetti and Roberts 2015). Wearing a monastic habit invited certain moods and motivations.[3] Specific clothing scenarios, such as being initiated and dressed in the habit, being deprived of it if expelled from the monastery, or dressing a dead body, triggered specific emotions. Because garments trigger associations and help to recall memories, inheriting them rekindled feelings of respect, dependence, and love. Tearing garments or hiding in them could be profoundly symbolic actions, at the same time as they aroused and expressed various, sometimes conflicting, emotions.

According to Peter Corrigan (2008: 5), "none of the senses . . . provide as many possibilities for fine distinctions and meaning-making as the sense of sight, which is primary to an understanding of clothing." This is true to a great extent; social distinctions are often based on visual interpretations of dress in rather intricate ways. However, the totality of the working of the senses should not be underestimated in the experience of clothes. Clothes are also felt, heard, and smelled.

The smell of clothes played a special role. Monastics and ascetics imagined paradise and salvation as sweet-smelling, and saintly ascetics were sometimes said to give off a sweet smell. Pambo "smelled the sweet fragrance" (*stinoufe*) of Pamoun a mile away from his home in the desert (Budge 1914: 130). This is not necessarily an exact description of the situation. The frequency of washing clothes differed between communities, and abstaining from bathing was characteristic of a successful ascetic; therefore, it is reasonable to assume that garments unmistakably smelled of their wearers, and also that "some hagiographical episodes seem to beg for olfactory consideration" (Harvey 2006: 205). A woman's garment had to be cleansed before Pachomius could touch it to heal her, indicating either dirtiness or stench or both. Generally speaking, clothes transmit the scent of their wearers, which implies that they embody them and make others recall them to mind. Although sounds that clothes made when monastics were moving are not mentioned, they might be imagined as rustling, while the sounds of destruction were heard when Shenoute tore his own garments or broke the belt of a lapsed monastic.

The feel of clothes and their intimate contact with the skin affect the wearer. Different materials, textures, and shapes feel differently. Touch is conspicuously present in the sources. A soft sheepskin was more comfortable than a goatskin and was hence forbidden (P 81; see also P 98). In the continuum of tactile influences of textiles on ascetic bodies, the polar opposite to the soft sheepskin was the itchy hair shirt. Merely touching a garment was sometimes thought to have a powerful effect, as when people touching the garment of a saintly monastic were healed. Healing by means of a garment is also a strong indication of how closely clothes were associated and integrated with their wearer.

The social dimension

The sensual and emotional dimension is closely connected to the material and social dimensions.[4] Accordingly, "the way we feel about and in our clothes is a relevant phenomenon with a definite impact on our social behaviour and ultimately on our social life" (Ruggerone 2017: 574). Clothes participated in cultural and social interactions between the monastics and their surroundings and were constantly present. Even when they were absent, nakedness was understood as a lack of clothing. Ideally, all habits were identical, although there were variations in real life. Both the monastics and their clothes were governed by norms, which means that clothes participated in the social control of the monastics.

Clothes create and reflect meanings and values, and interpreting dress is part of the social game. Dress reveals gender, class, ethnicity, and age. In ancient ascetics and monastics, it revealed the degree of intensity of their ascetic life, institutional belonging, and place in the monastic hierarchy. Because clothes are so closely connected to their wearers and their social groups, they are also apt tools in literary descriptions of how people appear and act.

The social world of ancient ascetics and monastics was intertwined with a mythological and ritual world of superhuman beings and actions, and clothes mediated between this world and the world of divine beings, demons, and biblical heroes; for instance, in the epilogue of the *Lausiac History*, bread from the world above is received in a sheepskin, and Elisha's cloak is supernaturally transferred to Shenoute according to Besa's *Life of Shenoute*.

The cognitive dimension

The phenomenological tradition emphasizes the significance of bodily existence and stresses that cognition is grounded in bodily experience. Merleau-Ponty's idea (1945) that perception is built on the body's experience of being in the world implies that because the body in the world is a dressed body, clothes influence perception and the production of meaning. Clothes are part of human-embodied identity and its embeddedness in the world and a source of cognition and conceptualization. While cognition can be seen as embodied, embedded, enactive, and possibly extended because it arises from an interplay between the brain, the body, and the world and through a dynamic interaction between humans and their environment[5]—it is frequently also enclothed (Adam and Galinsky 2012, 2019).

Clothes function as cognitive extensions because they carry information outside of the brain. The invention of a special monastic dress suggests that ascetic life took a material shape and became visible and palpable and that the ideology of this life was formed and developed through the habit. According to Steven Mithen (1998: 103), "religious ideas that are represented in material form gain survival value for the process of cultural transmission: they become easier to communicate and comprehend as their material form provides a second anchor in the human mind." Ascetic and monastic clothes became that sort of second anchor for cultural transmission. The habit was integrated with the body and its movements and intentions while storing and transmitting information as part of the external symbolic storage. Some of the cultural meanings transmitted by the habit were explicit, inscribed, and explained, while others were implicit, incorporated, and in flux.[6] The habit was an externalized symbol of monastic life interacting with internalized ideas and experiences of this type of life. While the main function of the monastic habit was to stress the collective and remove individuality, actual use must also have given each habit individual meanings, associations, and references, which means that it became part of the self.

When humans have grown into their clothes, moving in the world dressed filters their experience of the world and offers tools to think with. Dressed embodiment and enclothed cognition are reflected in language and communicated in discourse, myths, symbols, metaphors, and memories. The sensory experience of wearing clothes becomes a source of vestimentary metaphors (Cerulo 2019: 88).[7] In Christianity, the conceptual metaphor of the body as a garment is activated, and clothing metaphors are used to describe salvation.[8]

Conclusion

This study of ascetic and monastic clothes has attempted to demonstrate that clothes are integrated with their wearers. Clothes enable and restrict us; we are dependent on them and get entangled in them; we use them metaphorically when we try to conceptualize our being in the world and the meaning of our existence, as Paul so eloquently did. Clothes are situated at the intersection between us and our surroundings; they act on us and are experienced by us while at the same time being physically in contact with the world around us and representing us to it. Taken together, the dimensions of clothes listed above reflect the multiplicity of meanings, functions, and experiences of being the dressed species and point to the integration of clothes in our material, social, emotional, and cognitive interactions with the world.

To return to the crocodile one last time: even when it mistook the habit for the monastic, it perceptively understood the close connection between the wearer's identity and his clothes. It seems that it was focusing on something important: the significance of clothes in human life. What more can we ask of a talking reptile?

Notes

1 According to Troels Engberg-Pedersen, Paul's clothing metaphors presuppose "the first set of clothes being the body of flesh and blood and the second set the new form *of* that body" (2010: 225). He notes that in resurrection, a physical body of flesh and blood is transformed into a pneumatic body (48–50, 68–69; see also Campbell 2014; Kim 2004; Tappenden 2016).

2 Tappenden (2016: 123–125) also notes that Paul applies the conceptual metaphor CLOTHING IS CONTAINER, which points to the functional aspects of ancient clothing and suggests that clothes were something one moved in and out of—in other words, it indicates how they were used.

3 According to Joel Krueger (2016: 245),

> there does appear to be a tight link between the way we use material culture to organize and manipulate different spaces (home, work, and so on), and the sort of moods and emotions we routinely feel when we inhabit and negotiate these spaces.

The space of clothes can easily be added.

4 Elizabeth Wilson noted that "part of this strangeness of dress is that it links the biological body to the social being, and public to private." Dress in general seems "to fulfil a number of social, aesthetic and psychological functions; indeed it knots them together, and can express all simultaneously" (Wilson 1985: 2–3; see also Entwistle 2000; Hesselbein 2019).

5 Andy Clark points out that the extended mind "emerges at the productive interface of brain, body and social and material world" (2011: 218–219; see also Geertz 2010: 304). In their seminal article, Andy Clark and David Chalmers focused on things that contribute to human cognitive processes and self-stimulating activity, such as notebooks, cell phones, and pens: "The human organism is linked with an external entity in a two-way interaction, creating a *coupled system* that can be seen as a cognitive system in its own right" (1998: 8).

6 According to Merlin Donald (1998: 185),

> above all, the symbolic value of any artefact is not always evident in its appearance. The same object may have several functions, and several layers of symbolism in different times, places, and social classes, in the same society. It is only a node in a dynamic social-cognitive system. The system itself defines the role of such objects. It creates, changes, and enforces their precise functions. True, the objects themselves serve a storage function. But to know what symbols and artefacts store, and what kinds of specific cognition they might support, we must know a lot about the culture, and the mind, that uses them.

7 Douglas Cairns puts it aptly when he writes about garment metaphors in ancient Greece and describes the interaction between wearers, clothes, and language and expressions:

> Dress, even in its concrete, literal form, is laden with symbolism. In particular, dress extends, prosthetically, the body's capacity to express thought and emotion. These physical expressions are then available as symbols for the emotional concepts that they express. All the emotions for which garment metaphors exist can also be expressed or referred to metonymously by means of dress.
>
> (2016: 29)

8 Writing about ancient Syrian Christianity, Sebastian Brock argued that "the entire span of salvation history can be expressed in terms of clothing imagery" (Brock 1982: 11; see also Kim 2004; Daniel-Hughes 2011; Hunt 2012).

Bibliography

The abbreviations of the Shenoutean sources refer to *Shenoute's Literary Corpus* by Stephen Emmel (2004).

Abbreviations

A: *Apophthegmata Patrum* Alphabetical Collection
ACW: Ancient Christian Writers
ANF: Ante-Nicene Fathers
AP: *Apophthegmata Patrum*
BG: Berlin Papyrus Codex 8502, 2 (*Berlinus Gnosticus*)
CH: *Corpus Hermeticum*
G^1: *Life of Pachomius* (first Greek life)
HL: *Historia Lausiaca*
HM: *Historia Monachorum in Aegypto*
LCL: Loeb Classical Library
N: *Apophthegmata Patrum* Anonymous Collection
NHC: Nag Hammadi codex
NPNF1: Nicene and Post-Nicene Fathers, first series
NPNF2: Nicene and Post-Nicene Fathers, second series
P: *Praecepta*
S: *Apophthegmata Patrum* Systematic Collection
SBo: *Life of Pachomius* (Bohairic Life where lacunae have been filled in from Sahidic texts)

Primary Sources

Acts of Thomas. *The Introduction, Text, and Commentary*. Translated by A. F. J Klijn. 2nd ed. Leiden and Boston: Brill, 2003.

Ambrose of Milan. *On Repentance in Ambrose: Select Works and Letters*. Translated by H. de Romestin. NPNF2. Vol. 10. Edinburgh: T&T Clark, 1989.

Ambrose of Milan. "Concerning Virgins." In *Ambrose: Select Works and Letters*, translated by H. de Romestin. NPNF2. Vol. 10. Edinburgh: T&T Clark, 1989.

The Apocryphon of John. *Die Gnostischen Schriften des koptischen Papyrus Berolinensis 8502*. Edited by Walter C. Till and Hans-Martin Schenke. Berlin: Akademie Verlag, 1972.

The Apocryphon of John. *Synopsis of Nag Hammadi Codices II,1; III,1; and IV,1 with BG 8502,2.* Edited by Michael Waldstein and Frederik Wisse. Nag Hammadi and Manichaean Studies 33. 11–177. Leiden: Brill, 1995.

Apophthegmata Patrum. A: *The Alphabetic Collection.* Edited by J. P. Migne. Patrologia Cursus Completus, Series Graeca. Vol. 65, cols. 71–440. Paris: Migne, 1868.

Apophthegmata Patrum. S: *Les Apophthegmes des Pères: Collection Systématique. Inroduction, texte critique, traduction, et notes.* Translated into French by Jean-Claude Guy. Vol. 3. Paris: Éditions du Cerf, 1993, 2003, 2005.

Apophthegmata Patrum. A: *The Sayings of the Desert Fathers: The Alphabetical Collection.* Translated by Benedicta Ward. Kalamazoo, MI: Cistercian Publications, 1984 [1975].

Apophthegmata Patrum. S: *The Book of the Elders: Sayings of the Desert Fathers: The Systematic Collection.* Translated by John Wortley. Collegeville, MN: Liturgical Press, 2012.

Apophthegmata Patrum. N: *The Anonymous Sayings of the Desert Fathers: A Select Edition and Complete English Translation.* Translated by John Wortley. Cambridge: Cambridge University Press, 2013.

Apuleius. *Metamorphoses.* Edited and translated by J. Arthur Hanson. LCL. Cambridge, MA: Harvard University Press, 1989.

Athanasius. *Circular to Bishops of Egypt and Libya (Ad Episcopos Ægypti).* Translated by Miles Atkinson. NPNF 2. Vol. 4. Edinburgh: T&T Clark, 1991.

Athanasius. *Vie d'Antoine.* Translated into French by G. J. M. Bartelink. Sources Chrétiennes. Vol. 400. Paris: Éditions du Cerf, 1994.

Augustine. *On the Care to Be Had for the Dead.* Translated by H. Browne. NPNF1. Vol. 3. Edinburgh: T&T Clark, 1993a.

Augustine. *The Trinity.* Translated by Arthur West Haddam. NPNF1. Vol. 3. Edinburgh: T&T Clark, 1993b.

Augustine. *Exposition of the Psalms.* Translation and notes by Maria Boulding. The Works of Saint Augustine: A Translation for the 21st Century. Vol. III/15–20. New York, NY: New City Press, 2000–2004.

Augustine. "Praeceptum." In *Augustine of Hippo and His Monastic Rule,* edited and translated by George Lawless. 80–103. Oxford: Clarendon Press, 2010.

Augustine. *The City of God.* Translated by William Babcock. The Works of Saint Augustine: A Translation for the 21st Century. Vols. I/6–7. New York, NY: New City Press, 2012–2013.

Augustine. *On Genesis.* Translated by Edmund Hill. The Works of Saint Augustine: A Translation for the 21st Century. Vol. I/13. New York, NY: New City Press, 2013 (Includes *On Genesis: A Refutation of the Manichees; The Literal Meaning of Genesis*).

Aulus Gellius. *Noctes Atticae.* Translated by J. C. Rolfe. LCL. Vol. 3. London: Heinemann, 1961.

Basil of Caesarea. "The Long Rules." In *Ascetical Works,* translated by M. Monica Wagner. The Fathers of the Church. Vol. 9. Washington, DC: The Catholic University of America, 1962a.

Basil of Caesarea. *The Letters.* Translated by Roy J. Deferrari. LCL. London: Heinemann, 1962b.

Besa. *The Life of Shenoute.* Translated by David N. Bell. Kalamazoo, MI: Cistercian Publications, 1983.

Caesarius of Arles. *Regula ad virgines in Oevres monastiques.* Introduction, texte critique, traduction et notes par Adalbert de Vogüé and Joël Curreau. Sources Chrétiennes. Vol. 345. 170–272. Paris: Éditions du Cerf, 1988.

Charles, R. H., trans. *The Book of Jubilees*. London: Forgotten Books, 2007 [1917].

Chrysostom, John. *Homilies*. NPNF1. Vol. 10–14. Edinburgh: T&T Clark, 1989–1991.

Clement of Alexandria. *The Stromata, or Miscellanies*. Translated by Alexander Roberts and James Donaldson. ANF. Vol. 2. Edinburgh: T&T Clark, 1994.

Coptic Documentary Texts from Kellis. Vol. 1. Edited by Ian Gardner, Anthony Alcock, and Wolf-Peter Funk. Dakhleh Oasis Project: Monograph 9. Oxford and Philadelphia: Oxbow Books, 1999.

Coptic Documentary Texts from Kellis. Vol. 2. Edited by Ian Gardner, Anthony Alcock, and Wolf-Peter Funk. Dakhleh Oasis Project: Monograph 16. Oxford and Philadelphia: Oxbow Books, 2014.

Corpus Hermeticum in Hermetica. *The Greek Corpus Hermeticum and the Latin Asclepius in a New English Translation With Notes and Introduction*. Translated by Brian P. Copenhaver. Cambridge: Cambridge University Press, 1992.

Epic of Gilgamesh. *The Babylonian Gilgamesh Epic: Introduction, Critical Edition and Cuneiform Texts*. Edited and translated by A. R. George. Vol. 2. Oxford: Oxford University Press, 2003.

Epiphanius. *The Panarion of Epiphanius of Salamis*. Book I (Sects 1–46). Translated by Frank Williams. Nag Hammadi and Manichaean Studies. 2nd ed. Vol. 63. Leiden: Brill, 2009.

Epiphanius. *The Panarion of Epiphanius of Salamis*. Books II and III. De Fide. Translated by Frank Williams. Nag Hammadi and Manichaean Studies. 2nd ed. Vol. 79. Leiden: Brill, 2012.

Epiphanius. *Ancoratus* und *Panarion Haer*. 1–33. First edition by Karl Holl. Leipzig, 1915. Second edition by Marc Bergemann and Christian-Friedrich Collatz. Die Griechischen Christlichen Schriftsteller der Ersten Jahrhunderte. Berlin: De Gruyter, 2014.

Eusebius. *Ecclesiastical History*. Edited and translated by Kirsopp Lake (Vol. 1) and J. E. L. Oulton and H. J. Lawlor (Vol. 2). LCL. Vol. 2. Cambridge, MA: Harvard University Press, 1926–1932.

Evagrius of Pontus. *The Greek Ascetic Corpus*. Translated by Robert E. Sinkewicz. Oxford: Oxford University Press, 2003.

Festugière, A. J., ed. *Historia Monachorum in Aegypto*. Édition critique du texte grec. Subsidia Hagiographica. Vol. 53. Bruxelles: Societé des Bollandistes, 1961.

Genesis Rabbah. *Genesis in Two Volumes*. Translated by H. Freedman and M. Simon. London: Soncino, 1961.

Gerontius. *The Life of Melania the Younger*. Translated by Elizabeth A. Clark. Studies in Women and Religion. Vol. 14. New York, NY: The Edwin Mellen Press, 1984.

The Gospel of Philip. *Nag Hammadi Codex II, 2–7*. Edited by Bentley Layton. Translated by Wesley W. Isenberg. Nag Hammadi Studies 20. 142–215. Leiden: Brill, 1989.

The Gospel of Thomas. *Nag Hammadi Codex II, 2–7*. Edited by Bentley Layton. Translated by Thomas O. Lambdin. Nag Hammadi Studies 20. 52–93. Leiden: Brill, 1989.

The Interpretation of Knowledge (NHC XI, 1). *The Coptic Gnostic Library: A Complete Edition of the Nag Hammadi Codices*. Translated by John D. Turner. Vol. 5. Leiden: Brill, 2000.

The Investiture of the Archangel Michael. *Die Bücher der Einsetzung der Erzengel Michael und Gabriel.* Edited by C. Detlef G. Müller. Corpus Scriptorum Christianorum Orientalum. Vol. 225. Louvain: Secrétariat du Corpus SCO, 1962.

The Investiture of the Archangel Michael. "An Introduction and Translation by Hugo Lundhaug." In *New Testament Apocrypha; More Noncanonical Scriptures,* edited by Tony Burke. Vol. 2. 499–550. Grand Rapids, MI: Eerdmans Publishing, 2020.

Irenaeus. *Against the Heresies.* Translated by Dominic J. Unger and Matthew C. Steenberg. Ancient Christian Writers. Vols. 55, 64–65. London: Paulist Press, 1991, 2012.

Jerome. *Vita Sancti Pauli primae eremitae.* Edited by J. P. Migne. *Patrologia Latina.* Vol. 23. 17–60. Paris: Migne, 1850.

Jerome. "La Règle de S. Pachome, par L. Th. Lefort." In *Pachomiana Latina* par *Dom Amand Boon.* 13–52. Bruxelles: Éditions Nauwelaerts, 1932.

Jerome. *Letters and Select Works.* Translated by W. H. Freemantle. NPNF 2. Vol. 6. Edinburgh: T&T Clark, 1989a.

Jerome. *Life of Paul the First Hermit.* Translated by W. H. Freemantle. NPNF 2. Vol. 6. Edinburgh: T&T Clark, 1989b.

John Cassian. *Institutions cénobitiques/Jean Cassien.* Translated into French by Jean-Claude Guy. Sources Chrétiennes. Vol. 109. Paris: Éditions du Cerf, 1965.

John Cassian. *The Conferences.* Translated by Boniface Ramsey. ACW. Vol. 57. New York, NY: Paulist Press, 1997.

John Cassian. *The Institutes.* Translated by Boniface Ramsey. ACW 58. New York, NY: Paulist Press, 2000.

Kephalaia. *The Kephalaia of the Teacher: The Edited Coptic Manichaean Texts in Translation with Commentary.* Translated by Iain Gardner. Leiden: Brill, 1995.

Methodius. *Discourse on the Resurrection.* Translated by William R. Clark. ANF. Vol. 6. Edinburgh: T&T Clark, 1993.

Origen. *De Principiis.* Translated by Frederick Crombie. ANF. Vol. 4. Edinburgh: T&T Clark, 1994.

Origen. *Contra Celsum.* Translated by Henrich Chadwick. Cambridge: Cambridge University Press, 1953.

Origen. *Homilies on Leviticus.* Translated by Gary Wayne Barkley. The Fathers of the Church. Vol. 71. Washington: Catholic University of America Press, 1990.

Pachomian Koinonia. Vol. 1: *The Life of Saint Pachomius and His Disciples.* Vol. 2: *Pachomian Chronicles and Rules.* Vol. 3: *Instructions, Letters, and Other Writings of Saint Pachomius and His Disciples.* Translated by Armand Veilleux. Kalamazoo, MI: Cistercian Publications, 1980–1982.

Pachomius. *S. Pachomii vitae sahidice scriptae.* Edited by Louis Théophile Lefort. Corpus Scriptorum Orientalium. Vol. 99–100. Scriptores Coptici, ser. 3, t. 8. Paris: Typographeo Reipublicae (1933) 1965.

Pachomius. *S. Pachomii vita Bohairice scripta.* Edited by Louis Théophile Lefort. Vol. 2. Louvain: Officina Orientali et Scientifica, 1964, 1965 [1925/1936].

Pachomius. *The Life of Pachomius: Vita Prima Graeca.* Translated by Apostolos N. Athanassakis. Texts and Translations, no. 7: Early Christian Literature Series 2. Missoula, MT: Scholars Press, 1975.

Palladius of Apuna. *The Lausiac History of Palladius.* Edited by Dom Cuthbert Butler. Cambridge Library Collection. Vol. 2. Cambridge: Cambridge University Press, 1898–1904.

Palladius of Apuna. *The Lausiac History*. Edited and translated by John Wortley. Collegeville, MN: Liturgical Press, 2015.

Paphnutius. *Histories of the Monks of Upper Egypt and the Life of Onnophrius*. Edited and translated by Tom Vivian. Cistercian Studies. Vol. 140. Kalamazoo, MI: Cistercian Publications, 2000.

The Paraphrase of Shem. *Nag Hammadi Codex VII*. Edited by Birger A. Pearson. Translated by Frederik Wisse. Nag Hammadi and Manichaean Studies 30. 24–127. Leiden: Brill, 1996.

Philo. "Allegorical Interpretation." In *The Works of Philo: Complete and Unabridged; New Updated Version*, translated by C. D. Yonge. 25–79. Peabody, MA: Hendrickson Publishers, 2002a.

Philo. "On the Posteriority of Cain and His Exile." In *The Works of Philo: Complete and Unabridged; New Updated Version*, translated by C. D. Yonge. 132–151. Peabody, MA: Hendrickson Publishers, 2002b.

Philo. "Questions and Answers on Genesis." In *The Works of Philo: Complete and Unabridged; New Updated Version*, translated by C. D. Yonge, 791–863. Peabody, MA: Hendrickson Publishers, 2002c.

Plato. "Phaedrus." In *Plato: Euthyphro, Apology, Crito, Phaedo, Phaedrus*, translated by Harold North Fowler. LCL. Cambridge, MA: Harvard University Press, 1999.

Porphyry. *On Abstinence from Killing Animals*. Translated by Gillian Clark. London: Duckworth, 2000.

Pseudo-Athanasius. *The Canons of Athanasius of Alexandria*. Edited by Wilhelm Riedel and Walter Ewing Crum. London and Oxford: Williams and Norgate for the Text and Translation Society, 1904; reprinted in Amsterdam, 1973.

Quintilian. *The Orator's Education*. Translated by Donald A. Russell. LCL 124–127, 492. Vol. 5. Cambridge, MA: Harvard University Press, 2001.

Russel, Norman, trans. *The Lives of the Desert Fathers*. Kalamazoo, MI: Cistercian Publications, 1981.

Seneca, L. Annaeus. *Natural Questions*. Translated by Thomas H. Corcoran. LCL 450, 457. Cambridge, MA: Harvard University Press, 1971–1972.

Shenoute. *Shenoute's Literary Corpus*. Edited by Stephen Emmel. Corpus Scriptorum Christianorum Orientalium. Vol. 599–600. Louvain: Peeters, 2004.

Socrates. *Church History*. Translated by A. C. Zenos. NPNF2. Vol. 2. Edinburgh: T&T Clark, 1989.

Sozomen. *Church History*. Translated by Chester D. Hartranft, NPNF2. Vol. 2. Edinburgh: T&T Clark, 1989.

Sulpitius Severus. *The Works of Sulpitius Severus*. Translated by Alexander Roberts. NPNF2. Vol. 11. Edinburgh: T&T Clark, 1991.

The Teachings of Silvanus. *Nag Hammadi Codex VII*. Edited by Birger A. Pearson. Translated by Malcolm Peel and Jan Zandee. Nag Hammadi and Manichaean Studies 30. 24–127. Leiden: Brill, 1996.

Tertullian. *The Writings of Tertullian*. Edited by A. Cleveland Coxe. ANF. Vol. 3 (Includes *On Idolatry*; *On the Resurrection of the Flesh*; *The Shows, or De Spectaculis*). Edinburgh: T&T Clark, 1993.

Tertullian. *Tertullian, Minucius Felix, Commmodianus, Origen*. Edited by A. Cleveland Coxe. ANF. Vol. 4 (Includes *On the Apparel of Women*; *On Modesty*; *On the Pallium*; *On the Veiling of Virgins*). Edinburgh: T&T Clark, 1994.

Theodoret of Cyrrhus. "Historia Religiosa (Greek text)." In *Das Leben des heiligen Symeon Stylites*, edited by Hans Lietzmann. Texte und Untersuchungen zur Geschichte der altchristlichen Literatur. Vol. 32. 1–18. Leipzig: J.C. Hinrichs, 1908.

The Theodosian Code. *The Theodosian Code and Novels, and the Sirmondian Constitutions.* Translated by Clyde Pharr in collaboration with Theresa Sherrer Davidson and Mary Brown Pharr. New York, NY: Greenwood Press, 1969.

Trimorphic Protennoia. *Nag Hammadi Codices XI, XII, XIII.* Edited by Charles W. Hedrick. Translated by John D. Turner. Nag Hammadi Studies 28. 402–433. Leiden: Brill, 1990.

Virgil. *Aeneid.* Translated by H. Rushton Fairclough. LCL 63, 65. Cambridge, MA and London: Harvard University Press, 1999–2000.

Secondary Sources

Adam, Hajo, and Adam D. Galinsky. 2012. "Enclothed Cognition." *Journal of Experimental Social Psychology* 48: 918–925.

Adam, Hajo, and Adam D. Galinsky. 2019. "Reflection on Enclothed Cognition: Commentary on Burns et al." *Journal of Experimental Social Psychology* 83: 157–159.

Adamson, P. B. 1985. "Some Rituals Associated with Parturition in Antiquity." *Folklore* 96 (2): 176–183.

Amélineau, Émile. 1907–1914. *Oeuvres de Schenoudi: Texte copte et traduction française.* Vol. 2. Paris: Ernest Leroux.

Andrew, Thomas. 2009. "The Holy Fools: A Theological Enquiry." PhD diss., University of Nottingham.

Andrewes, Janet. 2004. *Bodywork: Dress as Cultural Tool; Dress and Demeanour in the South of Senegal.* Leiden: Brill.

Appadurai, Arjun, ed. 1986. *The Social Life of Things: Commodities in Cultural Perspective.* Cambridge: Cambridge University Press.

Assmann, Jan. 2006. *Religion and Cultural Memory.* Stanford: Stanford University Press.

Bagnall, Roger S. 1993. *Egypt in Late Antiquity.* Princeton, NJ: Princeton University Press.

Ball, Jennifer. 2009–2010. "Decoding the Habit of the Byzantine Nun." *Journal of Modern Hellenism* 27–28: 25–52.

Balter, Michael. 2009. "Clothes Make the (Hu) Man." *Science* 325: 1329.

Barber, Elizabeth Wayland. 1991. *Prehistoric Textiles: The Development of Cloth in the Neolithic and Bronze Ages with Special References to the Aegean.* Princeton, NJ: Princeton University Press.

Barber, Elizabeth Wayland. 1994. *Women's Work: The First 20,000 Years; Women, Cloth, and Society in Early Times.* New York, NY and London: Norton.

Bartelink, G. J. M. 1994. *Athanase d'Alexandre, Vie d'Antoine, Introduction, Critical Text, Translation, Notes et Index.* Sources Chrétiennes 400. Paris: Éditions du Cerf.

Barthel, Christian. 2019. "The Conversion of Pachomius Revisited." *Scrinium* 15 (1): 30–43.

Barthes, Roland. (1967) 2010. *The Fashion System.* London: Vintage Books.

Barthes, Roland. (1993–1995) 2013. *The Language of Fashion.* London: Bloomsbury.

Batten, Alicia J., Carly Daniel-Hughes, and Kristi Upson-Saia. 2014. "Introduction: What Shall We Wear?" In *Dressing Judeans and Christians in Antiquity*, edited by Kristi Uspon-Saia, Carly Daniel-Hughes, and Alicia J. Batten. 1–18. London: Routledge.

Belknap, Robert E. 2004. *The List: The Uses and Pleasures of Cataloguing*. New Haven, CT: Yale University Press.

Bell, Catrherine. 1992. *Ritual Theory, Ritual Practice*. Oxford: Oxford University Press.

Bianchi, Ugo, ed. 1985. *La tradizione dell'enkrateia: Motivazioni ontologiche e protologiche*. Rome: Edizioni dell'Ateneo.

Black, Prudence. 2009. "The Detail: Setting the Fashion System in Motion." *Fashion Theory* 13 (4): 499–510.

Blanchard, Monica J. 2007. "Sarabaitae and Remnouth: Coptic Considerations." In *The World of Early Egyptian Christianity; Language, Literature, and Social Context*, edited by James E. Goehring and Janet A. Timbie. 49–60. Washington, DC: The Catholic University of America Press.

Blanke, Louise. 2019. *An Archaeology of Egyptian Monasticism: Settlement, Economy and Daily Life at the White Monastery Federation*. Yale Egyptological Publications 2. New Haven, CT: Yale University Press.

Bodner, Keith. 2013. *Elisha's Profile in the Book of Kings: The Double Agent*. Oxford: Oxford University Press.

Bolman, Elizabeth S., Stephen J. Davis, and Gillian Pyke. 2010. "Shenoute and a Recently Discovered Tomb Chapel at the White Monastery." *Journal of Early Christian Studies* 18 (3): 453–462.

Boud'hors, Anne. 2009. "Le 'scapulaire' et la mélote: nouvelles attestations dans les textes coptes?" In *Études coptes XI; Treizième journée d'études* (Marseille, 7–9 juin 2007), edited by Anne Boud'hors and Catherine Louis. Cahiers de la Bibliothèque copte 17. 1–15. Paris: De Boccard.

Boulluec, Alain le. 1985. *La notion d'hérésie dans la littérature grecque*. Paris: Études Augustiniennes.

Bourdieu, Pierre. 1985. "The Market of Symbolic Goods." *Poetics* 14 (1–2): 13–44.

Bourdieu, Pierre. 1986. "The Forms of Capital." In *Handbook of Theory and Research for the Sociology of Education*, edited by J. Richardson. 241–258. New York, NY: Greenwood.

Bourdieu, Pierre. (1997) 2000. *Pascalian Meditations*. Oxford: Polity Press.

Brakke, David. 1998. *Athanasius and Asceticism*. New York, NY: Oxford University Press.

Brakke, David, and Andrew Crislip. 2018. *Selected Discourses of Shenoute the Great: Community, Theology, and Social Conflict in Late Antique Egypt*. Cambridge: Cambridge University Press.

Bremmer, Jan N. 1983. *The Early Greek Concept of the Soul*. Princeton, NJ: Princeton University Press.

Bremmer, Jan N. 1992. "Symbols of Marginality from Early Pythagoreans to Late Antique Monks." *Greece & Rome* (Second series) 39 (2): 205–214.

Bremmer, Jan N. 2002. *The Rise and Fall of the Afterlife*. London and New York, NY: Routledge.

Bremmer, Jan N. 2019. "Athanasius' *Life of Antony*: Marginality, Spatiality and Mediality." In *Marginality, Media and Mutations of Religious Authority in*

History of Christianity, edited by Laura Feldt and Jan N. Bremmer. Studies in the History and Anthropology of Religion 6. 23–45. Louvain: Peeters.

Bremmer, Jan N. 2020. "The City a Desert: The Case of Jerome's Paul the First Hermit." *Ephemerides Theologicae Lovanienses* 84.

Brennan, Brian. 1985. "Athanasius' 'Vita Antonii': A Sociological Interpretation." *Vigiliae Christianae* 39: 209–227.

Britt, Brian. 2002. "Prophetic Concealment in a Biblical Type Scene." *The Catholic Biblical Quarterly* 64 (1): 37–58.

Brock, Sebastian. 1982. "Clothing Metaphors as Means of Theological Expression in Syriac Tradition." In *Typus, Symbol, Allegorie bei den östlichen Vätern und ihren Parallelen im Mittelalter*, edited by Margot Schmidt. 11–38. Regensburg: Verlag Friedrich Pustet.

Brown, Peter. 1971. "The Rise and Function of the Holy Man in Late Antiquity." *The Journal of Roman Studies* 61: 80–101.

Brown, Peter. 1988. *The Body and Society: Men, Women, and Sexual Renunciation in Early Christianity*. New York, NY: Columbia University Press.

Brown, Peter. 2012. *The Rise of Western Christendom: Triumph and Diversity, A. D. 200–1000*. London: John Willey & Sons.

Brown, Peter. 2016. "Wealth, Work and the Holy Poor: Early Christian Monasticism Between Syria and Egypt." *Irish Theological Quarterly* 81 (3): 233–245.

Budge, E. A. Wallis. 1914. *Coptic Martyrdoms etc. in the Dialect of Upper Egypt*. London and New York, NY: AMS Press.

Bull, Christian. 2018. *The Tradition of Hermes Trismegistus: The Egyptian Priestly Figure as a Teacher of Hellenized Wisdom*. Leiden: Brill.

Burns, Dylan M. 2014. *Apocalypse of the Alien God: Platonism and the Exile of Sethian Gnosticism. Divinations: Rereading Ancient Religions*. Philadelphia, PA: University of Pennsylvania Press.

Burns, Dylan M. 2015. "μίξεώς τινι τέχνῃ κρείττονι: Alchemical Metaphor in the *Paraphrase of Shem* (NHC VII,1)." *Aries* 15: 81–108.

Burns, Devin M., Elizabeth L. Fox, Michael Greenstein, Gayla Olbright, and DeMaris Montgomery. 2019. "An Old Task in New Clothes: A Preregistered Direct Replication Attempt of Enclothed Cognition Effects on Stroop Performance." *Journal of Experimental Social Psychology* 83: 150–156.

Burrus, Virginia. 2000. *"Begotten, Not Made": Conceiving Manhood in Late Antiquity*. Stanford, CA: Stanford University Press.

Bynum, Caroline Walker. 1995. *The Resurrection of the Body in Western Christianity, 200–1336*. New York, NY: Columbia University Press.

Cain, Andrew. 2016. *The Greek Historia Monachorum in Aegypto: Monastic Hagiography in the Late Fourth Century*. Oxford: Oxford University Press.

Cairns, Douglas. 2016. "Mind, Body, and Metaphor in Ancient Greek Concepts of Emotion." *L'Atelier du Centre de recherches historiques* 16. https://doi.org/10.4000/acrh.7416.

Cameron, Averil. 1999. "On Defining the Holy Man." In *The Cult of Saints in Late Antiquity and the Middle Ages: Essays on the Contributions of Peter Brown*, edited by James Howard-Johnston and Paul Antony Hayward. 27–43. Oxford: Oxford University Press.

Campbell, Constantine R. 2014. "Metaphor, Reality, and Union with Christ." In *'In Christ' in Paul*, edited by Michael J. Thate, Kevin J. Vanhoozer, and Constantine

R. Campbell. Wissenscaftliche Untersuchungen zum Neuen Testament 2. Vol. 384. 72–86. Tübingen: Mohr Siebeck.

Caner, Daniel 2002. *Wandering, Begging Monks: Spiritual Authority and the Promotion of Monasticism in Late Antiquity*. Berkeley and Los Angeles: University of California Press.

Carroll, R. P. 1969. "The Elijah-Elisha Sagas: Some Remarks on Prophetic Succession in Ancient Israel." *Vetus Testamentum* 19 (4): 400–415.

Carter, Michael. 2012. "Stuff and Nonsense: The Limits of the Linguistic Model of Clothing." *Fashion Theory: The Journal of Dress, Body & Culture* 16 (3): 343–353.

Carter, Michael. 2017. *Being Prepared: Aspects of Dress and Dressing*. Sydney: Puncher and Wattman.

Castel, Georges. 1979. "Étude d'une momie copte." In *Hommages à Serge Sauneron, II: Égypte post-pharaonique*, edited by J. Vercoutter. 121–143. Cairo: Institut Français d'archéologie orientale du Caire.

Cerulo, Karen A. 2019. "Embodied Cognition: Sociology's Role in Bridging Mind, Brain and Body." In *The Oxford Handbook of Cognitive Sociology*, edited by Wayne H. Brekhus and Gabe Ignatow. 81–100. Oxford: Oxford University Press.

Choat, Malcolm. 2013. "The Life of Antony in Egypt." In *Ascetic Culture: Essays in Honor of Philip Rousseau*, edited by Blake Leyerle and Robin Darling Young. 50–74. Notre Dame, IN: University of Notre Dame Press.

Choat, Malcolm. 2015. "From Letters to Letter-Collections: Monastic Epistolography in Late-Antique Egypt." In *Collecting Early Christian Letters: From the Apostle Paul to Late Antiquity*, edited by Bronwen Neil and Pauline Allen. 82–93. Cambridge: Cambridge University Press.

Choat, Malcolm. 2017. "Monastic Letters on Papyrus from Late Antique Egypt." In *Writing and Communication in Early Egyptian Monasticism*, edited by Malcolm Choat and Maria Chiara Giordia. 17–72. Leiden: Brill.

Clark, Elizabeth A. 1992. *The Origenist Controversy: The Cultural Construction of an Early Christian Debate*. Princeton, NJ: Princeton University Press.

Clark, Elizabeth A. 1999. *Reading Renunciation: Asceticism and Scripture in Early Christianity*. Princeton, NJ: Princeton University Press.

Clark, Andy. 2011. *Supersizing the Mind: Embodiment, Action, and Cognitive Extension*. Oxford: Oxford University Press.

Clark, Andy, and David Chalmers. 1998. "The Extended Mind." *Analysis* 58 (1): 7–19.

Clarysse, Willy, and Dorothy J. Thompson. 2006. *Counting the People in Hellenistic Egypt*. Cambridge: Cambridge University Press.

Colombetti, Giovanna, and Joel Krueger 2015. "Scaffoldings of the Affective Mind." *Philosophical Psychology* 28 (8): 1157–1176.

Colombetti, Giovanna, and Tom Roberts. 2015. "Extending the Extended Mind: The Case for Extended Affectivity." *Philosophical Studies* 172: 1243–1263.

Connerton, Paul. 1989. *How Societies Remember*. Cambridge: Cambridge University Press.

Coon, Lynda L. 1997 *Sacred Fictions: Holy Women and Hagiography in Late Antiquity*. Philadelphia, PA: University of Pennsylvania Press.

Copenhaver, Brian P. 1992. *The Greek Corpus Hermeticum and the Latin Asclepius in a New English Translation with Notes and Introduction*. Cambridge: Cambridge University Press.

Corrigan, Peter. 2008. *The Dressed Society: Clothing, the Body and Some Meaning of the World*. London: Sage Publications.

Crum, Walter E. 1962. *Coptic Dictionary*. Oxford: Oxford University Press.

Daniel-Hughes, Carly. 2011. *The Salvation of The Flesh in Tertullian of Carthage: Dressing for Resurrection*. New York, NY: Palgrave Macmillan.

Daniel-Hughes, Carly. 2017. "Belief." In *A Cultural History of Dress and Fashion in Antiquity*, edited by M. Harlow. 71–85. New York, NY: Bloomsbury.

Davies, Glenys, and Lloyd Llewellyn-Jones. 2017. "The Body." In *A Cultural History of Dress and Fashion in Antiquity*, edited by M. Harlow. 49–69. New York, NY: Bloomsbury.

Davis, Stephen J. 2002. "Crossed Texts, Crossed Sex: Intertextuality and Gender in Early Christian Legends of Holy Women Disguised as Men." *Journal of Early Christian Studies* 10 (1): 1–36.

Demacopoulos, George E. 2007. *Five Models of Spiritual Direction in the Early Church*. Notre Dame, IN: University of Notre Dame Press.

Dietz, Maribel. 2005. *Wandering Monks, Virgins, and Pilgrims: Ascetic Travel in the Mediterranean World, A:D. 300–800*. University Park, PA: Pennsylvania State University.

Dihle, Albrecht. 1979. "Das Gewand des Einseidlers Antonius." *Jahrbuch für Antike und Christentum* 22: 22–29.

Donald, Merlin. 1991. *Origins of the Modern Mind: Three Stages in the Evolution of Culture and Cognition*. Cambridge, MA: Harvard University Press.

Donald, Merlin. 1998. "Material Culture and Cognition: Concluding Thoughts." In *Cognition and Material Culture: The Archaeology of Symbolic Storage*, edited by Colin Renfrew and Chris Scarre. McDonald Institute Monographs. 181–187. Cambridge: McDonald Institute for Archaeological Research.

Donald, Merlin. 2001. *A Mind so Rare: The Evolution of Human Consciousness*. New York, NY: W.W. Norton & Company.

Draguet, R. 1944. "Le chapitre de HL sur les Tabennésiotes dérive-t-il d'une source copte?" *Muséon* 57: 53–145.

Draguet, R. 1945. "Le chapitre de HL sur les Tabennésiotes dérive-t-il d'une source copte?" *Muséon* 58: 15–95.

Driver, Steven D. 2002. *John Cassian and the Reading of Egyptian Monastic Culture*. London: Routledge.

Dunand, Françoise. 2007. "Between Tradition and Innovation: Egyptian Funeral Practices in Late Antiquity." In *Egypt in the Byzantine World 300–700*, edited by Roger S. Bagnall. 163–184. Cambridge: Cambridge University Press.

Durkheim, Emile. 1915. *The Elementary Forms of the Religious Life*. Translated by Joseph Ward Swaine. London: George Allen & Unwin Ltd.

Elm, Susanna. 1994. *"Virgins of God": The Making of Asceticism in Late Antiquity*. Oxford: Oxford University Press.

Emmel, Stephen. 2004. *Shenoute's Literary Corpus*. Vol. 1 (Corpus Scriptorum Christianorum Orientalium 599). Louvain: Peeters.

Emmel, Stephen. 2016. "Editing Shenute, Old Problems, New Prospects: The Death of Shenoute's Death." In *Coptic Society, Literature and Religion from Late Antiquity to Modern Times: Proceedings of the Tenth International Congress of Coptic Studies, Rome, September 17th–22nd, 2012, and Plenary Reports of the Ninth International Congress of Coptic Studies, Cairo, September 15th–19th,*

2008, edited by Paola Buzi, Alberto Camplani, and Federico Contardi. Orientalia Lovaniensia Analecta 247. Vol. 2. 937–944. Leuven: Peeters.

Endsjø, Dag Øistein. 2008. *Primordial Landscapes, Incorruptible Bodies: Desert Asceticism and the Christian Appropriation of Greek Ideas on Geography, Bodies, and Immortality.* New York, NY: Peter Lang.

Endsjø, Dag Øistein. 2012. "'The Truth Is Out There': Primordial Lore and Ignorance in the Wilderness of Athanasius' Vita Antonii." In *Wilderness in Mythology and Religion: Approaching Religious Spatialities, Cosmologies, and Ideas of Wild Nature*, edited by Laura Feldt. 114–129. Berlin: Walter de Gruyter.

Engberg-Pedersen, Troels. 2010. *Cosmology & Self in the Apostle Paul: The Material Spirit.* Oxford: Oxford University Press.

Entwistle, Joanne. 2000. "Fashion and the Fleshy Body: Dress as Embodied Practice." *Fashion Theory: The Journal of Dress, Body & Culture* 4 (3): 323–347.

Entwistle, Joanne. 2015. *The Fashioned Body: Fashion, Dress and Modern Social Theory.* London: Polity Press.

Farag, Mary K. 2018. "Pachomius Outside the Shadow of the *Vita Antonii*." *Harvard Theological Review* 111 (4): 516–540.

Feldt, Laura. 2012. *The Fantastic in Religious Narrative from Exodus to Elisha.* Sheffield: Equinox.

Feldt, Laura. 2013. "Wild and Wondrous Men: Elijah and Elisha in the Hebrew Bible." In *Credible, Incredible: The Miraculous in the Ancient Mediterranean*, edited by Tobias Nicklas and Janet E. Spittler. 323–351. Berlin: Mohr Siebeck.

Feldt, Laura. 2015. "Ancient Wilderness Mythologies—The Case of Space and Religious Identity Formation in the Gospel of Matthew." *Archiv für Religionsgeschichte* 16 (1): 163–192.

Feldt, Laura, and Susanne Koch. 2011. "A Life's Journey—Reflections on Death in the Gilgamesh Epic." In *Akkade Is King: A Collection of Papers by Friends and Colleagues Presented to Aage Westenholz on the Occasion of his 70th Birthday 15th of May 2009*, edited by Gojko Barjamovic, Jacob L. Dahl, Ulla Susanne Koch, Walter Sommerfeld, and Joan Goodnick Westenholz. PIHANS. Vol. 118. 111–134. Leiden: Nederlands Instituut voor het Nabije Oosten.

Fetherolf, Christina Marie. 2017. "Elijah's Mantle: A Sign of Prophecy Gone Awry." *Journal for the Study of the Old Testament* 42 (2): 199–212.

Fine, Steven. 2013. "How Do You Know a Jew When You See One? Reflections on Jewish Costume in the Roman World." In *Fashioning Jews: Clothing, Culture, and Commerce*, edited by Leonard J. Greenspoon. 19–27. West Lafayette, IN: Purdue University Press.

Fischhaber, Gudrun. 1997. *Mumifizierung im koptischen Ägypten: Eine Untersuchung zur Körperlichkeit im 1. Jahrtausend n. Chr.* Wiesbaden: Otto Harrassowitz Verlag.

Fluck, Cäcilia. 2008. "Akhmim as a Source of Textiles." In *Christianity and Monasticism in Upper Egypt*, edited by G. Takla. 211–224. Cairo and New York, NY: American University in Cairo Press.

Flügel, J. C. (1930) 1950. *The Psychology of Clothes.* London: Hogarth.

Foster, Benjamin R. 2005. *Before the Muses: An Anthology of Akkadian Literature.* University Park, PA: Pennsylvania State University Press.

Foucault, Michel. 1982. "Afterword: The Subject and Power." In *Michel Foucault: Beyond Structuralism and Hermeneutics*, edited by Hubert L. Dreyfus and Paul Rabinow. 208–226. New York, NY: Harvester Wheatsheaf.

Foucault, Michel. 1984. *The History of Sexuality*. Harmondsworth: Penguin.

Fowler, Kimberley A. 2018. "Reading Gospel of Thomas 100 in the Fourth Century: From Roman Imperialism to Pachomian Concern Over Wealth." *Vigiliae Christianae* 72 (4): 421–446.

Frank, Karl Suso. 1964. *Angelikos Bios: Begriffsanalytische und begriffsgeschichtliche Untersuchungen zum "engelgleichen Leben" im frühen Mönchtum*. Beitrage zur Geschichte des alten Mönchtums und des Benediktinerordens. Vol. 26. Münster: Aschendorffsche Verlagsbuchhandlung.

Frankfurter, David. 1990. *Elijah in Upper Egypt: Studies in the History and Composition of the Coptic Elijah Apocalypse*. Princeton, NJ: Princeton University Press.

Frankfurter, David. 2018. *Christianizing Egypt: Syncretism and Local Worlds in Late Antiquity*. Princeton, NJ: Princeton University Press.

Franzmann, Majella. 2013. "Augustine and Manichaean Almsgiving: Understanding a Universal Religion with Exclusivist Practices." In *Augustine and Manichaean Christianity: Selected Papers from the First South African Conference on Augustine of Hippo, University of Pretoria, 24–26 April 2012*, edited by Johannes van Oort. 37–49. Leiden: Brill.

Frazer, James. (1922) 1950. *The Golden Bough: A Study in Magic and Religion*. New York, NY: Palgrave Macmillan.

Freiberger, Oliver. 2009. *Der Askesediskurs in der Religionsgeschichte: Eine Vergleichende Untersuchung Brahmanischer und Frühchristlicher Texte*. Studies in Oriental Religions. Wiesbaden: Otto Harrassowitz Verlag.

Freiberger, Oliver. 2010. "Locating the Ascetic's Habitat: Towards a Microcomparison of Religious Discourses." *History of Religions* 50 (2): 162–192.

Freiberger, Oliver. 2019. *Considering Comparison: A Method for Religious Studies*. Oxford: Oxford University Press.

Gathercole, Simon. 2014. *The Gospel of Thomas: Introduction and Commentary*. Leiden: Brill.

Geertz, Armin. 2010. "Brain, Body and Culture: A Biocultural Theory of Religion." *Method & Theory in the Study of Religion* 22: 304–321.

Gennep, Arnold van. 1960. *The Rites of Passage*. Translated by Monika B. Vizedom and Gabrielle L. Caffe. London: Routledge and Keagan Paul.

George, Andrew. 1999. *The Epic of Gilgamesh*. London: Penguin.

George, Andrew. 2003. *The Babylonian Gilgamesh Epic: Introduction, Critical Edition and Cuneiform Texts*. Vol. 2. Oxford: Oxford University Press.

Gilhus, Ingvild Sælid. 2018a. "How Things Make Monks: Objects and Artifacts in the Pachomian Rules." In *Religion, Law, and Justice: Seven Essays*, edited by Håkan Rydving and Stefan Olsson. 43–66. Oslo: Novus Forlag.

Gilhus, Ingvild Sælid. 2018b. "Sheepskins, Hair Shirts and Tunics of Palm Leaves: Charismatic Authority and Monastic Clothing in Egypt in Late Antiquity." *Temenos* 54 (1): 79–102.

Gilhus, Ingvild Sælid. 2019. "Enclothed Cognition and Ancient Monasticism." In *Evolution, Cognition, and the History of Religions: A New Synthesis; Festschrift in Honour of Armin W. Geertz*, edited by Anders Klostergaard Petersen, Ingvild Sælid Gilhus, Luther H. Martin, Jeppe Sinding Jensen, and Jesper Sørensen. 527–561. Leiden: Brill.

Gilhus, Ingvild Sælid. 2020. "Braiding Ropes, Weaving Baskets: The Narrative Culture of Ancient Monasticism." In *Narrative Cultures and the Aesthetics of*

Religion, edited by Dirk Johannsen, Anja Kirsch, and Jens Kreinath. 249–269. Leiden: Brill.

Gilligan, Ian. 2007. "Clothing and Farming Origins: The Indo-Pacific Evidence." *The Bulletin of the Indo-Pacific Prehistory Association* 27: 12–21.

Gilligan, Ian. 2010a. "The Prehistoric Development of Clothing: Archaeological Implications of a Thermal Model." *Journal of Archaeological Method and Theory* 17 (1): 15–80.

Gilligan, Ian. 2010b. "Clothing and Modern Human Behaviour in Australia." *Bulletin of the Indo-Pacific Prehistory Association* 30: 54–69.

Gilligan, Ian. 2019. *Climate, Clothing, and Agriculture in Prehistory: Linking Evidence, Causes, and Effects.* Cambridge: Cambridge University Press.

Giorda, Maria Chiara. 2011. "Does the Cowl Make the Monk? A Monastic Accessory during the First Centuries of Egyptian Monasticism." In *Dress Accessories of the 1st Millennium AD from Egypt: Proceedings of the 6th Conference of the Research Group "Textiles from the Nile Valley" Antwerp, 2–3 October 2009*, edited by Antoine De Moor and Cäcilia Fluck. 182–187. Lanoo: Tielt.

Giorda, Maria Chiara. 2015. "Familles du 'monde', familles monastiques: Une économie du capital dans l'Égypte chrétienne (Vᶜ–VIIᶜ siècles)." *Archives de sciences sociales des religions* 171: 265–288.

Goehring, James E. 1986. *The Letter of Ammon and Pachomian Monasticism.* Berlin and New York, NY: de Gruyter.

Goehring, James E. 1999. *Ascetics, Society, and the Desert: Studies in Egyptian Monasticism.* Studies in Antiquity and Christianity. London and New York, NY: Continuum.

Goehring, James E. 2000. "The First Sahidic Life of Pachomius." In *Religions of Late Antiquity in Practice*, edited by Richard Valantasis. 19–33. Princeton, NJ: Princeton University Press.

Goehring, James E. 2008. "Pachomius and the White Monastery." In *Christianity and Monasticism in Upper Egypt, Vol. 1: Akhmim and Sohag*, edited by Gawdat Gabra and Hany N. Takla. 47–57. Cairo and New York, NY: The American University in Cairo Press.

Goehring, James E. 2020. "Producing Pachomius: The Role of Lower Egypt in the Creation, Reception, and Adaption of the Pachomian *Vita* Tradition." In *Wisdom on the Move: Sayings and Stories in Multicultural Conversation. Essays in Honor of Samuel Rubenson*, edited by Susan Ashbrook Harvey, Thomas Arentzen, Henrik Rydell Johnsén, and Andreas Westergren. 35–53. Leiden: Brill.

Goodrich, Richard J. 2007. *Contextualizing Cassian: Aristocrats, Asceticism, and Reformation in Fifth-Century Gaul.* Oxford Early Christian Studies. Oxford: Oxford University Press.

Goody, Jack. 1978. *The Domestication of the Savage Mind.* Cambridge: Cambridge University Press.

Gosden, Chris, and Lambros Malafouris. 2015. "Process Archaeology (P-Arch)." *World Archaeology* 47 (5): 701–717.

Graiver, Inbar. 2016. "The Paradoxical Effects of Attentiveness." *Journal of Early Christian Studies* 24 (2): 199–227.

Graiver, Inbar. 2017. "'I Think' vs. 'The Thought Tells Me': What Grammar Teaches Us About the Monastic Self." *Journal of Early Christian Studies* 25 (2): 255–279.

Graiver, Inbar. 2018. "Possible Selves in Late Antiquity: Ideal Selfhood and Embodied Selves in Evagrian Anthropology." *The Journal of Religion* 98 (1): 59–89.

Griggs, C. Wilfred. 2005. "Early Christian Burials in the Fayoum." In *Christianity and Monasticism in the Fayoum Oasis*, edited by Gawdat Gabra. 185–195. Cairo and New York, NY: The American University in Cairo Press.

Grumett, David, and Rachel Muers. 2010. *Theology on the Menu: Asceticism, Meat and Christian Diet*. London: Routledge.

Gurney, Daniel J., Neil Howlett, Karen Pine, Megan Tracey, and Rachel Moggridge. 2017. "Dressing Up Posture: The Interactive Effects of Posture and Clothing on Competency Judgements." *British Journal of Psychology* 108 (2): 436–451.

Guy, Jean-Claude. 1993, 2003, 2005. *Les Apophthegmes des Pères: Collection Systématique. Inroduction, texte critique, traduction, et notes*. Vol. 3. Paris: Éditions du Cerf.

Halkin, François, ed. 1932. *Sancti Pachomii Vitae Graecae*. Subsidia Hagiographica. Vol. 19. Brussels: Societé des Bollandistes.

Hansen, Karen Tranberg. 2004. "The World in Dress: Anthropological Perspectives on Clothing, Fashion, and Culture." *Annual Review of Anthropology* 33: 369–392.

Harlow, Mary. 2017. *Introduction to a Cultural History of Dress and Fashion in Antiquity*, edited by Mary Harlow. 1–11. New York: Bloomsbury.

Harmless, William. 2004. *Desert Christians: An Introduction to the Literature of Early Monasticism*. Oxford: Oxford University Press.

Harvey, Susan Ashbrook. 2006. *Scenting Salvation: Ancient Christianity and the Olfactory Imagination*. Berkeley, CA: University of California Press.

Hedstrom, Darlene L. Brooks. 2009. "The Geography of the Monastic Cell in Early Egyptian Monastic Literature." *Church History* 78 (4): 756–791.

Hedstrom, Darlene L. Brooks. 2017. *The Monastic Landscape of Late Antique Egypt: An Archaeological Reconstruction*. Cambridge: Cambridge University Press.

Henshilwood, Christopher, Francesco d'Errico, Karen L. van Niekerk, Laure Dayet, Alain Queffelec, and Luca Pollarolo. 2018. "An Abstract Drawing from the 73,000-Year-Old Levels at Blombos Cave, South Africa." *Nature* 652: 115–118.

Hermkens, Anna Karina. 2010. "Clothing as Embodied Experience of Belief." In *Religion and Material Culture: The Matter of Belief*, edited by David Morgan. 231–246. London and New York, NY: Routledge.

Hesselbein, Chris. 2019. "Walking the Catwalk: From Dressed Body to Dressed Embodiment." *Fashion Theory: The Journal of Dress, Body & Culture* 23: 1–16.

Horsfield, Peter. 2015. *From Jesus to the Internet: A History of Christianity and Media*. Oxford: Wiley Blackwell.

Hoss, Stefanie. 2012. "The Roman Military Belt." In *Wearing the Cloak: Dressing the Soldier in Roman Times*, edited by Marie-Louise Nosch. Ancient Textiles Series, Vol. 10. 28–44. Oxford and Oakville, CT: Oxbow Books.

Howlett, Neil, Karen J. Pine, İsmail Orakçıoğlu, and Ben C. Fletcher. 2012. "The Influence of Clothing on First Impressions: Rapid and Positive Responses to Minor Changes in Male Attire." *Journal of Fashion Marketing and Management* 17 (1): 38–48.

Howlett, Neil, Karen J. Pine, Natassia Cahill, İsmail Orakçıoğlu, and Ben C. Fletcher. 2015. "Unbuttoned: The Interaction Between Provocativeness of Female Work Attire and Occupational Status." *Sex Roles* 72: 105–116.

Hunt, Hannah. 2012. *Clothed in the Body: Asceticism, the Body, and the Spiritual in the Late Antique Era*. Studies in Philosophy and Theology in Late Antiquity. London: Routledge.

Ihde, Don, and Lambros Malafouris. 2019. "*Homo faber* Revisited: Postphenomenology and Material Engagement Theory." *Philosophy and Technology* 32: 195–214.

Innemée, Karel C. 1992. *Ecclesiastical Dress in the Medieval Near East.* Leiden: Brill.

Ivanov, Sergey A. 2006. *Holy Fools in Byzantium and Beyond.* Oxford: Oxford University Press.

Jablonski, Nina G. 2004. "The Evolution of Human Skin and Skin Color." *Annual Review of Anthropology* 33: 585–623.

Jenkins, Richard. 1992. *Pierre Bourdieu.* Key Sociologists. London: Routledge.

Joest, Christoph. 2009. "Die sog. 'Règlements' als Werk des Pachomianers Horsiese." *Vigiliae Christianae* 63 (5): 480–492.

Joest, Christoph. 2012. "Die Leges Pachoms und die Mönchsregeln der Pachomianer." *Vigiliae Christianae* 66 (2): 160–189.

Jones, Arnold Hugh Martin. 1960. "Church Finances in the Fifth and Sixth Centuries." *The Journal of Sociological Studies* 11 (1): 84–95.

Jones, Ann Rosalind, and Peter Stallybrass. 2000. *Renaissance Clothing and the Materials of Memory.* Cambridge: Cambridge University Press.

Jussen, Bernhard. 2001. *Ordering Medieval Society: Perspectives on Intellectual and Practical Modes of Shaping Social Relations.* Philadelphia, PA: University of Pennsylvania Press.

Katos, Demetrios S. 2011. *Palladius of Helenopolis: The Origenist Advocate.* Oxford: Oxford University Press.

Kim, Jinha. 2002. "The Spiritual Anthropology of John Cassian." PhD diss., University of Leeds.

Kim, Jung Hoon. 2004. *The Significance of Clothing Imagery in the Pauline Corpus.* Library of New Testament Studies. London and New York, NY: T & T Clark.

Kim, Young R. 2015. *Epiphanius of Cyprus: Imagining an Orthodox World.* Ann Arbor, MI: University of Michigan Press.

Klijn, A. F. J. 2003. *The Acts of Thomas: Introduction, Text, and Commentary.* 2nd ed. Leiden and Boston: Brill, 2003.

Kloss, Sinah Theres. 2016. *Fabrics of Indianness: The Exchange and Consumption of Clothing in Transnational Guyanese Hindu Communities.* New York, NY: Palgrave Macmillan.

Köhlmoos, Melanie. 2019. "Tearing One's Clothes and Rites of Mourning." In *Clothing and Nudity in the Hebrew Bible*, edited by Christoph Berner, Manuel Schäfer, Martin Schott, Sarah Schuntz, and Martina Weingärtner. 303–313. London: T&T Clark.

Krawiec, Rebecca. 2002. *Shenoute and the Women of the White Monastery.* Oxford: Oxford University Press.

Krawiec, Rebecca. 2008. "The Role of Female Elder in Shenoute's White Monastery." In *Christianity and Monasticism in Upper Egypt*, edited by Gawdat Gabra and Hany N. Takla. 59–71. Cairo and New York, NY: The American University in Cairo Press.

Krawiec, Rebecca. 2009. "'Garments of Salvation': Representations of Monastic Clothing in Late Antiquity." *Journal of Early Christian Studies* 17 (1): 125–150.

Krawiec, Rebecca. 2014. "The Holy Habit and the Teachings of the Elders: Clothing and Social Memory in Late Antique Monasticism." In *Dressing Judeans and*

Christians in Antiquity, edited by Kristi Upson-Saia, Carly Daniel-Hughes, and Alicia J. Batten. 53–73. London: Routledge.

Krueger, Derek. 1997. "Typological Figuration in Theodoret of Cyrrhus's Religious History and the Art of Postbiblical Narrative." *Journal of Early Christian Studies* 5 (3): 393–419.

Krueger, Derek. 2001. *Writing and Holiness: The Practice of Authorship in the Early Christian East*. Philadelphia, PA: Philadelphia University Press.

Krueger, Joel. 2016. "Extended Mind and Religious Cognition." In *Mental Religion: The Brain, Cognition, and Culture*, edited by Niki Kasumi Clements. 237–254. New York, NY: Palgrave Macmillan.

Kuefler, Mathew. 2001. *The Manly Eunuch: Masculinity, Gender Ambiguity, and Christian Ideology in Late Antiquity*. Chicago, IL: Chicago University Press.

Kugel, James L. 1998. *The Traditions of the Bible: A Guide to the Bible as It Was at the Start of the Common Era*. Cambridge, MA: Harvard University Press.

Lakoff, George, and Mark Johnson. 1980. *Metaphors We Live by*. Chicago, IL: Chicago University Press.

Lampe, G. W. H., ed. 1997. *A Patristic Greek Lexicon*. Oxford: Oxford University Press.

Larsen, Lillian. 2016. "Early Monasticism and the Rhetorical Tradition: Sayings and Stories as School Texts." In *Education and Religion in Late Antique Christianity: Reflections, Social Contexts and Genres*, edited by Peter Gemeinhardt, Lieve Van Hoof, and Peter Van Nuffelen. 13–33. London: Routledge.

Latour, Bruno. 1991. "Technology is Society Made Durable." In *A Sociology of Monsters: Essays on Power, Technology and Domination*, edited by J. Law. 101–131. London: Routledge.

Layton, Bentley. 2007. "Rules, Patterns, and the Exercise of Power in Shenoute's Monastery: The Problem of World Replacement and Identity Maintenance." *Journal of Early Christian Studies* 15 (1): 45–73.

Layton, Bentley. 2014. *The Canons of our Fathers: Monastic Rules of Shenoute*. Oxford Early Christian Studies. Oxford: Oxford University Press.

Layton, Richard A. 2013. "Didymus the Blind and the *Philistores*: A Contest over *Historia* in Early Christian Exegetical Argument." In *New Approaches to the Study of Biblical Interpretation in Judaism of the Second Temple Period and in Early Christianity*, edited by Gary A. Anderson, R. A. Clements, and David Satran. Studies on the Texts of the Desert of Judah. Vol. 106. Leiden: Brill.

Lefort, Louis Théophile, ed. 1965. *Pachomii vita Bohairice scripta*. Louvain: Officina Orientali et Scientifica.

Leyerle, Blanche. 2005. "Monks and Other Animals." In *The Cultural Turn in Late Ancient Studies: Gender, Asceticism, and Historiography*, edited by Dale B. Martin and Patricia Cox Miller. 150–173. Durham, NC and London: Duke University Press.

Leyser, Conrad. 2000. *Authority and Asceticism from Augustine to Gregory the Great*. Oxford: Clarendon Press.

López, Ariel G. 2013. *Shenoute of Antripe and the Uses of Poverty: Rural Patronage, Religious Conflict, and Monasticism in Late Antiquity*. The Transformation of the Classical Heritage. Vol. 50. Berkeley, CA, Los Angeles, CA and London: University of California Press.

López-Pérez, Belén, Tamara Ambrona, Ellie L. Wilson, and Marina Khalil. 2016. "The Effect of Enclothed Cognition on Empathic Responses and Helping Behavior." *Social Psychology* 47 (4): 223–231.

Lösch, Sandra, Estelle Hower-Tilmannn, and Albert Zink. 2013. "Mummies and Skeletons from the Coptic Monastery Complex Deir el-Bachit in Thebes-West, Egypt." *Anthropologischer Anzeiger* 70 (1): 27–41.

Lundhaug, Hugo. 2010. *Images of Rebirth: Cognitive Poetics and Transformational Soteriology in the Gospel of Philip and the Exegesis of the Soul.* Leiden: Brill.

Lundhaug, Hugo. 2011. "Baptism in the Monasteries of Upper Egypt: The Pachomian Corpus and the Writings of Shenoute." In *Ablution, Initiation, and Baptism: Late Antiquity, Early Judaism, and Early Christianity*, edited by David Hellholm, Tor Vegge, Øyvind Norderval, and Christer Hellholm. 1347–1380. Berlin: Walter de Gruyter.

Lundhaug, Hugo. 2013. "Begotten, Not Made, to Arise in This Flesh: The Post-Nicene Soteriology of the Gospel of Philip." In *Beyond the Gnostic Gospels: Studies Building on the Work of Elaine Pagels*, edited by Eduard Iricinschi, Lance Jenott, Nicola Denzey Lewis, and Philippa Townsend. Studies and Texts in Antiquity and Christianity 82. 236–265. Tübingen: Mohr Siebeck.

Lundhaug, Hugo. 2017. " 'Tell Me What Shall Arise': Conflicting Notions of the Resurrection Body in Fourth- and Fifth-Century Egypt." In *Coming Back to Life: The Permeability of Past and Present, Mortality and Immortality, Death and Life in the Ancient Mediterranean*, edited by Frederick S. Tappenden and Carly Daniel-Hughes. 215–236. Montreal, QC: McGill University Library.

Lundhaug, Hugo, and Lance Jenott 2015. *The Monastic Origins of the Nag Hammadi Codices.* Tübingen: Mohr Siebeck.

MacCoull, Leslie S. B. 1998. "Prophethood, Texts, and Artifacts: The Monastery of Epiphanius." *Greek, Roman, and Byzantine Studies* 39: 307–324.

Maguire, Eunice Dauterman. 2003. "Dressed for Eternity: A Prelude." In *Living for Eternity: The White Monastery and Its Neighbourhood; Proceedings of a Symposium at the University of Minnesota, Minneapolis, March 6–9, 2003*, edited by P. Sellew. 39–69. Minneapolis, MN. http://egypt.umn.edu/Egypt/1-pb%20pdfs/maguire.pdf.

Malafouris, Lambros. 2010. "The Brain-Artefact Interface (BAI): A Challenge for Archaeology and Cultural Neuroscience." *Social Cognitive and Affective Neuroscience* 5: 264–273.

Malafouris, Lambros. 2013. *How Things Shape the Mind: A Theory of Material Engagement.* Cambridge, MA and London: The MIT Press.

Malafouris, Lambros, and M. D. Koukouti. 2018. "How the Body Remembers Its Skills: Memory and Material Engagement." *Journal of Consciousness Studies* 25 (7–8): 158–180.

Martinez, Mariá Jesús Albarrán. 2008. "El hábito monástico femenino en Egipto (siglos IV-VI)." *Collectanea Christiana Orientalia* 5: 23–34.

McClure, Judith. 1979. "Handbooks Against Heresy in the West from the Late Fourth to the Late Sixth Centuries." *The Journal of Theological Studies* 30 (1): 186–197.

McCracken, Grant D. 1985. "Clothing as Language: An Object Lesson in the Study of the Expressive Properties of Material Culture." In *Material Anthropology: Contemporary Approaches to Material Culture*, edited by Barrie Reynolds and Margaret A. Stott. 103–128. Lanham, MD: University Press of America.

McCracken, Grant D., and Victor J. Roth. 1989. "Does Clothing Have a Code? Empirical Findings and Theoretical Implications in the Study of Clothing as a

Means of Communication." *International Journal of Research in Marketing* 6: 13–33.

McDonnell, Myles. 1991. "The Introduction of Athletic Nudity: Thucydides, Plato, and the Vases." *The Journal of Hellenic Studies* 111: 182–193.

Merleau-Ponty, Maurice. 1945. *Phénoménologie de la perception*. Paris: Gallimard.

Meyer, Birgit. 2009. "Introduction: From Imagined Communities to Aesthetic Formations: Religious Mediations, Sensational Forms, and Styles of Binding." In *Aesthetic Formations: Media, Religion, and the Senses*, edited by B. Meyer. 1–28. New York, NY: Palgrave Macmillan.

Mihas, Elena. 2012. "Bodily-Based Conceptual Metaphors in Ashénika Perené Myths and Folk Stories." In *Endangered Metaphors*, edited by Anna Idström and Elisabeth Piirainen. 149–159. Amsterdam and Philadelphia, PA: John Benjamins Publishing Company.

Mikaelsson, Lisbeth. 1980. "Sexual Polarity: An Aspect of the Ideological Structure in the Paradise Narrative Genesis 2:4–3:24." *Temenos, Nordic Journal of Comparative Religion* 16: 84–91.

Mikaelsson, Lisbeth. 1999. "Tenk rikt! Bli rik!" In *Myte, magi og mirakel i møte med det modern*, edited by Bente Gullveig Alver, Ingvild Sælid Gilhus, Lisbeth Mikaelsson, and Torunn Selberg. 200–213. Oslo: Pax.

Miller, Patricia Cox. 1994. "Desert Asceticism and 'The Body from Nowhere'." *Journal of Early Christian Studies* 2 (2): 137–153.

Miller, Daniel. 2010. *Stuff*. Cambridge: Polity Press.

Miola, Maria del Fiat. 2018. "Permitted and Prohibited Textiles in the Regula Virginum: Unweaving the Terminology." *Early Medieval Europe* 26 (1): 90–102.

Mithen, Steven. 1998. "The Supernatural Beings of Prehistory and the External Storage of Religious Ideas." In *Cognition and Material Culture: The Archaeology of Symbolic Storage*, edited by Colin Renfrew and Chris Scarre. McDonald Institute Monographs. 97–106. Cambridge: Short Run Press.

Mobley, Gregory. 1997. "The Wild Man in the Bible and the Ancient Near East." *Journal of Biblical Literature* 116 (2): 217–233.

Morgan, Faith Pennick. 2018. *Dress and Personal Appearance in Late Antiquity: The Clothing of the Middle and Lower Classes*. Leiden: Brill.

Moss, Candida R. 2019. *Divine Bodies: Resurrecting Perfection in the New Testament and Early Christianity*. Yale: Yale University Press.

Mossakowska-Gaubert, Maria. 2004. "Les origines des tuniques à manches courtes et sans manches utilisées par les moines égyptiens (IVe–début du VIIe siècle)." *Antiquité Tardive* 12: 153–167.

Mossakowska-Gaubert, Maria. 2015. "Alimentation, hygiène, vêtements et sommeil chez les moines égyptiens (IVe–début du VIIe siècle); L'état des sources archéologiques et écrites." In *La vie quotidienne des moines en Orient et en Occident (IVe–Xe siècle), Vol. I: L'état des sources*, edited by Olivier Delouis and Maria Mossakowska-Gaubert. 23–49. Cairo and Athens: Institut français d'archéologie orientale and École française d'Athènes.

Mossakowska-Gaubert, Maria. 2017. "Tunics Worn in Egypt in Roman and Byzantine Times: The Greek Vocabulary." In *Textile Terminology from the Orient and the Mediterranean and Europe, 1000 BC to 1000 AD*, edited by Salvatore Gaspa, Cécile Michel, and Marie-Louise Nosch. 321–345. Lincoln, NE: Zea Books.

Muc, Agnieszka. 2009. "Some Remarks on the Egyptian Monastic Dress in the Context of Literary Sources and Funerary Finds." *Studies in Ancient Art and Civilization* 13: 183–188.

Muehlberger, Ellen. 2008. "Ambivalence About the Angelic Life: The Promise and Perils of an Early Christian Discourse on Asceticism." *Journal of Early Christian Studies* 16 (4): 447–478.

Muehlberger, Ellen. 2013. *Angels in Late Ancient Christianity*. Oxford: Oxford University Press.

Neufeld, Dietmar. 2005. "Under the Cover of Clothing: Scripted Clothing Performances in the Apocalypse of John." *Biblical Theology Bulletin* 35: 67–76.

Oden, Robert A. 1987. "Grace or Status? Yahweh's Clothing of the First Humans." In *The Bible Without Theology: The Theological Traditions and Alternatives to It*, edited by Robert A. Oden. 92–105. San Francisco, CA: Harper & Row.

Ogden, Daniel. 2004. *Greek and Roman Necromancy*. Princeton, NJ: Princeton University Press.

Olson, Kelly. 2017. *Masculinity and Dress in Roman Antiquity*. London: Routledge.

Olson, Kelly. 2018. "Toga and Pallium: Status, Sexuality, Identity." In *Sex in Antiquity: Exploring Gender and Sexuality in the Ancient World*, edited by Mark Masterson, Nancy Sorkin Rabinowitz, and James Robson. 422–448. London: Routledge.

Orakçıoğlu Mehlika, İsmail Orakçıoğlu, and Ben C. Fletcher, 2016. "Enclothed Cognition and Hidden Meanings in Important Ottoman Textiles." *Textile; Cloth and Culture* 14 (3): 360–375.

Orlandi, Tito. 1985. *Shenute contra Origenistas*. Corpus dei manoscritti copti letterari. Rome: C.I.M.

Patrich, Joseph. 1995. *Sabas, Leader of Palestinian Monasticism: A Comparative Study in Eastern Monasticism, Fourth to Seventh Centuries*. Washington, DC: Dumbarton Oaks Research Library and Collection.

Pearson, Birger, and James E. Goehring, eds. 1986. *The Roots of Egyptian Christianity*. Minneapolis, MN: Augsburg Press.

Petersen, Anders Klostergaard. 2016. "The Difference Between Religious Narratives and Fictional Literature: A Matter of Degree Only." *Religion* 46 (4): 500–520.

Plesa, Alexandra D. 2017. "Religious Belief in Burial: Funerary Dress and Practice at the Late Antique and Early Islamic Cemeteries at Matmar and Mostagedda, Egypt (Late Fourth—Early Ninth Centuries CE)." *Ars Orientalis* 47: 18–42.

Pöllänen, Sinikka Hannele. 2015. "Crafts as Leisure Based Coping: Craft Makers' Descriptions of Their Stress-Reducing Activity." *Occupational Therapy in Mental Health* 20 (3): 58–78.

Presley, Stephen O. 2015. *The Intertextual Reception of Genesis 1–3 in Irenaeus of Lyons*. Leiden: Brill.

Pyschny, Katharina. 2019. "Concepts and Contexts of Female and Male Nudity in the Iconography of the Southern Levant." In *Clothing and Nudity in the Hebrew Bible*, edited by Christoph Berner, Manuel Schäfer, Martin Schott, Sarah Schulz, and Martina Weingärtner. 127–184. London: T&T Clark.

Ramsey, Boniface. 2000. *John Cassian: The Institutes*. ACW 58. New York, NY: Paulist Press, 2000.

Rantala, Markus J. 2007. "Evolution of Nakedness in Homo sapiens." *Journal of Zoology* 273: 1–7.

Rapp, Claudia. 2005. *Holy Bishops in Late Antiquity: The Nature of Christian Leadership in an Age of Transition*. The Transformation of the Classical Heritage. Vol. 37. Berkeley, CA, Los Angeles, CA and London: University of California Press.

Reaves, Pamela Mullins. 2019. "John the Baptist and the Jordan River: The Arrival of the Son of Man in *the Testimony of Truth* (NHC IX,3) and Parallels in the *Paraphrase of Shem* (NHC VII,1)." *Journal of Early Christian Studies* 27 (1): 55–83.

Rebillard, Éric. 2003. "The Cult of the Dead in Late Antiquity: Towards a New Definition of the Relation Between the Living and the Dead." *Acta ad archaeologiam et artium historiam pertinentia* 17: 47–55.

Rebillard, Éric. 2013. *Transformations of Religious Practices in Late Antiquity*. Farnham: Ashgate.

Reed, David L. et al. 2015. "The Study of Primate Evolution from a Lousy Perspective." In *Parasite Diversity and Diversification: Evolutionary Ecology Meets Phylogenetics*, edited by Serge Morand, Boris R. Krasnov, and D. Timothy J. Littlewood. 202–214. Cambridge: Cambridge University Press.

Reuling, Hanneke. 2006. *After Eden: Church Fathers and Rabbis on Genesis 3:16–21*. Leiden: Brill.

Rice, Gene. 2006–2007. "Elijah's Requirement for Prophetic Leadership (2 Kings 2: 1–18)." *Journal of Religious Thought* 59–60: 1–12.

Riedel, Wilhelm, and Walther Ewing Crum, eds. 1904. *The Canons of Athanasius of Alexandria*. The Arabic and Coptic versions edited and translated with introductions, notes and appendices. London: Williams and Norgate.

Riesebrodt, Martin. 1999. "*Charisma* in Max Weber's Sociology of Religion." *Religion* 29: 1–14.

Riggs, Christina. 2014. *Unwrapping Ancient Egypt*. New York, NY: Bloomsbury Academic.

Riley, Jill. 2008. "Weaving an Enhanced Sense of Self and a Collective Sense of Self Through Collective Textile-Making." *Journal of Occupational Science* 15 (2): 63–73.

Rollason, N. K. 2016. *Gifts of Clothing in Late Antique Literature*. London and New York, NY: Routledge.

Römer, Thomas. 2012. "Abraham Traditions in the Hebrew Bible Outside the Book of Genesis." In *The Book of Genesis: Composition, Reception, and Interpretation*, edited by Craig A. Evans, Joel N. Lohr, and David L. Petersen. 159–180. Leiden: Brill.

Rousseau, Philip. (1985) 1999. *Pachomius: The Making of a Community in Fourth-Century Egypt*. The Transformation of the Classical Heritage. Vol. 6. Berkeley, CA, Los Angeles, CA and London: The University of California Press.

Rousseau, Philip. (1978) 2010. *Ascetics, Authority, and the Church in the Age of Jerome and Cassian*. Notre Dame, IN: Notre Dame University Press.

Rubenson, Samuel. 1995. *The Letters of St. Antony: Monasticism and the Making of a Saint*. Minneapolis: Fortress Press.

Rubenson, Samuel. 2009. "'As Already Translated to the Kingdom While Still in the Body': The Transformation of the Ascetic in Early Egyptian Monasticism." In *Metamorphoses: Resurrection, Body and Transformative Practices in Early Christianity*, edited by Turid Karlsen Seim and Jorunn Økland. Ekstasis: Religious Experience from Antiquity to the Middle Ages. Vol. 1. 271–289. Berlin: Walter de Gruyter.

Rubenson, Samuel. 2013a. "Apologetics of Asceticism: The *Life of Antony* and Its Political Context." In *Ascetic Culture: Essays in Honor of Philip Rousseau*, edited by Blake Leyerle and Robin Darling Young. 75–96. Notre Dame, IN: Notre Dame University Press.

Rubenson, Samuel. 2013b. "To Tell the Truth: Fact and Fiction in Early Monastic Sources." *Cistercian Studies Quarterly* 48 (3): 317–324.

Rubenson, Samuel, ed. 2013c. *Early Monasticism and Classical Paideia. Vol. 3 of Studia Patristica LV: Papers Presented at the Sixteenth International Conference of Patristic Studies Held at Oxford 2011*. Edited by Markus Vinzent. Leuven: Peeters.

Rubenson, Samuel. 2015. "The Letter-Collections of Antony and Ammonas: Shaping a Community." In *Collecting Early Christian Letters: From the Apostle Paul to Late Antiquity*, edited by Bronwen Neil and Pauline Allen. 68–79. Cambridge: Cambridge University Press.

Rubenson, Samuel. 2017. "Textual Fluidity in Early Monasticism: Sayings, Sermons and Stories." In *Snapshots of Evolving Traditions: Jewish and Christian Manuscript Culture, Textual Fluidity, and New Philology*, edited by Liv Ingeborg Lied and Hugo Lundhaug. 178–200. Berlin: Walter de Gruyter.

Ruggerone, Lucia. 2017. "The Feeling of Being Dressed: Affect Studies and the Clothed Body." *Fashion Theory* 21 (5): 573–593.

Russell, Nancy Ukai. 2014. "Aspects of Baby Wrappings: Swaddling, Carrying, and Wearing." In *Wrapping and Unwrapping Material Culture: Archaeological and Anthropological Perspectives*, edited by Susanna Harris and Laurence Douny. 43–58. Walnut Creek, CA: Left Coast Press.

Rydén, Lennart. 1981. "The Holy Fool." In *The Byzantine Saint*, edited by Sergei Hackel. 106–113. London: University of Birmingham.

Salisbury, Joyce E. 1997. *Perepetua's Passion: The Death and Memory of a Young Roman Woman*. London: Routledge.

Schiek, Annette Paetz gen. 2012. "A Late Roman Painting of an Egyptian Officer and the Layers of Its Perception: On the Relations Between Images and Textile Finds." In *Wearing the Cloak: Dressing the Soldier in Roman Times*, edited by Marie-Louise Nosch. Ancient Textiles Series. Vol. 10. 85–108. Oxford and Oakville, CT: Oxbow Books.

Schott, Martin. 2019. "Elijah's Hairy Robe and the Clothes of the Prophets." In *Clothing and Nudity in the Hebrew Bible*, edited by Christoph Berner, Manuel Schäfer, Martin Schott, Sarah Schuntz, and Martina Weingärtner. 477–489. London: T&T Clark.

Schroeder, Caroline T. 2007. *Monastic Bodies: Discipline and Salvation in Shenoute of Antripe*. Philadelphia, PA: University of Pennsylvania Press.

Schroeder, Caroline T. 2015. "In the Footsteps of Shenoute: Caroline T. Schroeder on Bentley Layton's *The Canons of Our Fathers*." In *Marginalia Review of Books*. http://marginalia.lareviewofbooks.org/in-the-footsteps-of-shenoute-caroline-t-schroeder.

Shaw, Teresa M. 1997. "Wolves in Sheeps' Clothing: The Appearance of True and False Piety." *Studia Patristica* 29: 127–133.

Sheridan, Mark. 2015. "Early Egyptian Monasticism: Ideals and Reality, or: The Shaping of the Monastic Ideal." *Journal of the Canadian Society for Coptic Studies* 7: 9–24.

Siegal, Michael Bar-Asher. 2013. *Early Christian Monastic Literature and the Babylonian Talmud*. Cambridge: Cambridge University Press.

Slepian, Michael L., Simon N. Ferber, Joshua M. Gold, and Abraham M. Rutchick. 2015. "The Cognitive Consequences of Formal Clothing." *Social Psychology and Personal Science* 6 (6): 661–668.

Smith, Jonathan Z. 1966. "The Garments of Shame." *History of Religions* 5 (2): 217–238.

Smith, Duane E. 2015. "The Divining Snake: Reading Genesis 3 in the Context of Mesopotamian Ophiomancy." *Journal of Biblical Literature* 134 (1): 31–49.

Sontag, Suzanne M., and Jean Davis Schlater. 1982. "Proximity of Clothing to Self: Evolution of a Concept." *Clothing and Textiles Research Journal* 1: 1–8.

Sontag, Suzanne M., and Jongnam Lee. 2004. "Proximity of Clothing to Self." *Clothing and Textiles Research Journal* 22 (4): 161–177.

Sotiriou, Eleni. 2015. " 'Monasticizing the Monastics': Religious Clothes, Socialization and the Transformation of Body and Self Among Greek Orthodox Nuns." *Italian Journal of Sociology of Education* 7 (3): 140–166.

Speidel, Michael Alexander. 2012. "Dressed for the Occasion: Clothes and Context in the Roman Army." In *Wearing the Cloak: Dressing the Soldier in Roman Times*, edited by Marie-Louise Nosch. Ancient Textiles Series. Vol. 10. 1–12. Oxford and Oakville, CT: Oxbow Books.

Stallybrass, Peter. 1993. "Worn Worlds: Clothes, Mourning, and the Life of Things." *Yale Review* 81 (2): 35–50.

Sterk, Andrea. 2009. *Renouncing the World yet Leading the Church: The Monk-Bishop in Late Antiquity*. Cambridge, MA: Harvard University Press.

Stevenson, Alice, and Michael W. Dee. 2016. "Confirmation of the World's Oldest Woven Garment: The Tarkhan Dress." *Antiquity* Project Gallery 90 (349). http://antiquity.ac.uk/projgall/stevenson349.

Stroumsa, Guy. 2016. "Modes of Scriptural and Personal Authority in Late Antique Religion." In *Submerged Literature in Ancient Greek Culture, Vol. 3: The Comparative Perspective*, edited by Andrea Ercolani and Manuela Giordano. 169–182. Berlin: Walter de Gruyter.

Sutton, John. 2007. "Spongy Brains and Material Memories." In *Environment and Embodiment in Early Modern England*, edited by Mary Floyd-Wilson and Garrett A. Sullivan, Jr. 14–32. London: Palgrave Macmillan.

Sutton, John. 2008. "Material Agency, Skills and History: Distributed Cognition and the Archaeology of Memory." In *Material Agency: Towards a Non-Anthropocentric Approach*, edited by Carl Knappett and Lambros Malafouris. 37–55. New York, NY: Springer.

Szakolczai, Arpad. 2000. *Reflexive Historical Sociology*. London: Routledge.

Tappenden, Frederick S. 2016. *Resurrection in Paul: Cognition, Metaphor, and Transformation*. Atlanta, GA: SBL Press.

Taylor, Joan E. 2018. *What Did Jesus Look Like?* London: Bloomsbury.

Teigen, Håkon F. 2018. "Limbs of the Light Mind: The Social World of a Manichaean Community in Fourth-Century Egypt." PhD diss., University of Bergen.

Thelamon, Françoise. 1994. "Sociabilité, travail et loisir dans le monachisme antique." *Archives de sciences sociales des religions* 86: 183–197.

Thomas, Thelma K. 2012. "Mimetic Devotion and Dress in Some Monastic Portraits from the Monastery of Apa Apollo at Bawit." *Coptica* 11: 37–79.

Thomas, Thelma K. 2019. "The Honorific Mantle as Furnishing for the Household Memory Theater in Late Antiquity: A Case Study from the Monastery of Apa Apollo at Bawit." In *Catalogue of the Textiles in the Dumbarton Oaks Byzantine Collection*, edited by Gudrun Bühl and Elizabeth Dospěl Williams. www.doaks.org/resources/textiles/essays/thomas.

Thomassen, Einar. 2005. *The Spiritual Seed: The Church of the "Valentinians".* Nag Hammadi and Manichaean Studies. Leiden: Brill.

Thomassen, Einar. 2009. "Valentinian Ideas About Salvation as Transformation." In *Metamorphoses: Resurrection, Body and Transformative Practices in Early Christianity*, edited by Turid Karlsen Seim and Jorunn Økland. Ekstasis: Religious Experience from Antiquity to the Middle Ages. Vol. 1. 169–186. Berlin: Walter de Gruyter.

Tilley, Maureen. 2018. "Caesarius's *Rule* for Unruly Nuns: Permitted and Prohibited Textiles in the Monastery of St. John." *Early Medieval Europe* 26 (1): 83–89.

Tovar, Sofia Torallas. 2007. "The Terminology of Egyptian Monastic Garments." In *Material Culture and Well-Being in Byzantium (400–1453): Proceedings of the International Conference (Cambridge, 8–10 September 2001)*, edited by Michael Grünbart, Ewald Kislinger, Anna Muthesius, and Dionysios Ch. Stathakopoulos. 219–224. SOS Free Stock. www.austriaca.at/3602-6inhalt.

Tradigo, Alfredo. 2006. *Icons and Saints of the Eastern Orthodox Church*. Los Angeles, CA: J. Paul Getty Museum.

Turner, Terence S. (1980) 2012. "The Social Skin." *HAU: Journal of Ethnographic Theory* 2 (2): 486–504.

Turner, Victor W. 1969. *The Ritual Process*. Chicago, IL: Aldine.

Undheim, Sissel. 2018. *Borderline Virginities: Sacred and Secular Virgins in Late Antiquity*. London: Routledge.

Undheim, Sissel, and Vladimir Ivanovici. 2019. "Consecrated Virgins as Living Reliquaries in Late Antiquity." *RIHA Journal*. www.riha-journal.org/articles/2019/0222-0229-special-issue-paradigms-of-corporeal-iconicity/0228-ivanovici-and-undheim.

Upson-Saia, Kristi. 2011. *Early Christian Dress: Gender, Virtue, and Authority*. London: Routledge.

Upson-Saia, Kristi. 2014. "Hairiness and Holiness in the Early Christian Desert." In *Dressing Judeans and Christians in Antiquity*, edited by Kristi Upson- Saia, Carly Daniel Hughes, and Alicia J. Batten. 155–172. London: Routledge.

Upson-Saia, Kristi, Carly Daniel Hughes, and Alicia J. Batten, eds. 2014. *Dressing Judeans and Christians in Antiquity*. London: Routledge.

Urban, Hugh. 2003. "Sacred Capital: Pierre Bourdieu and the Study of Religion." *Method & Theory in the Study of Religion* 15 (4): 354–389.

Utriainen, Terhi. 2004. "Naked and Dressed: Metaphorical Perspective to the Imaginary and Ethical Background of the Deathbed Scene." *Mortality* 9 (2): 132–149.

Valantasis, Richard. 1997. *The Gospel of Thomas*. New Testament Readings. London: Routledge.

Veblen, Thorstein. (1899) 2007. *The Theory of the Leisure Class*. Oxford World's Classics. Oxford: Oxford University Press.

Veilleux, Armand. 1968. *La liturgie dans le cenobitisme Pachomien au quatrieme siècle*. Studia Anselmiana, Vol. 57. Rome: Herder.

Veilleux, Armand. 1980. *Pachomian Koinonia. Vol. 1: The Life of Saint Pachomius and His Disciples*. Kalamazoo, MI: Cistercian Publications.

Veilleux, Armand. 1981. *Pachomian Koinonia. Vol. 2: Pachomian Chronicles and Rules*. Kalamazoo, MI: Cistercian Publications.

Veilleux, Armand. 1982. *Pachomian Koinonia. Vol. 3: Instructions, Letters, and Other Writings of Saint Pachomius and His Disciples*. Kalamazoo, MI: Cistercian Publications.

Vogt, Kari. 1987. "La moniale folle du monastère des tabennésiotes: Une interpretation du chapitre 34 de l'*Historia Lausiaca* de Pallade." *Symbolae Osloensis* 53: 95–108.

Ward, Benedicta. 1980. *Introduction to the Lives of the Desert Fathers*. Edited and translated by Norman Russell. Cistercian Studies. Vol. 34. Kalamazoo, MI: Cistercian Publications.

Ware, Kallistos. 1998. "The Way of the Ascetics: Negative or Affirmative?" In *Asceticism*, edited by Vincent L. Wimbush and Richard Valantasis. 3–15. Oxford: Oxford University Press.

Weber, Max. (1922) 1968. *Economy and Society*. Edited by Guenther Roth and Claus Wittich. Vol. 3. New York: Bedminster Press.

Weber, Max. (1948) 2007. *From Max Weber: Essays in Sociology*. Edited and translated by H. H. Gerth and C. Wright Mills. London: Routledge.

Wilson, Elizabeth. 1985. *Adorned in Dreams: Fashion and Modernity*. London: Virago Press.

Winlock, Herbert E., and Walter E. Crum. 1926. *The Monastery of Epiphanius at Thebes*. New York: Metropolitan Museum of Art.

Wipszycka, Ewa. 2009. *Moines et communautés monastiques en Égypte (IVe-VIIIe siècles)*. JJP supplement 11. Warsaw: Journal of Juristic Papyrology.

Wipszycka, Ewa. 2011. "Resources and Economic Activities of the Egyptian Monastic Communities (4th–8th Century)." *The Journal of Juristic Papyrology* 41: 159–263.

Wisse, Frederik. 1970. "The Redeemer Figure in the Paraphrase of Shem." *Novum Testamentum* 12 (2): 130–140.

Woolf, Virginia. (1928) 1977. *Orlando*. London: Triad Grafton.

Wortley, John. 2012. *The Book of the Elders: Sayings of the Desert Fathers: The Systematic Collection*. Collegeville, MN: Liturgical Press, Cistercian Publications.

Young, Dwight W. 2000. "Five Leaves from a Copy of Shenoute's *Third Canon*." *Muséon* 113 (3–4): 263–294.

Young, Robin Darling. 2007. "Notes on Divesting and Vesting in the Hymn of the Pearl." In *Reading Religions in the Ancient World: Essays Presented to Robert McQueen Grant on His 90th Birthday*, edited by David E. Aune and Robin Darling Young. 199–214. Leiden: Brill.

Zecher, Jonathan L. 2014. "Antony's Vision of Death? Athanasius of Alexandria, Palladius of Helenopolis, and Egyptian Mortuary Religion." *Journal of Late Antiquity* 7 (1): 159–176.

Zwickel, Wolfgang. 2019. "Fabrication, Functions, and Uses of Textiles in the Hebrew Bible." In *Clothing and Nudity in the Hebrew Bible*, edited by Christoph Berner, Manuel Schäfer, Martin Schott, Sarah Schuntz, and Martina Weingärtner. 177–215. London: T&T Clark.

Index

Note: Page numbers in **bold** indicate a table on the corresponding page.

Printed in the United States
By Bookmasters